OPEN ROAD'S BEST OF
Las Vegas

by Jay Fenster
– plus 53 pages of gaming tips
by gambling guru Avery Cardoza

**Open Road Travel Guides – designed for the
amount of time you *really* have for your trip!**

Open Road Publishing

Open Road's new travel guides cut to the chase.
You don't need a huge travel encyclopedia – you need a *selective guide* to steer you right. If you're going on vacation for a few weeks or less, get a guide that brings you the *best* of any destination for the amount of time you *really* have for your trip!

Open Road – the guide you need for the trip you want.

The New Open Road *Best Of* Travel Guides.
Right to the point.
Uncluttered.
Easy.

Text Copyright © 2008 by Jay Fenster & Avery Cardoza
- All Rights Reserved -
ISBN 10: 1-59360-107-7
ISBN 13: 978-1-59360-107-2
Library of Congress Control No. 2007942858

Maps by DesignMaps.com except map on page 13. Photos © ShutterStock.com except as noted below: *The following photos are from flickr.com*: p. 1: aNgeLinRicHmoNd; p. 7 left: flattop341; p. 7 right: Shoshanah; p. 21: tinou bao; p. 25: tlianza; p. 26: iluvzurich; p. 31: ulybug; p. 38: AMagill; p. 39: foxgirl; p. 42: kevint3141;° p. 45: Super Starfish; p. 53: terren in Virginia; p. 71: mackenzieeeee; p. 72: vibin; p. 79: Argyleist; p. 84: StuSeeger; p. 100: paper or plastic?; pp. 113, 264: http2007; pp. 116, 129: airgap; p. 119: lookslikeamy; p. 130: Foxgirl; p. 135: FotoDawg; p. 136: bludgeoner86; p. 137: hirondellecanada; p. 145: jay.tong; p. 151: mil8; p. 152: jrgcreations; p. 157: Jack_Dawkins; p. 168: miss karen; p. 185: jamesguhe; p. 218: palmsrick; p. 268: larrykang. *The following photos are from wikimedia commons*: p. 92: Kjkolb; p. 93: Grombo; p. 121: Pamela McCreight; p. 127: Urban; p. 142: Lvtalon; p. 143: Flicka; p. 245: David Singleton; p. 261: mikerussell.

CONTENTS

Maps

Open Road's Best Of
LAS VEGAS

1. INTRODUCTION

Las Vegas is a city of dreamers, and of dreams. It is a glimmering beacon in the desert that embraces the eccentric and liberates the inhibited. Las Vegas is a place that will let you be whoever you are – or whoever you want to be. Perhaps no other city in the world offers such breathtaking diversity and limitless potential to its visitors. In the pages that follow, we'll sort out the options and show you how to get the most out of your Vegas visit – whether you're here for just a day, a long weekend or a week or two.

When most people think of Las Vegas, the first thought that comes to mind is gambling. Which, of course, stands to reason. If you're planning on gambling, we'll help maximize your chance of beating the house. This is the only Las Vegas guidebook offering **advice from gaming guru Avery Cardoza**. Want to know where to find the best craps odds in town, full-pay video poker, and the newest poker rooms? Read on. We'll show you

which games to play, which bets to avoid, and how to get comps.

Our advice doesn't end on the Strip. We'll take you downtown for that old-school Vegas vibe and share the very best of the locals' casinos, hidden gems offering better value than the tourist-oriented Strip hot spots.

The world's most renowned and in-demand fashion designers operate boutique shops in some of the finer hotels, but we'll also show you where to find outlet-center bargains. Chefs aren't celebrities until they open a Vegas eatery, and we'll show you the best places for culinary greatness. Indulgent spas and challenging golf courses beckon during the day. Superclubs, ultralounges and marvelous production shows let the night take you just about anywhere.

Sin City is many things to many people. It's the Wonka factory with more calories. It's the corner of Bourbon Street and Collins Avenue. It's the excess of Ibiza, the glamour of Hollywood and the chic of Manhattan rolled up into one. It's Disneyland with lap dances. Las Vegas is truly a place where anything can happen. Follow the advice in this book to ensure that what happens in Vegas, gets bragged about when you get home.

There's a world of things to do here that have nothing to do with gambling. We'll lead you to places like Red Rock Canyon and the Valley of Fire, showcases of Las Vegas' natural beauty. We'll visit Bonnie Springs and the Neon Graveyard if you're interested in he city's rowdy and colorful history. Area 51, the Hoover Dam, and the Grand Canyon are easily accessible. If you're so inclined, we'll even get you on a snowboard.

2. OVERVIEW

The first golden age of Las Vegas was defined by larger-than-life personalities. Mobster Bugsy Siegel, who owned the Flamingo. Rat Packers Frank Sinatra, Dean Martin and Sammy Davis Jr. performed at the Sands and Dunes while filming *Ocean's Eleven*. Elvis Presley's residency at the International is Las Vegas lore.

The second golden age of Las Vegas has been defined by larger-than-life mega-resorts with great restaurants, plush accommodations and sumptuous facilities, starting in 1989, when Steve Wynn opened the Mirage. Over the next decade, the gaming equivalent of a nuclear arms race ensued, as the world's largest hotels opened on the Strip in quick succession – the MGM Grand and Treasure Island in 1993, Monte Carlo in 1996, New York-New York in 1997, the Bellagio in 1998, Paris Las Vegas, the Venetian and Mandalay Bay in 1999. Each of these places is a destination attraction in its own right.

Things came full circle with the 2005 opening of the breathtaking Wynn Las Vegas, and the construction of resorts like Palazzo, Encore, CityCenter and Echelon.

Gambling
Las Vegas' biggest draw is legal gambling. There are over 40 casinos on the Strip and over 200 across town. With a little knowledge and preparation, even a rookie can get thrills and excitement on the casino floor. **Slots are the most popular** and ubiqui-

tous games in town, providing great fun in spite of relatively poor odds. We'll show you how to get the most out of these casino cash cows. If table games are more your cup of tea, we've got you covered there too. We'll show you how to maximize your chances of winning and the best places to play your game of choice, including blackjack, craps, poker, roulette, and baccarat. We'll also give you tips on video poker, sports betting, keno and all the rest.

The Strip

Las Vegas Boulevard South, best known as the Strip, is dotted with gigantic neon-clad hotel towers. Many are elaborately themed, with architecture and décor recreating some of the world's most recognizable places. Some unthemed hotels are even more spectacular.

The five-star **Bellagio** boasts a must-see dancing fountain show, indoor conservatory, art museum, and elite dining. The Strip's best-known hotel, however, is **Caesars Palace**, iconic since 1966. The $2.7 billion **Wynn Las Vegas** provides a level of service and sophistication matched by few hotels in the world, and has the awards to back that up. Wynn's two previous mega-resorts, the **Mirage** and the adjacent **Treasure Island**, are spectacles in their own right, each equal parts tourist trap and chic adult playground. Adjacent to his eponymous project is Wynn's newest hotel and mirror image, **Encore**, slated to open in 2009.

Another opulent pair of properties right next door is the brand-new **Palazzo** and its older sister, the **Venetian** - which duplicates in amazing detail the famous landmarks of the canal city. **Paris Las Vegas** and **New York-New York** duplicate their cities' landmarks as well. **Luxor** has toned down the Egyptian theming and evolved into one of the hipper spots on the Strip. Finally, **Mandalay Bay** anchors the south end of the Strip with one of the most incredible swimming pools in the world. While all of these hotels are high-end, there are worthwhile Strip spots that won't break the bank.

Downtown, Off-Strip, & Neighborhood Casinos

For those willing to forsake the bright lights and easy access to the Strip, the rewards can include lower room rates and more player-

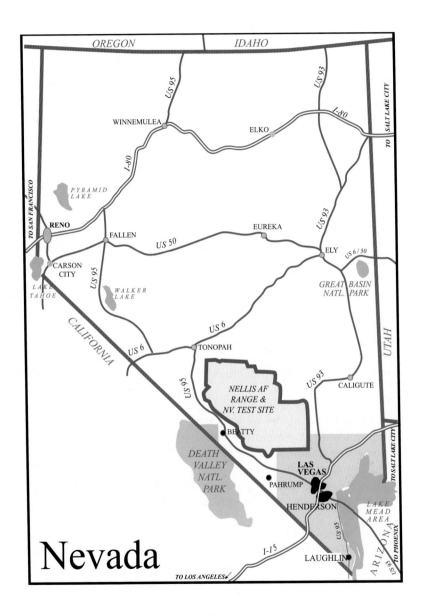

Nevada

friendly gambling. The most famous off-Strip casino is the **Palms**, home of MTV's 2003 Real World season and its 2007 Video Music Awards. A similarly young and celebrity-spotting crowd is drawn to the **Hard Rock**.

For a taste of Vegas history, head downtown, where casinos like the **Golden Nugget** and **Binion's** recall "Old Vegas." When the sun goes down, downtown is transformed by the **Fremont Street Experience**, a high-tech sound-and-light extravaganza. All across the metro area are neighborhood casinos luring locals with generous players' clubs, valuable promotions and favorable odds. Two locals casinos with strong visitor appeal are Station Casinos' otherworldly **Red Rock** and the Tuscan-style **Green Valley Ranch**.

Great Eats

In recent years, Las Vegas has become one of the top dining destinations in America. Twenty years ago it was unthinkable, but the days of tasteless $2 steak and drab hospital-food buffets are long gone. Now, the name of the game is oneupsmanship. **Celebrity chefs** are status symbols, flaunted by hotels. Recently, French cuisine demigods Joël Robuchon and Guy Savoy opened their first American restaurants. TV personalities Bobby Flay, Emeril Lagasse, Wolfgang Puck and Mario Batali are represented, as are many other culinary superstars.

Perhaps nothing exemplifies Las Vegas' renaissance like the transformation of the all-you-can-eat experience. **Buffets** are dining events, with gourmet preparation, exotic menu items, interactive stations, and on weekends, champagne. More casual and less gluttonous eats are found at the casinos' 24-hour cafés. There are still great dining bargains to be found if you're willing to look. We'll clue you in on specials you won't find on any menu.

Nightlife & Entertainment

Though casinos are open 24 hours, take some time to *spend* your winnings. The best DJs in the world routinely play at the city's many plush clubs. If you suffer from lack of rhythm but still want that velvet rope vibe, equally chic bars called ultralounges might be more your scene. Our tips will help you get in.

Why not take in a show? Choose from no less than five Cirque du Soleil shows, headliners, Broadway musicals and magic. Of course, this is Vegas, so topless revues and beefcake shows abound too. If you prefer your nudity without culture, strippers are almost as ubiquitous in this town as slot machines. Some strip clubs rank among the most opulent spots in town.

Day Trips & Excursions

Among the excursions that can be easily undertaken from Las Vegas are the landmark **Hoover Dam** and adjacent **Lake Mead Recreation Area**. The **Grand Canyon** is within day trip distance, while helicopter tours can make it a quicker visit. Within easier driving distance are the towns of **Laughlin, Mesquite, Primm** and **Pahrump**. They each have something to offer, like Colorado River views in the case of Laughlin, or legal prostitution in Pahrump.

Sports & Recreation

Less than an hour from the Strip, **Lee Canyon** offers winter sports. Tennis and bowling are represented, as are extreme sports like bungee jumping and skydiving. Hiking and mountain biking are popular pastimes at **Red Rock Canyon** and **Valley of Fire**, two of the best spots around to take in Nevada's stunning natural beauty. Lake Mead is a destination for water sports and fishing. Golf is popular, with over three dozen courses in the area.

Swimming is an adventure at many casinos, with lush, feature-packed facilities. Spas are similarly over-the-top, and like the advent of the celebrity chef, they are a recent phenomenon that's part and parcel of the upscaling of Las Vegas.

Shopping

In retrospect, you have to wonder why it took Vegas so long to offer so many ways for its visitors to spend money. High-end shopping is natural fit, as evidenced by the array of boutiques from haute designers, like Chanel, Prada, Hermes, Manolo Blahnik, Jimmy Choo, Oscar de la Renta, Jean-Paul Gaultier and more. Many casinos have elaborately themed malls – the **Forum Shops at Caesars** (*see photo below*) and the **Grand Canal Shoppes** at the Venetian are legitimate attractions in and of themselves. But you don't have to be a high roller to shop in Vegas – we'll show you outlets with name brands for less.

Websites in this Book

All casino and hotel web sites are given in Chapter 6, *Best Sleeps & Eats*. For any other business or facility listed in this book, we've compiled all those websites for you at **www.thebestoflasvegas.us**.

3. GREAT ONE-DAY PLANS

We've organized three **one-day plans** to help you experience the absolute best, no matter how long you're spending in Sin City. We'll show you how to see the best of the Strip or vintage Vegas in a single day. Whatever brings you here, spending a single day will only leave you begging for more.

Nonetheless we've put together several quick itineraries guaranteed to wow you. These one-day plans focus on sightseeing, a full day's worth of fun without necessitating a single wager. You can gamble whenever the mood hits, of course, but remember that extended sessions limit your ability to see everything in a single day.

THE VERY BEST OF LAS VEGAS

If you haven't been to Vegas before, **start here**. This itinerary can be enjoyed on foot, by taxi, or in your car, although we prefer walking, weather permitting. There's too much to see to worry about driving perpetually-congested Las Vegas Blvd., and taxis use back roads that save time at the expense of Strip views.

Start your day in Sin City at the **Paris Las Vegas**. Out of all the Vegas casinos paying homage to another city, none embraces its theme with such *joie de vivre*. It's an excellent choice for breakfast. Le Village Buffet ($12.95) offers hand-made crêpes, while JJ's Boulangerie, Le Notre and Le Creperie all have heavenly pastries. City landmarks like L'Arc de Triomphe and the Louvre are recreated inside and out. Skip the Eiffel Tower Experience; the view from the top, while impressive, is neither the best in town nor the cheapest – especially during the day. The wait is usually too long to justify this if you only have one day in town. *Info: Paris Las Vegas* - 3655 Las Vegas Blvd. S., between Flamingo and Harmon. Tel. 702/946-7000.

Head south to the New York-New York. Follow signs to the **Roller Coaster at New York-New York**. This 4,777-foot coaster is a thriller, reaching a top speed of 67mph as it swoops and zooms around the faux skyscrapers of the hotel towers. It'll put the fear of God in you with a 180-degree heartline twist, a 540-degree spiral and a harrowing 144-foot drop. This intense ride is also quite long – two minutes and 45 seconds. After you ride, consider

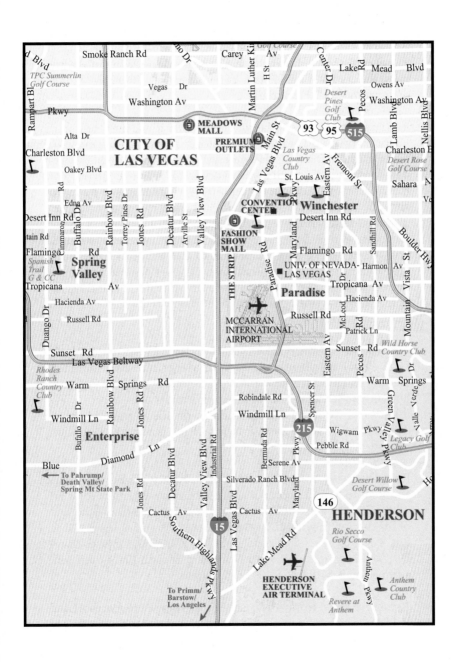

an inexpensive lunch at the **ESPN Zone**. *Info: New York-New York* - 3790 Las Vegas Blvd. S. at Tropicana. Tel. 702/740-6969. Roller Coaster open 11am-11pm Sun-Thu, 10:30am-midnight Fri-Sat. Tickets are $14 for the first ride, $7 for re-rides, $25 for an all-day pass. Riders must be 54" tall. *ESPN Zone* (Tel. 702/933-3776) is open from 11am-11pm daily.

Your next stop is the **Bellagio**. There's a lot to see here, but your top priority should be the Conservatory – an inviting atrium with leaping fountains and elaborately themed floral displays updated, refreshed, and changed every week or two. Be in front of the hotel on the half hour for the must-see **Fountains of Bellagio show**. In this $40 million technological masterpiece, dancing jets of water are synchronized with music: some of it cheesy, some of it evocative. *Info: Bellagio* - 3600 Las Vegas Blvd. S. at Flamingo. Tel. 702/693-7111. Free admission to Conservatory and Fountains of Bellagio. Conservatory open 24 hours. Fountains feature performances every half hour from 3pm-8pm Mon-Fri and 12pm-8pm Sat-Sun, with additional performances nightly every 15 minutes from 8pm-midnight.

Cab it about 3/4 mi. north to your next stop, the stunning **Wynn Las Vegas**. Partially obscured behind a large, forested mountain, Steve Wynn's latest opus has all the class and elegance of Bellagio, but with an understated sophistication all its own. Worth a few minutes of your time is the hotel's on-site Ferrari/Maserati dealership. Cars here are regularly sold for as much as $1 million in cash.

If you're ready to eat, consider the Country Club, which has excellent food and golf course views. Otherwise, relax for a bit with a drink at Pasasol Up/Down, a two-level bar facing the side of the mountain with the waterfalls. *Info: Wynn Las Vegas* - 3131 Las Vegas Blvd. S. at Sands. Tel. 702/770-7000. Penske-Wynn Ferrari Maserati is open 10am-9pm Mon-Sat and 10am-6pm Sun. Admission is $10, free for Ferrari owners.

Across the street from Wynn is the Strip's newest megaresort, the **Palazzo**. The Venetian's sister property was still in the process of opening at the time of writing, but should definitely be worth a few moments of your time for a walk-through, a browse through Barney's New York or one of 50 other shops or a game at the 40/40 Club. *Info: Palazzo Las Vegas* – 3325 Las Vegas Blvd. S. at Sands.

As day turns to night, cross the street to the **Mirage**. Daylight enhances the hotel's tropical atrium and aquarium. After dark it's not nearly the same. Once the sun goes down, stake out a close view of the volcano, about 10 or 15 minutes before the top of the hour. When it erupts, you'll feel the heat from the 100-foot high flames. The volcano is one of the city's signature attractions, and it's slated to get even better in 2008. Engineers are currently at the drawing board redesigning it to feature taller fireballs and more realistic lava.

If your stomach is rumbling, the Carnegie Deli offers gluttonous sandwiches. *Info: Mirage* - 3400 Las Vegas Blvd. S., between Flamingo and Spring Mountain. Tel. 702/791-7111. Volcano

ALTERNATIVE PLAN

Many casino malls offer highly coveted brand names, unique showcase restaurants, and sometimes even a free attraction or two. They're a great way to witness the excess of Las Vegas while avoiding the desert heat. The highest of the high-end shopping can be found at Via Bellagio and the Wynn Esplanade. Accessible and eye-popping, the Forum Shops at Caesars Palace feature an animatronic fountain show and practically bottomless caverns for retail spelunkers. The Grand Canal Shoppes at the Venetian (*see photo below*) feature strolling musicians, gondola rides, and convincing "living statues." And since $180 for a nighttime Strip ride is a lot – you can also ride the Deuce, a double-decker circulator bus giving bird's-eye views for just $2 per ride, or $5 for an all-day pass.

erupts at the top of every hour from 6, 7 or 8 pm (depending on season) until midnight. Free admission.

Next door at **Treasure Island** is another one of Vegas' best-known attractions: *The Sirens of TI*. While it is admittedly "meh" compared to the pirate battle that preceded it, it's still fun, combining pyrotechnics, song, dance, acrobatics and gorgeous, scantily clad "sirens" who seduce a wayward pirate and his shipmates four times nightly. Check this out if time permits, but if a show's just ended, it's not worth waiting around an hour-plus for the next one. *Info: Treasure Island* – 3300 Las Vegas Blvd. S. at Spring Mountain. Tel. 702/894-7111. Show is performed nightly, every 90 minutes between 7 and 11:30pm. Free admission.

No trip to Vegas is complete without an awe-inspiring nighttime cruise down shimmering Las Vegas Boulevard. It's usually traffic-choked, partly due to rubbernecking. Open Road supports safe gawking, so let someone else do the driving. Renting a limo to tour the Strip is a viable option that can be cost-effective if you're with a group. LookTours lets you and up to five friends cruise the Strip or downtown in stretched-out luxury with a complimentary bottle of champagne. *Info: Neon Nights Limousine Tour* – Tel. 866/807-4697. Two-hour tours offered nightly Sun-Fri. Cost is $75 per person.

THE HOT SPOTS

As spectacular as the Strip is, some of the hottest party spots in town are elsewhere. That's really saying something in a town considered a 24/7 party. If you're content to leave the volcano and the fountains to the sunburned tourists in favor of **more contemporary adventures**, this is your day in Las Vegas. This itinerary is best enjoyed with your own transportation, as very few of the places you'll be visiting are within walking or cheap taxi distance. Designate a driver if you decide to take this tour pub-crawl style.

This great day starts at **Green Valley Ranch**, the stately suburban resort featured in Discovery Channel's fascinating *American Casino* reality show. It's five minutes east of the airport off I-215 (take Green Valley Pkwy. S. and make a quick right on  Paseo Verde). The Original Pancake House is a great place to fuel up for the day, as is **GVR's Feast Buffet**, one of the best buffet values in Vegas. Enjoy the pristinely manicured grounds and Tuscan influenced public areas. *Info: Green Valley Ranch* - 2300 Paseo Verde Pkwy., Henderson. Tel. 702/617-7777.

Just off I-15 on Tropicana Ave. is the **Orleans**, possibly Vegas' best-kept secret. The festive and well-executed Mardi Gras theme translates well, and the hotel appeals to locals and tourists alike with good rooms, attention to detail and diverse entertainment including touring headliners like George Carlin and Dennis Miller. Public areas are filled with murals and statues depicting Crescent City's tableaus and costumed revelers. The casino is decorated with masks and plaques from the city's many Mardi Gras krewes. Grab a drink at Big Al's Oyster Bar, the Mardi Gras Bar, or Brendan's Irish Pub. *Info: Orleans* - 4500 W. Tropicana Ave., 1 1/2 mi. west of the Strip. Tel. 702/365-7111.

Head east to Paradise and Harmon, where the **Hard Rock** awaits. This is one of the hippest and most hedonistic hotels in town, even though like the cheesy theme restaurants of the same name, the walls are plastered with obscure memorabilia like Kurt Cobain's heroin spoon. But don't let that scare you off. This place is seriously upscale and seriously debauched. Its unusual casino is round and fairly intimate, although the tradeoff is limited variety in games. The **Center Bar** is elevated to give a great vantage point for celebrity spotting. The **Pink Taco** is an excellent place to grab a fajita or margarita made from one of 60 different

ALTERNATE PLAN

One of the best restaurants in town totally overlooked by tourists is the moderately-priced Hash House A Go Go, Their innovative and improvisational twists on classic comfort dishes are served in massive portions. Keep heading west for the newest must-see Las Vegas hot spot, Red Rock, 10 miles west of the Strip in nearby Summerlin (off the 215 Beltway, exit 22). The $1 billion resort opened in April 2006 with stunning views of the Spring Mountains and the Strip. The décor is sleek and modern while embracing and repeating the strata of rock found in the mountains to the west. *Info: Hash House A Go Go* – 6800 W. Sahara Ave. Tel. 702/804-4646. *Red Rock* - 11011 W. Charleston Blvd. at the 215. Tel. 702/797-7777.

tequilas. *Info: Hard Rock* - 4455 Paradise Rd. at Harmon, 3/4 mi. east of the Strip. Tel. 702/693-5000.

Back west on Flamingo are the last two stops on this tour, right across the street from one another. First up is the Carnivale-themed **Rio**. The casino is centered around **Masquerade Village**, a shopping, dining and entertainment area. Overhead is the *Masquerade in the Sky* show, which consists of over 40 high-energy singers, dancers and acrobats performing on stage and on elaborate floats traveling 900 feet around the perimeter of the room. This is among the best free shows in Vegas, but hardly the most amazing spectacle: take the elevator up to the 51st floor to the Rio's **rooftop VooDoo Lounge**. The flair bartenders can make you a Witch Doctor, a potent potable combining four rums and tropical fruit juices. The view from here is perhaps even more striking from that of the 110-story Stratosphere tower. *Info: Rio* - 3700 W. Flamingo Rd., 3/4 mi. west of the Strip. Tel. 702/777-7777. *Masquerade in the Sky* performances are every hour from 6pm to midnight. Free admission. *VooDoo Lounge*, Tel. 702/777-7800, is open 5pm-3am, with a cover of $20 Sun-Wed, $30 Thu-Sat.

The **Palms** is among the top choices of the celebrity A-list. But there's more to the Palms than paparazzi. This is one of the best places in town to play slots, perennially winning piles of awards from the *Las Vegas Review-Journal*. You're probably not enough of a high roller to stay in the 2,900 sq. ft. **Real World Suite**, but there are some slightly less exclusive adventures here. **ghostbar**, on the  55th floor, offers 180 degree Strip views (*see photo above*).

Atop the Fantasy Tower is the world's only **Playboy Club** casino, which is admittedly more appealing in concept than execution. There's also a nightclub called **Moon** with a retractable roof and one of the hottest Tuesday parties in town. *Info: Palms* - 4321 W. Flamingo Rd., 1 mi. west of the Strip. Tel. 702/942-7777. *ghostbar* opens 8pm. Admission is $10 Sun-Thu, $25 Fri-Sat. *Playboy Club* opens at 8pm nightly. *Moon* opens at 10:30 pm Thursday through Sunday and Tuesday. Admission to both is $20-40, depending on the night.

OLD SCHOOL

Nostalgia is a powerful driving force in Las Vegas. How else can you explain Barry Manilow, Wayne Newton and all those Elvis impersonators? One by one, the venerable casinos of old have taken their final bows. While the Dunes has given way to the Bellagio and the Sands to the Venetian, there are still places where you can enjoy the **Las Vegas of days past**. Hope you were able to enjoy it while it lasted; the Stardust and New Frontier fell in 2007, with rumors constantly swirling about who's next. No car is necessary for this itinerary.

With the demise of the Stardust and Frontier in 2007 , there's not much history left on the Strip, as places like the Riviera and

Sahara don't offer much in the way of curb appeal or sightseeing. So the majority of this tour is along Fremont Street. While the Strip wants to be NYC, Rome, Paris and Venice, downtown Vegas simply wants to be Vegas.

One of the city's old-school joints, owned and operated by a true pioneer, is Jackie Gaughan's **El Cortez**. It doesn't look like much from the outside, and ok, let's be honest, it doesn't look like much from the inside either, although $20 million in recent renovations have helped. But this place has loyalists, emphasis on the loyal – it's one of the few places in town that still bears the imprint of its owner's character. Easy room offers, dirt cheap dining and player-friendly blackjack and video poker make this dive worth a recommend. *Info: El Cortez* – 600 E. Fremont St. Tel. 702/385-5200.

Downown's crown jewel, the **Golden Nugget**, has been a beacon for the past 50 years. Steve Wynn transformed it from a sawdust-

on-the-floors place to the high roller's paradise that's captured the AAA Four Diamond award every year for the past three decades. In recent years the Nugget has been sold repeatedly, yet through it all the **grand dame of Fremont Street** has maintained its impeccable reputation. Its current owners have pumped $100 million in improvements and renovations into the place, including The Tank, a stunning new swimming pool with a swim-through aquarium with sharks. *Info: Golden Nugget* - 129 E. Fremont St. Tel. 702/385-7111.

Just across Fremont Street is **Binion's**, a legendary place that's seen better days. Harrah's bought the debt-ridden casino briefly, only to strip it of the World Series of Poker and the Horseshoe brands. This place is steeped in history. Benny Binion broke ground in ways most gamblers take for granted today, including casino carpeting, comped drinks and high-limit tables. The recently-renovated casino is the draw here, epitomizing old-school Vegas. This is still one of the best spots in town to play poker, but only if you're good at it. You can enjoy a classic, classy old-Vegas dinner at **Binion's Ranch Steakhouse**, which offers better value than Strip steakhouses, a total old-school vibe and a phenomenal view. *Info: Binion's* -128 E. Fremont St. Tel. 702/380-0952. Open 24 hours. Free admission.

At the end of this four-block pedestrian paradise is the **Plaza**, a fairly historic spot.

You Won't Get the *Rain Main* Suite!

Remember in *Swingers* when Trent and Mikey try to get comped by playing dress up? Sadly, it's part of the Vegas myth. You're not going to fool the casinos just by wearing a suit. Not in the digital age, when the casinos know exactly what to give you based on how much action you give them. **Plug into this system by getting rated** when you play table games and by joining player's clubs and using the card whenever you play machine games. Keep in mind, you still won't get something for nothing.

In an absolutely awesome vantage overlooking the center of Fremont Street is **The Dome Ultra Sports Lounge**, featured in the movie *Casino* in its former incarnation as the Center Stage restaurant. The Dome offers some of the city's strongest parlay cards, a full betting station and 16 big-screen televisions. They've also got an unusual shop specializing in beef jerky. *Info: Plaza* – 1 Main Street. Tel. 702/386-2110.

Is the sun down yet? If so, be sure to catch the **Fremont Street Experience**. Sure, this tour is about the Vegas Old School, but downtown has gone back to the future with this one-of-a-kind show. All the lights in Glitter Gulch go out, and a wild six-to-nine minute themed light show is displayed on a 1,400-foot long canopy of synchronized LED modules, towering 90 feet high over a four-block length of Fremont Street. A 550,000-watt system delivers sound effects and music. *Info: Fremont Street Experience* - 111 S. 4th St. Tel. 702/678-5600. Shows every hour on the hour between 7pm and midnight.

Head back to the Strip in time for the 10pm performance of *Legends in Concert* at the semi-retro **Imperial Palace**. The IP, a bustling party joint, has a lot to offer visitors, including low limits, inexpensive rooms and the Dealertainers, celebrity impersonators who deal blackjack. But they are only a teaser for "Legends," whose rotating cast includes singing, dancing, instrument-playing versions of Elvis, Madonna, Prince, Michael Jackson and the Blues Brothers. *Info: Imperial Palace* - 3535 Las Vegas Blvd. S. between Flamingo and Sands. Tel. 702/731-3311. *Legends in Concert* (Tel. 888/777-7664) has 7:30 and 10pm shows Mon-Sat. Tickets are $49.95-59.95 adults, $34.95-44.95 kids.

End your evening in style across the street at **Caesars Palace**. In 1966 it set the standard for A-list supercasinos, with an opulent, decadent Roman Empire theme. Caesars has never looked back, expanding and modernizing to retain its elite status for four decades. Table minimums are high (the VIP Palace Court has some of the highest in the city), so low rollers should play elsewhere. But you can certainly gorge your eyes with splendor. It's like the Roman Empire never fell, with gleaming white marble statues and columns everywhere. The domed ceilings of the Palace Casino date back to the hotel's earliest days. Find your way to the perennial favorite, **Cleopatra's Barge**, for a nightcap and a rousing game of spot-the-hooker. *Info: Caesars Palace* - 3570 Las Vegas Blvd. S. at Flamingo. Tel. 702/731-7110.

4. FANTASTIC WEEKENDS IN VEGAS

A two- to four-day weekend is an optimal length of time to spend in Vegas. It's enough time to see and do a whole bunch. Vegas weekends are packed with potential, regardless of what's bringing you here. Whether a romantic getaway, a bachelor party, or a shopping binge, these suggested itineraries will help you get the most out of every minute.

Each getaway assumes Friday evening arrival and a Sunday evening departure. Three- and four-day weekends offer a king-size slice of the Vegas experience. After each Friday-Sunday plan, you'll find a **Long Weekend** section offering day and night ideas to keep you entertained beyond the first 48 hours.

Hotel Rates

In Las Vegas, room rates fluctuate wildly from one day to the next, driven by citywide occupancy trends and gaming revenue needs, since these 3,000-room-plus behemoths are filing cabinets for gamblers moreso than lodging for tourists. Weekends, special events, conventions and holidays all drive up the price of a room.

It's hard to give an accurate picture of what you'll pay in such a dynamic market, but we'll give you an idea what your *best-case scenario* is. **$** hotels can often be booked for less than $50 per night. **$$** hotels frequently go for less than $100 per night. **$$$** hotels usually start in the $100-150 range, while **$$$$** hotels rarely have rates below $150.

RECOMMENDED PLAN: Choose wisely when booking your hotel. You definitely want something comfortable and convenient. Since **weekends are busier**, expect to pay significantly more, not just for your hotel room, but at the tables. $5 minimums are rare on the Strip on weekends, and some higher-end places jack their minimums up to $15 or $20. Many of these plans can be executed much more cheaply during the week without missing out, so consider taking a few days off from work for your visit if your wallet can't handle a weekend.

VEGAS ESSENTIALS WEEKEND

What happens in Vegas stays in Vegas. You've seen the commercials. It's a mantra. And yet, ironically enough, somebody's told you wild stories of what happened to them in Vegas. And now you've decided to experience it firsthand. And while Las Vegas has an anything-can-happen vibe, if you leave every detail of your trip to luck you will likely not have a great trip. Preparation is key! Play it safe and book hotels and shows in advance.

First-time Vegas visitors should **book a casino hotel on the Strip**. There's just something about being in the middle of all the action. Despite the overall upward trend of the Vegas lodging market, there are rooms in every price range on the Strip. Our top recommendations in each price range for first-time visitors are **Caesars Palace** ($$$$),

Don't Miss...

- **Fountains of Bellagio**
- **Mirage Volcano**
- **Forum Shops at Caesars**
- **The Strip after dark**
- **A big production show**
- **Wynn Las Vegas**
- **Fremont Street Experience** (for a long weekend stay)

Mirage ($$$), **Mandalay Bay** ($$$), **Flamingo** ($$) and **Imperial Palace** ($).

After checking in and stashing your stuff, explore the hotel. Find the buffet, the 24-hour coffee shop, and the exit! Casino exits are notoriously difficult to find, and you'll lose valuable time if you wander around lost every time you want to catch a taxi.

Once you get settled in, check out the Strip on foot. Be sure to catch a performance of the **Fountains of Bellagio** show. It's

particularly worthwhile at night, adding light to the synchronized mix of music and water. Head back to your hotel and change into something nice, because you're going out on the town.

Strip hotels feature lounges, bars, performers and nightclubs, often under the same roof. If you've got the money, a great way to spend your first night in town is to grab a few drinks at a lounge, play some craps or blackjack to get into a social mood, and then visit a burlesque club. This **new Vegas trend** combines the elegance of a cabaret,

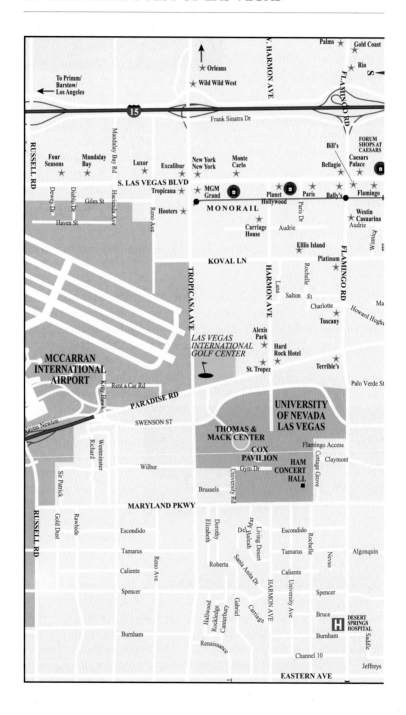

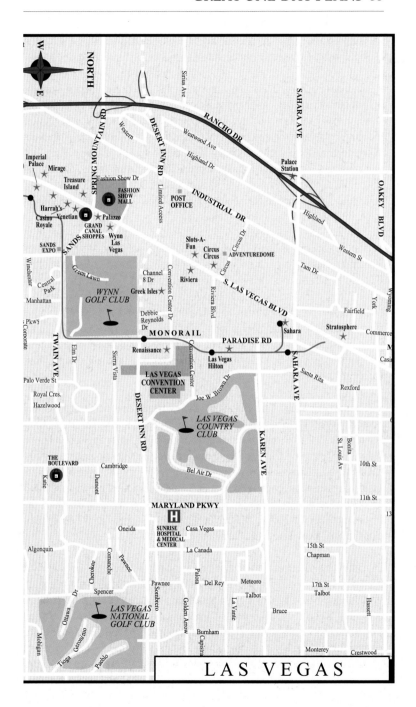

the sex appeal of a strip joint and the social potential of a dance club. Some of the best choices for this kind of evening are:

• **Mandalay Bay.** Red Square, with its headless Lenin statue, offers 100 different kinds of vodka and every imaginable martini. Classy, intimate and deliciously retro, Ivan Kane's Forty Deuce features DJs and classically trained dancers whose striptease is accompanied by a three-piece jazz band every 90 minutes. It's easy to miss, by design, located behind the escalators to Mandalay Place. *Info: Mandalay Bay* – 3950 Las Vegas Blvd. S. at Russell. Tel. 702/632-7777. *Ivan Kane's Forty Deuce* (Tel. 702/632-9442) is open 10pm 'til dawn Thu-Mon. Cover is $25.

• **ti – Treasure Island.** While many bemoan the scrubbing of Treasure Island's pirate motif, we like the party vibe here. The Breeze Bar features Bobby Barrett's dead-on Sinatra impersonation. The always-packed Tangerine offers burlesque shows every hour from 10:45pm to 1:15am. Its outdoor patio boasts a fantastic view of the Strip. *ti – Treasure Island* – 3300 Las Vegas Blvd. S. at Spring Mountain, Tel. 702/894-7111. *Tangerine* is open 5:30pm-4am Tue-Sat. Cover is $20 for men, $10 for women, free for hotel guests.

• **Caesars Palace.** The Shadow Bar tantalizes with silhouetted dancers who gyrate toplessly behind curtains and talented flair bartenders. The Pussycat Dolls Lounge at PURE nightclub is the Vegas outpost of the Hollywood burlesque whose cast has featured virtually every known celebrity with two Y chromosomes. They demonstrate the art of the tease every half hour from 10:30pm on. *Info: Caesars Palace* – 3570 Las Vegas Blvd. S. at Flamingo Tel. 702/731-7110. *PURE* and *Pussycat Dolls Lounge* are open 8pm-4am Tue-Sat. Cover is $20.

Hopefully you made it to your room not much worse for wear, as it's easy to get caught in the moment your first night in Vegas. If you're not hurting your first morning, you weren't trying hard enough. Recovery, like most things, is better at poolside. Vegas pools are generally open from March to November, but some are year round. During the day, they are usually the hotels' centers of activity. The Mandalay Bay, Mirage and Flamingo all have beautiful tropically land-scaped pools. Be sure to stay hydrated! At some point you'll to be ready to refuel. The casino coffee shops offer casual dining at all hours. Grab a bite at the one at your hotel, or venture elsewhere if you want to check out the competition.

Ease back into life by visiting one of the Strip's many themed shopping malls. The first stop should be the recently-expanded **Forum Shops** at Caesars Palace. The Forum Shops are impressive, with decadent, ornate Roman touches throughout, a trompe l'oeil ceiling and 160 shops. Head all the way down to the Fall of Atlantis Show. Ev-

Best Vegas Podcast

iTunes users embrace the brave new world of podcasts, MP3s posted on the Internet for on-demand listening. Of several podcasts covering Las Vegas, one is clearly the best of the bunch: **Five Hundy By Midnight**, hosted by a charming, soft-spoken, and offbeat couple from the Twin Cities. This show includes everything from Vegas news and trip reports to late-night hooker hunts and fantasy concepts like their beloved "Monkey Poker Dome." It's hard to describe and even harder to resist. Download their show from iTunes or on their website, www.fivehundybymidnight.com.

ery hour on the hour this fountain and 50,000 gallon salt-water aquarium comes alive with a special effects-laden battle between *les enfants terribles* of King Atlas over the fate of the sunken city. *Info: Forum Shops at Caesars Palace* - 3500 Las Vegas Blvd. S. at Flamingo. Tel. 702/893-4800. Open 10am-11pm Sun-Thu and 10am-midnight Fri-Sat. *Fall of Atlantis* – shows are every hour on the hour. Free admission.

While you're here you should take in one of the big-production extravaganzas for which Vegas is known. The first name in the business is Cirque du Soleil. And of its five Vegas shows, **Mystère** is a great place to start. Cirque began 20 years ago as a humble troupe of bohemian street performers in Montreal, and while each subsequent show goes further over the top, this is probably the Strip's purest iteration of Cirque's original vision. Mystère has won "Best Production Show" honors from the *Review-Journal*

"The $20 Trick"

If you're interested in upgrading your room, try the so-called "$20 Trick." When you're checking in, tuck a folded $20 bill under your credit card as you hand it to the clerk. Ask if any upgrades are available. If affirmative, you just got upgraded for a mere $20, and looked smooth doing it. If there's nothing available, you keep your money and dignity. Supply and demand determine the outcome, so don't expect an upgrade to a popular hotel's suite on a holiday weekend. If you have your heart set on a particular room, don't leave it to chance. Book what you want since this trick is no guarantee!

eight times, but thanks to the novelty of the newer productions, tickets are usually easier to get than for KÀ and O. *Info: Treasure Island* - 3300 Las Vegas Blvd. S. at Spring Mountain. *Mystère* (Tel. 800/392-1999) performances are 7 and 9:30pm Sat-Wed. Tickets are $60, $75 and $95.

Another show worth checking out is the **Blue Man Group**. This trio of mute but meticulous musicians captures the colorful, imaginative and downright weird vibe that defines Vegas. They make art or music out of virtually anything. The show is a dizzying sensory overload that inspires love-it-or-hate-it reactions, but open minds usually appreciate it. This high-energy act freshened up in 2005 when it moved into a custom-built 1,760 seat theatre at the Venetian. *Info: Venetian* – 3355 Las Vegas Blvd. S. at Sands. *Blue Man Group* (Tel. 866/641-SHOW) performances at 7 and 10pm Mon, Tues, Fri, Sat, 8pm performances on Wed, Thu, Sat. Tickets are $71.50, 93.50 and $121.

Before blue men and contor-

Line Passes

If you've managed to hang on at the tables for an hour or more, ask the pit boss for a **line pass to the nightclub**. Line passes, mostly available for nightspots, coffeeshops and buffets, are among the easiest comps to get. Casinos don't mind giving them out, because they don't cost them anything.

tionists invaded the strip, Las Vegas nightlife was dominated by headliners like Siegfried and Roy, Elvis Presley and Liberace. Now, two are dead, one got eaten by a tiger. But **Barry Manilow** has still got it. The "Music and Passion" show at the Hilton is the kind of nostalgia performance that actually makes you understand the artist's original appeal. Manilow has aged far better than Wayne Newton. Don't forget to check out the Elvis statue by the main entrance. It was here that the King held court for the last seven years of his life. *Info: Las Vegas Hilton* – 3000 Paradise Rd., between Desert Inn and Sahara, 3/4 mi. east of the Strip. Tel. 800/222-5361. *Barry Manilow: Music and Passion* shows are at 8pm on selected nights. Check the Hilton website for show dates. Ticket prices are $95-225.

No matter what you got into last night, now is not the time to start repenting. Go get some brunch. Champagne Sunday brunches are offered by most casinos, but there is no brunch finer than **Bally's Sterling Brunch**. This sumptuous spread includes lobster, shrimp, crabs, sushi, caviar, and attentively poured Evian water and premium champagne. *Info: Bally's Las Vegas* – 3645 Las Vegas Blvd. S. at Flamingo. Tel. 702/967-7999. *Sterling Brunch* starts at 9:30am, last seating is at 1:30pm. Cost is $65 per person plus tax and tip.

Before you leave town, you've got to see Steve Wynn's newest megaresort: the opulent **Wynn Las Vegas**. Unlike the streetside attractions he built at Bellagio, Mirage and Treasure Island, you have to step inside to see the cool attractions on offer here. Enjoy the view at **Parasol Up/Down**, a beautiful two-level bar named for the colorful umbrellas hanging from the ceiling. It looks directly across the Lake of Dreams into a waterfall. *Info:Wynn Las Vegas* - 3131 Las Vegas Blvd. S. at Sands. Tel. 702/693-7111.

If you still have some time left before you need to get to the airport or hit the road, check out the **Bellagio Conservatory** or the **Flamingo Habitat.**

LONG WEEKEND

It's not a bad idea to extend a Vegas trip beyond a 48-hour banzai run, especially if this is your first time. There's a lot to see here, and while three days only scratch the surface, you see a lot more of the town at a much more leisurely pace. An extra day also gives you more freedom to explore beyond the Strip. Add these stops to your list for a third day.

At the **Rio**, every corner turned provides new opportunities for entertainment. There's a pit where bikini-clad dealers deal black-jack games. There are Bevertainers, cocktail servers who burst into song and dance routines every 20 minutes or so. If all that seems a little passive for your taste, there's the **Masquerade in the Sky parade**. You can participate, put on a costume and join performers aboard the floats. *Info: Rio* - 3700 W. Flamingo Rd., 3/4 mi. west of the Strip. Tel. 702/777-7777. *Masquerade in the Sky* performances are every hour from 6pm to midnight. Viewing the show is free, riding costs $12.95. Riders must be 36" tall.

While a few of the hotels in Vegas are more plain on the inside than their wild exteriors would indicate, the **New York-New York** delivers in evocative detail. Recreations of Central Park, Grand Central Station and the Financial District are particularly faithful, as are the 300-foot Brooklyn Bridge and 150-foot Statue

 of Liberty that face the Strip. The **Roller Coaster at New York-New York** is a thrilling way to tour the outside of the ho-tel, as the track loops around the twelve skyscrap-ers that mimic landmarks like the Chrysler Building

and the Empire State Building. *Info: New York-New York* - 3790 Las Vegas Blvd. S. at Tropicana. Tel. 702/740-6969. *Roller Coaster* open 11am-11 pm Sun-Thu, 10:30am-midnight Fri-Sat. Tickets are $14 for the first ride, $7 for re-rides, $25 for an all-day pass. Riders must be 54" tall.

A bonus night in Vegas allows a trip downtown. Do this after you've seen the Strip, so you can appreciate the differences. The *Viva Vision* show at the **Fremont Street Experience** is the most intense sensory stimulation this town has seen since Hunter S. Thompson flipped out on adrenochrome. The canopy displays different shows every hour, ranging from psychedelic to patriotic.

At the area's east end, the **Neon Museum** offers a self-guided outdoor walking tour of Vegas' unique contribution to Americana, with eleven signs displayed including the old Aladdin genie lamp and the Hacienda's Horse and Rider. Also popular are guided tours at noon and 2pm Tue-Fri. Reservations are a must! *Info: Fremont Street Experience* - Fremont St. between Main St. and Las Vegas Blvd. Tel. 702/678-5600. Shows every hour on the hour between 7pm and midnight. Free admission. *Neon Museum* – 702/387-NEON. Open 24 hours, free admission. Guided tours are a suggested $15 donation per person.

LOVE, VEGAS-STYLE WEEKEND

Las Vegas is the "marriage capital of the world." Everyone from Warren Beatty to Elvis Presley has married here. Some of them have worked out better than others. But you don't need to say "I do" to take advantage of all Sin City's opportunities for *amore*. Most Vegas hotels offer **Jacuzzi suites**, perfect for lovers. Some of these fantastic rooms even boast great Strip views right from the tub. The most romantic hotels in town are Paris Las Vegas ($$$), Venetian ($$$$), Bellagio ($$$$), Red Rock ($$$$) and Mandalay Bay ($$$).

Paris Las Vegas is one of the most beautiful spots in town, inside and out. Walk through the lovely shopping arcades inside the hotel, and outside through iconic landmarks like 2/3-scale Arc de Triomphe and the Louvre. The half-scale **Eiffel Tower Experience** gives a remarkable 360 degree Strip view, right from its

center. Take the elevator up 460 feet, where tour guides answer questions and point out landmarks. The 11th floor restaurant features Continental cuisine and sweeping fountain views. Want to pop the question here? You wouldn't be the first, but what a way to get a "yes." *Info: Paris Las Vegas* - 3655 Las Vegas Blvd. S., between Flamingo and Harmon. Tel. 702/946-7000. *Eiffel Tower Experience* open 9:30am-12:30am, weather permitting. Admission is $9, $7 for seniors and kids 6-12.

The **Bellagio** offers plenty for romantics. The Fountains are a no-brainer, but the main lobby reveals **Fiori Di Como**, a massive 70'x30' Dale Chihuly sculpture containing over 2,000 hand-blown glass flowers. The **Bellagio Gallery of Fine Art** rotates pieces from its $300 million permanent collection. This is a serious gallery. Recent exhibitions have featured the work of Warhol, Monet, Picasso and Van Gogh. *Info: Bellagio* - 3600 Las Vegas Blvd. S. at Flamingo. Tel. 702/693-7871. *Bellagio Gallery of Fine Art* (Tel. 702/693-

7871) is open 10am-6pm Sun-Thu, 10 am-9 pm Fri-Sat. Admission is $17, $14 for students, seniors and Nevada residents.

If the Eiffel Tower view isn't dynamic enough, you have options. Flying from McCarran, **Papillon** offers 8-10 minute helicopter rides over the Strip and Downtown. A more pricey option is a private flight including champagne and hotel pickup. *Info: Papillon* – 275 E. Tropicana Ave., 1 mi. east of the Strip. Tel. 702/736-7243. Flights leave between 6:30pm and 10:30pm. Cost is $82, $39 for kids. A private flight for up to 4 people is $375.

Don't Miss...

- **Eiffel Tower Experience**
- **Gondola rides**, either at the Venetian or on Lake Las Vegas
- **The Strip by helicopter**
- A spectacular **gourmet dinner**
- A **couples' massage**

Get up early and enjoy breakfast in bed if room service appeals to you. You don't have to wait til Sunday for a **champagne brunch** – most of the resorts, including the Paris, Planet Hollywood and Bellagio each offer this indulgence all weekend long.

The **Venetian's** romantic appeal is obvious. The canal city's Vegas namesake features many of its most recognized sights, built to full scale, plus free performances from strolling musicians and opera singers. The **Grand Canal Shoppes** feature 500,000 sq. ft. of premium shopping around a winding canal. You can take a gondola ride through the complex, though you never forget that you're inside a mall. Too bad the rides offered outdoors are kind of underwhelming as well. Quite riveting, how-

ever, are the talented **Living Statues**, who perform daily in St. Mark's Square and next to Ann Taylor. (If you're here for three days, skip the gondola ride here and take one on Lake Las Vegas instead.) *Info: Venetian* – 3355 Las Vegas Blvd. S. between Sands and Flamingo. Tel. 702/414-4469. *Grand Canal Shoppes* (Tel. 702/414-4500) open from 10am-11pm Sun-Thu and 10am-midnight Fri-Sat. Admission and entertainment are free. Living Statues perform noon-8pm daily. Gondola rides (Tel. 702/414-4300) are $12.50 outdoors, $15 indoors. Private 2-passenger rides are $50 and $60 respectively.

Part of the Vegas renaissance is the emergence of **luxurious spas**, which have popped up at all of the major casino resorts and many of the smaller ones too. Visit one of these world-class spas for an intimate couple's massage. The Venetian's **Canyon Ranch Spa** offers two-by-two aromatherapy, stone, Ayurvedic or Shirodhara massages. Tel. 702/414-3600. Other top choices include:

• Paris for Lovers ($450) at **Mandara Spa** (Paris), a 2-hour package offering a silkening body polish, pastry service while you soak in the whirlpool, and an Aromatique massage. *Info:* 3655 Las Vegas Blvd. S. Tel. 702/946-4366.

• The signature Pittura Festa ($475 per couple) treatment at the off-Strip **WELL Spa** at the new **Platinum Hotel**, which includes dual body glows and a private body painting party. *Info:* 211 E. Flamingo Road at Koval Lane. Tel. 702/636-2424.

Best Views in Vegas

• **VooDoo Lounge**, Rio
• **ghostbar**, Palms
• **Stratosphere Tower**, Stratosphere
• **Eiffel Tower Experience**, Paris
• **MIX**, THEhotel at Mandalay Bay

• The Ceremony of Love ($300-495 per couple) at **Planet Hollywood Spa by Mandara**, which combines the massage of your choice with an exotic jasmine flower bath. *Info:* 3667 Las Vegas Blvd. S. Tel. 702/758-5SPA.

Don't fret if these prices seem steep. Some **mid-market casino spas** offer some kind of couple's massage for about half the cost. Check out the Orleans, Tropicana, Imperial Palace or Euphoria – a highly rated local chain of day spas.

Las Vegas' wide array of **gourmet restaurants** includes many with enough intimacy and charm to appeal to couples. Don't miss out on the opportunity to dine in lavish surroundings unlike any you'll find at home. See the sidebar below for my top picks.

Quite a few of Las Vegas **shows** lift your heart and tantalize your nether regions. Your tastes may vary, but the three shows we suggest below are great for couples. **Zumanity** may be the best-suited of the bunch. Cirque du Soleil's productions are sensual enough to begin with, and this cabaret-style show spotlights human sexuality in all of its colors and kinks, to stimulating effect. The sublime and erotic show is not for every body, so if you are

---

Most Romantic Restaurants

• **Picasso**, Bellagio
• **Alizé**, Palms
• **Eiffel Tower Restaurant**, Paris Las Vegas
• **SW Steakhouse**, Wynn Las Vegas
• **Mix**, THEhotel

offended by topless women, transvestites, unnaturally large codpieces and dildo jugglers, move on. Best of all are the **Duo Sofas**, loveseats that offer some of the best vantage points in the house plus the chance to snuggle. *Info: New York-New York* - 3790 Las Vegas Blvd. S. at Tropicana. *Zumanity* (Tel. 702/740-6815) showtimes are 7:30 and 10:30pm Tue, Wed, Fri-Sun. Tickets are $69, $79 and $99. Duo Sofas are $129 per person.

Folies Bergère has been a Vegas fixture since 1959, featuring beautiful showgirls, elaborate sets and lavish costumes. Featured acts rotate over the years, but the general idea remains the same: beautiful dancers performing fast-paced and seamless production numbers. Its setting in Tropicana's Tiffany Theater is definitely showing its age, and it lacks the technical wizardry of some other productions. There is something to be said for traditions though. Note that there are topless and covered versions of the show. *Info: Tropicana* - 3801 Las Vegas Blvd. S. at Tropicana. *Folies Bergère* (Tel. 800/829-9034) is performed at 8:30pm Tue, Fri and at 7:30 and 10pm Mon, Wed, Thu, and Sat. 7:30pm performances are not topless. Tickets are $64.90-75.90.

The MGM Grand's skin show, **Crazy Horse Paris**, is one of the aforementioned technological marvels. This Parisian import, not to be confused with the Crazy Horse Too strip club, uses an astrological construct as its excuse to display the dancers' natural breasts in finely choreographed unison. Besides skimpy costumes, you'll get creative lighting, intricate set pieces, and special effects. This show is more high-brow than you'd expect. *Info: MGM Grand* – 3799 Las Vegas Blvd. S. at Tropicana. *Crazy Horse Paris* (Tel. 877/880-0880) is performed at 8 and 10:30pm Wed-Mon. Tickets are $49-59.

No Clocks Here ...

... Still, all of the **production shows in Las Vegas start promptly**. Plan accordingly, as it sucks maneuvering through a row of people cursing your inconsiderate name. Allow time for traffic, parking, and walking to the theater. Erring on the side of caution preserves your karma and gives you the chance to enjoy a pre-show drink.

On your last day in town, you'll be a little more comfortable and well-versed in the Strip's offerings. This is a good opportunity to explore some of the other Strip hotels. The **Mirage** is particularly lovely. Behind the check-in is a 20,000 gallon aquarium filled with over 1,000 colorful, unusual creatures, including sharks. Across the way is an atrium whose 90 ft. high glass dome houses a lush paradise recreating a tropical rainforest. The South Seas theme is carried out in many areas of the hotel's beautiful interior, including the elaborate casino. *Info: Mirage* - 3400 Las Vegas Blvd. S., between Flamingo and Spring Mountain. Tel. 702/791-7111.

LONG WEEKEND

Return to the **Bellagio.** See the Conservatory if you haven't already. Follow the smell of heaven to **Jean-Philippe Patisserie**. There you'll find the world's largest chocolate fountain, pump-

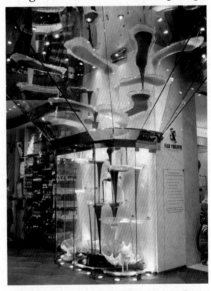

ing over two tons of molten white, milk and dark chocolate from the ceiling to the floor, through a series of 25 hand-crafted bowls. It's safely behind glass, so don't even think about pulling an Augustus Gloop. You can, however grab a decadent dessert or savory snack from interactive stations that will satisfy any unholy craving the fountain inspires in you. Or, visit the new **Payard Patisserie & Bistro** at Caesars Palace for the city's only dessert tasting menu. *Info: Bellagio* - 3600 Las Vegas Blvd. S. at Flamingo. Tel. 702/693-7111. *Jean-Philippe Patisserie* is open 7am-11pm, until midnight on Friday and Saturday. *Caesars Palace* – 3570 Las Vegas Blvd. S. at Flamingo. *Payard Patisserie* (Tel. 877/346-4642) hours were not available at press time. The restaurant is open for breakfast, lunch and dinner.

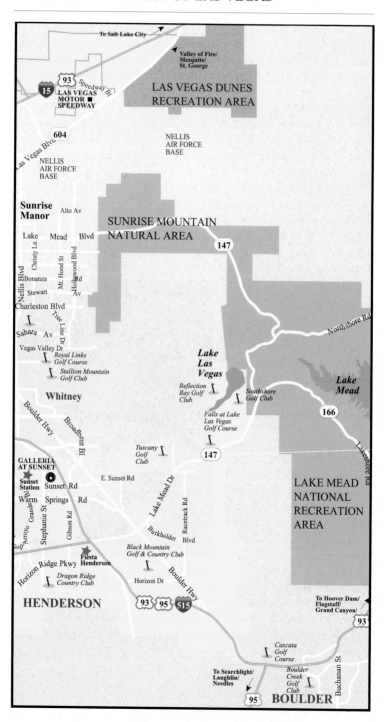

A half hour's drive from the Strip is **Lake Las Vegas**. This full resort community has Tuscan-inspired architecture, lush green fairways and multi-million dollar homes surrounding the placid 320-acre lake. Its views are some of the best in the entire valley. The resort includes golf, tennis, and gambling, but lovers will appreciate the **gondola rides**. The gondolas at the Venetian are all well and good, but you're in the middle of a chlorinated mall fountain. The open sky, serene water and mountain scenery make this a much more authentic experience. Book a gourmet dinner cruise, and you'll enjoy a savory meal served on the finest crystal, china and silver. Picnic cruises, as well as champagne and chocolate cruises, are also available.

Admittedly, Lake Las Vegas is fairly remote, but the presence of **free live jazz on the waterfront on weekends** sweetens the deal. *Info: Gondolas at Lake Las Vegas* – 220 Grand Mediterra, Henderson. Tel. 877/4-GONDOLA. Open 11am-midnight daily. Cruises are $135-395 per couple.

Gentlemen, you've sold your significant other on a Las Vegas vacation by playing up its fantastic shopping. Why not suck it up and join her for some of it? The **Esplanade** at the Wynn is haute couture at its haughtiest: the only stateside retail establishments of Oscar de la Renta and Jean-Paul Gaultier can be found here, along with a veritable who's who of fashion. The benefit of taking her shopping at the Esplanade is that its prices are so insanely high that you probably won't have to actually buy anything. If you're actually looking to take something home, the **Forum Shops** (*photo at right*)and **Grand Canal Shoppes** are high-end, but accessible. The Stratosphere recently renovated and renamed its 107th-floor lounge, **Romance at Top of the World**. The sweeping view alone lends itself to amorous ambitions, and they've enhanced it with mood lighting and candles. Live jazz trios and DJs provide tunes.

For true intimacy, private seating is available with Strip views and plush couches, perfect for bottle service and snuggling. *Info: Stratosphere* – 2000 Las Vegas Blvd S. north of Sahara. *Romance at Top of the World* (Tel. 702/380-7764) is open from 4pm-1am Sun-Thu, until 2am Fri-Sat. No cover.

If a day at Lake Las Vegas and shopping isn't your thing, how about this? If you can handle a pre-dawn wakeup, a short drive can yield an unforgettable view. Pack binoculars, champagne and OJ and take Lake Mead Blvd. (Highway 147) east to the edge of the Las Vegas Valley. The road curves through switchbacks, rising to pass between **Sunrise** and **Frenchman Mountains**. From these desert peaks 4,052 feet up, you can sip mimosas with your sweetheart while watching the early morning sun paint the casinos in colors you'll never see another time of day.

In the evening, head to **Peppermill's Fireside Lounge**, named **one of the top ten makeout bars in the country** by *Nerve* magazine. The low-lit and cozy atmosphere focuses on the eponymous fire pit. Lovers of a certain age can relive their adolescence at the last drive-in movie theater in town, the **Century Las Vegas 6**, near Fiesta Rancho. *Info: Peppermill's Fireside Lounge* – 2985 Las Vegas Blvd. S., at Convention Center. Tel. 702/735-4177. Open 24 hours. Free admission. *Century Las Vegas 6 Drive-In* – 4150 W. Carey Ave., North Las Vegas. Tel. 702/646-3565. Showtimes vary. Admission is $6, $4 on Tuesdays.

MAXIMUM PARTY WEEKEND

Las Vegas is to inhibitions what prom night is to virginity: things get lost. Las Vegas is a place to go off-script and get out of character. For many people, this means spending the weekend in a state of intoxication, **partying from dusk til dawn**. With Vegas' open container laws and 24-hour liquor licenses, you can understand why! Read on to find Sin City's best parties.

Many of the hot party places are located off-Strip, but you're still going to want easy Strip access, so avoid the neighborhood casinos. Off-strip or downtown hotels are OK. A cab ride is a cab ride, and you certainly won't be driving on this trip. The **best party hotels** in Vegas are the Palms ($$$), Hard Rock ($$$), Rio ($$), Treasure Island ($$) and the Stratosphere ($).

> ## Don't Miss ...
>
> • **Rehab pool party** at the Hard Rock
> • Harrah's **Carnaval Court**
> • Your choice of **A-list nightclubs**

If you get into Vegas before the sun goes down, **happy hour** is in order. One of the best ways to party on the cheap in this town is to take advantage of SpyOnVegas.com's Open Bar series, where every weekday a different bar hosts an event with a sponsored bar, where drinks featuring a particular liquor are on the house. The lineup changes every week, but the summer tends to feature pool parties with big-name performers at the Hard Rock's pool. *Info:* Check SpyOnVegas.com for details.

Some of our other favorites include **McCormick & Schmick's** (335 Hughes Center Dr., just off Flamingo and Paradise. Tel. 702/836-9000) for its renowned $1.95 bar menu, the **Triple 7 Brewpub** (Main Street Station, 200 N. Main St. Tel. 702/387-1896) for its microbrews, and **Firefly on Paradise** (3900 Paradise Rd., between Flamingo & Sands. Tel. 702/369-3971) for half price drinks to accompany the best tapas in the city.

Further down the stretch of Flaming known as Restaurant Row, **The Tillerman** (2245 E. Flamingo. Tel. 702/731-4036) offers half price bottles of wine and bar food. The Hard Rock's **Pink Taco** (4455 Paradise Rd. at Harmon): has deals on beers, margaritas and appetizers.

Check into your hotel and explore. While it's tempting to start throwing down money and quaffing the free drinks ASAP, you don't want to be burned out, blotto and broke before midnight. Pre-game but pace yourself. You've got a lot of weekend ahead of you! And tonight, you need to be 100%, because you're going

Best Ways Past the Velvet Rope

• The most iron-clad way to ensure entrance is to **reserve bottle service.**
• **Dress to impress.** No jeans, sneakers, t-shirts, athletic wear, Timberlands, baseball caps, etc., although the dress code varies by club and night. Call beforehand to verify.
• **Bring girls.** The prettier, the better. Groups of men have a real hard time getting into most places. Clubs aim for a 4:1 ratio in favor of females.
• **Arrive early.** As clubs fill up, doormen are more selective.
• If you're gambling where you'll be clubbing, **ask the pit boss or host for a line pass.**
• "Front-of-line" passes, which truthfully only get you into a shorter line, are available on VEGAS.com. You'll pay a $20 premium. Do not, however, buy line passes from a cabbie.
• **Don't club-hop.** $20-30 covers and long lines make this a really bad idea.
• If all else fails, you can try **tipping the bouncer.** Don't even think about trying this with less than a $20.

to one of the hottest clubs in the city. If you've got the scratch, consider taking advantage of **bottle service.** For $300 and up, depending on the club and the beverage, you can reserve your own table for four, complete with liquor, mixers and accoutrements. It may seem like a lot of money, but it can be a real conversation starter and attention getter if you're trying to flaunt and flirt.

The newest celebrity-approved hotspot in town is **Social House,** an overpriced but ultrachic sushi restaurant with prime real estate on the edge of the Treasure Island lagoon. The Palms maintains its Hollywood cache, as always, with the new **Playboy Club.** And some of the world's most in-demand DJs perform at the Hard Rock's **Body English,** especially at the Godskitchen party promoted by London's Ministry of Sound on Wednesdays. Friday and Sunday parties feature especially attractive promos for ladies. *Info: Treasure Island* – 3300 Las Vegas Blvd. S. at Spring Mountain. *Social House* (Tel. 702/894-7223) is open 5pm-midnight, with late night dining until 2am Thu-Sun. *Palms* - 4321 W.

Flamingo Rd., 1 mi. west of the Strip. *Playboy Club* (Tel. 702/942-6832) opens at 8pm nightly. Admission is $20-40, depending on the night, and may include Moon admission as well. *Body English* (Tel. 702/693-4000) at the Hard Rock Hotel, 4455 Paradise Rd. at Harmon, is open 10:30pm-4am Wed -Sun. Cover is $30 for men, $20 for women.

You can't talk about Vegas nightlife without discussing the **Palms**, home to wildest nightspots in town. George Maloof's hip off-Strip casino has long been another favorite with the celebrity elite. **Rain** is the Palms' signature nightclub. Pyrotechnics and special lighting effects dazzle onlookers, and surprises here include an infamous night where Britney Spears showed up and shocked by getting on stage to debut "I'm a Slave 4 U." Ah, those innocent days when Britney shocked us with her music. *Info: Palms* - 4321 W. Flamingo Rd., 1 mi. west of the Strip. *Rain* (Tel. 702/940-7246) opens 11pm Thu-Sat. Admission to each is $10 Thu, $25 Fri-Sat.

The Venetian's entry into the superclub sweepstakes is the ambitious and popular **Tao**, a 42,000 sq. ft. complex with a great restaurant, hip ultralounge, banging nightclub with two rooms of music and a lushly landscaped outdoor terrace with a pool. The décor is just as pan-Asian as the food, with the lounge boasting a hand-carved Buddha statue and a Koi-filled infinity pool. *Info: Venetian* – 3355 Las Vegas Blvd. S. between Sands and Flamingo. *Tao* (Tel. 702/388-8588) lounge opens at 5pm nightly, nightclub opens at 10pm Thu-Fri, 9:30pm Sat. Cover for the nightclub is $20, $30 for men.

Plan to sleep in and sleep it off. A couple glasses of water before bed will ease the morning after. Still, draw the shades unless you want to spontaneously combust at the unforgiving desert sunrise. Spend some time by the pool if that'll make you feel better. The Palms and Hard Rock are fantastic examples of aquatic excess, each featuring lounging hardbodies galore and swim-up blackjack tables. (Note that both pools, like most in this town, shutter up during the winter months.)

Ready to venture out into the public again? Time for some *al fresco* dining and drinking. One of our favorite places to sit and sip is **Carnaval Court** at Harrah's. This festive, brightly colored open-air venue features flair bartenders and diverse live music including Vegas legend Cook E. Jarr. Its casual menu is one of the Strip's most affordable options, with just about everything under ten bucks. *Info: Harrah's Las Vegas* – 3475 Las Vegas Blvd. S. between Flamingo and Sands. Tel. 702/369-5000. *Carnaval Court* is open from 1pm-2am.

The newest party bar in town is right next door at the Imperial Palace. **Rockhouse bar & nightclub** opened at this space right on the sidewalk during summer 2006. Rockhouse features a Strip-side daiquiri bar, cheap bottles and a mechanical bull and bird-cage where attention whores and bachelorette parties can debase themselves. *Info: Imperial Palace* – 3535 Las Vegas Blvd. S. between Flamingo and Sands. *Rockhouse bar & nightclub* (Tel. 702/691-2909) is open from 10am-4am daily. $10 cover charge applies after 9pm Thu-Sun. $20 cover after midnight Thu-Sun.

Ultralounges may seem on the surface like every other nightclub, but generally these are better environments for mingling, chatting, and general socializing. Perhaps the highest profile ultralounge is **ghostbar**, on the 55th floor of the Palms Tower. This sleek, retro-chic nightspot features a white, silver and green palette, with lots of chrome and even a little Astroturf. ghostbar takes full advantage of its height, offering a 180 degree view from inside the club, and 270 degrees from the patio. What's more, it's surfaced with reinforced glass, allowing you a view straight down to the pool. This is one of the most difficult spots in town to get into, so arrive early. *Info: Palms* - 4321 W. Flamingo Rd., 1 mi. west of the Strip. *ghostbar* (Tel. 702/942-6832) opens 8pm nightly. Admission is $15 Sun-Thu, $25 Fri-Sat.

Even though it's a hefty cab fare from North Strip, the **Whiskey** at **Green Valley Ranch** is another highly recommended nightspot, popular with your Clooneys and DiCaprios, plus locals from upscale Henderson. Outside, the 8-acre Whiskey Beach pool area offers Strip views, fresh air and quiet conversation, even during the winter months, when it's heated. *Info: Green Valley Ranch* - 2300 Paseo Verde Pkwy., Henderson, about 10 miles southeast of the Strip. *The Whiskey* (Tel. 702/617-7560) is open 5pm-2am Sun-Thu, 6pm-3am Fri-Sat. No cover.

There are, of course, ultralounge options on the Strip. We recommend the one that started it all: **Tabú**. Open since 2002, it's still a standard bearer. This sophisticated, happening venue features distinctive touches you won't find in any ordinary bar. Things like hostess/models who mix drinks at tableside and change costumes throughout the evening. Tables with morphing images projected onto them. Bottles presented inside a large block of ice. Every nightclub likes to paint itself as revolutionary, but Tabú is genuinely innovative. And speaking of innovative, check out the new **eyecandy sound lounge & bar** at Mandalay Bay. This place features interactive lighting, visuals and messaging, plus upscale cocktail lounge chic. *Info: MGM Grand* - 3799 Las Vegas Blvd. S. at Tropicana. *Tabú* (Tel. 702/891-7254) opens at 10pm Tue-Sat. Cover is $20 Sun, Tue, Wed, Thu; and $25 Fri-Sat. *Mandalay Bay* – 3950 Las Vegas Blvd. S. at Russell. Tel. 702/632-7777. *eyecandy* is open from 6 pm to 4 am.

No self-respecting night of Las Vegas excess is complete without a drunken meal at the **Peppermill**, the landmark North Strip restaurant featured in the movie *Casino*. While this place could get by on reputation and atmosphere alone, the food is great, especially when you've got a stomach full of alcohol. Breakfast is served 24 hours, but this is hardly a greasy spoon. It's not just retro, it's vintage. *Info: Peppermill* – 2985 Las Vegas Blvd. S. at Convention Center. Tel. 702/735-4177. Open 24 hours.

Champagne brunches are a dime a dozen, but if that's a little frou frou, head down to the outstanding **Garduño's** at the Palms.

This value-priced New Mexican restaurant offers an all-you-can-eat Sunday brunch featuring breakfast food, unlimited margaritas, and a fajita bar. *Info: Palms* - 4321 W. Flamingo Rd., 1 mi. west of the Strip. *Garduño's* (Tel. 702/938-2666) serves brunch from 10:30am-3pm Sun. Cost is $14.99 per person. Note: brunch is not served at the Fiesta Rancho location.

There's only one truly appropriate way to round out a weekend of drunken madness. Go to **Rehab**. On Sundays the **Hard Rock** opens its pool to the general public for a shindig favored by the fabulous. Tanned, trim and nearly threadless girls and guys drink, dance and dive at this party, which is as wild as anything that happens here after dark. Cabanas offer misters, shade and attentive drink service, plus you get the same kind of attention you get from ordering bottle service. *Info: Hard Rock* - 4455 Paradise Rd. at Harmon, 3/4 mi. east of the Strip. Tel. 702/693-5000. *Rehab* is on Sundays during pool season (usually Apr-Oct) from noon-8pm. Cover is $30 for men, $20 for women.

LONG WEEKEND

If you're getting in on Thursday, and you'd rather sneak in a little happy-hour action at the tables than at the bar, the quiet, modern **Westin Casuarina** is your go-to. Its normal $5 minimums drop to $3 on the craps table and 25 cents on the roulette wheel. Of course, this happy hour special also includes free cocktails. *Info: Westin Casuarina* – 160 E. Flamingo, 1/2 mi. east of the Strip. 702/836-9775. Happy hour is Mon-Thu from 5-8pm.

Be sure to take advantage of Vegas' liberal open container laws while you're here. Grab a frozen daiquiri at **Fat Tuesday** and wander the Strip. Its locations include the Stratosphere, MGM Grand, Miracle Mile, and the Forum Shops at Caesars. Downtown, the otherwise unremarkable **La Bayou** has a daiquiri bar serving lethally potent frozen drinks in footballs and yards. *Info: La Bayou* – 15 E. Fremont St. Tel. 702/385-4250.

If you'll be in town til Tuesday, you'll discover that Mondays are quiet. One notable exception is the **Foundation Room**, the House of Blues' exclusive, members-only club situated high atop the Mandalay Bay. This exotic, classy, and cozy room is open to the public only once a week, and the public takes full advantage, braving long lines and exorbitant beverage prices in exchange for chill conversation and stunning Strip views. Mirage's **JET** is another worthwhile Monday option, with a popular industry night. This state of the art pleasure palace includes cryogenics, lasers, and killer sound. *Info: Mandalay Bay* – 3950 Las Vegas Blvd. S. at Russell. *Foundation Room* (Tel. 702/632-7600) is open to the public 11pm-5am Mon. Admission is $30. *Mirage* - 3400 Las Vegas Blvd. between Flamingo and Spring Mountain. *Jet* (Tel. 702/693-8300) is open 10:30pm-4:30am Fri, Sat, Mon. Admission is $30.

If none of the above fits the bill, try hipster hangouts like the **Ice House Lounge** and the **Beauty Bar** (the latter a centerpiece of the bustling new Fremont East entertainment district), as well as more esoteric spots like the eclectic **Art Bar** and neighborhood-style **Dino's Lounge**. *Info: Ice House Lounge* – 650 S. Main St. Tel. 702/315-2570. Open 10am-2am Mon-Fri, 11am-2am Sat. Cover Sat only, $10 before 11pm, $20 after. *Beauty Bar* – 517 S. Fremont St. Tel. 702/598-1965. Open 9pm-4am Sat, Sun, Tue. Open 5pm-4am Wed-Fri. Cover is $5 Fri-Sat. *Art Bar* – 1511 S. Main St. Tel. 702/437-2787. Open 2pm-6am daily. *Dino's Lounge* – 1516 Las Vegas Blvd. S. Tel. 702/382-3894. Open 24 hours.

LAST WEEKEND OF FREEDOM

Las Vegas is also the **bachelor party capital** of the world. Bottomless booze. Topless dancers. Walls of big-screen TVs showing sports. And there's even a little gambling. If there's any better place for a group of guys to send someone off in style, we'd like to know about it. A bachelor party takes preparation and leadership. If you're the best man, be prepared for some cat herding as you keep your boys on schedule and on plan.

Quite a few bachelor parties will pack a bunch of guys into a single room. You're going to need a solid base of operations with plenty of space. (The standard rooms at the **Rio** ($$), **Venetian**

Don't Miss ...

• Lap dances for the groom at one of the hottest strip clubs in the world
• The full-on **Vegas steakhouse experience**
• The game of your choice at the **ESPN Zone**

($$$$), **Palazzo** ($$$$) and **THEhotel at Mandalay Bay** ($$$$) are well suited for this use.) Be aware that most hotels have an occupancy limit of 4 people to a room, but odd man out won't necessarily have to sleep on the floor. Call the front desk and ask for a rollaway. No budget-priced Vegas hotels are a great choice for a bachelor party.

Before you leave, make a dinner reservation for your first night in town. If everyone's on different flights, schedule it late enough that everyone can attend. Vegas overflows with gourmet rooms, and these steakhouses are an excuse to get dressed up and consume large cuts of red meat. Astoundingly, the best in town is the **Circus Circus Steak House**. Ordinarily a bachelor party wouldn't be caught dead in this garish Raoul Duke nightmare of screaming children and terrifying clowns, but its steakhouse is an oasis of Old Vegas class, serving up big cuts of juicy, perfectly-prepared steak at surprisingly low prices. *Info: Circus Circus* – 2880 Las Vegas Blvd. S., between Convention Center and Sahara. *The Steak House* (Tel. 702/794-3767) is open 5-10pm Sun-Fri, 5-11pm on Sat.

If you're trying to go in the opposite direction and eat the most over-the-top steak dinner imaginable, head to **Michael's** at the South Point, transplanted when Harrah's bought the Barbary Coast. Under stained glass, this velvet and mahogany 50-seat gourmet room complements its steaks with crudités, flashy tableside preparation, and chocolate-dipped fruit brought after the meal. The chateaubriand is a signature, and you're unlikely to find a better one anywhere. This meal is a once-in-a-lifetime experience, and certainly a better meal than anything your buddy's fiancée can make. *Info: South Point* – 9777 Las Vegas Blvd. S., at Silverado Ranch. Tel. 702/796-7111. *Michael's* offers two seatings nightly, at 6 or 6:30 and 9 or 9:30pm.

Have some BAM! with your beef at Emeril's **Delmonico Steakhouse** at the Venetian. Patiently aged beef is Creole-seasoned. Try the signature bone-in rib, or start with superb French onion soup – topped with a homemade English muffin and Swiss cheese. Now that's multilateralism for you. Great desserts are Emeril's trademark. The restaurant's wine cellar boasts over 17,000 bottles and has received the Award of Excellence from *Wine Spectator* magazine. *Info: Venetian* – 3355 Las Vegas Blvd. S. at Sands. Tel. 702/414-3737. *Delmonico Steakhouse* serves dinner from 5-10pm Sun-Thu, closing a half hour later on weekends. Lunch is also served from 11:30am-2pm daily.

After the tenderloin, it's time for breasts. No bachelor party would be complete without strippers, and luckily, Las Vegas has almost as many places to see "shoe models" as places to buy shoes. Whichever you choose, bring lots of $20s for lap dances and lots of singles for tips. Have the cash in hand prior to arrival. Strip club ATM surcharges run $6-8.

There seems to be a consensus about the city's best strip club: **Spearmint Rhino.** An unlimited supply of gorgeous women, plus a full menu. **Scores** draws a loyal following thanks to its notoriety from its NYC location. Claiming to be the world's largest strip club, **Sapphire** is an upscale option with a more understated feel than the Rhino, aimed more at conventioneers. **Minxx** opened recently with strong synergy with pornmakers Vivid Video, but achieved more notoriety as the site of the Pacman Jones shooting. *Info: Spearmint Rhino* – 3344 Highland Dr., 1/2 mi. west of the Strip, between Sahara & Spring Mountain. Tel. 702/796-3600. Open 24 hours. Cover is $20. *Scores* – 3355 Procyon St. at Desert Inn, 1/2 mi. west of the Strip. Tel. 702/367-4000. Open 24 hours. Cover is $30. *Sapphire* – 3025 S. Industrial Rd., 1/2 mi. west of the Strip,

between Sahara and Spring Mountain. Tel. 702/892-9458. Open 24 hours. Cover is $30. *Minxx* – 4636 Wynn Rd. between Tropicana and Flamingo. Tel. 702/889-6469. Open 24 hours. Cover is $30.

Hopefully you still have some money left, and have washed most of the glitter and stripper perfume off yourself. Grab breakfast or lunch and visit a **sports book**. Games from all sports are displayed on multiple screens, and you can bet on just about any of them. Put $11 down to win $10 on the game of your choice, get a drink ticket and sit down to watch. Some of the best sports books in town include the MGM Grand's massive facility, with 44 TVs (including three 12'x16' behemoths). The Hilton and Caesars books have also been consistent favorites for years. The Mandalay Bay is another great book, thanks to the wide array of prop bets and high betting limits.

Just Say No to Cabbies

Often when you tell a cab driver to take you to a particular strip club, he'll try to change your mind (with some ridiculous BS story) and lure you to a strip club of his recommendation. **Always insist on your original choice!** These cabbies get big kickbacks from those strip clubs for each guest they bring, and it's usually seedy little places that bribe cabbies.

There are places other than the book to watch sports. Head over to the **ESPN Zone** at the New York-New York. It features comfortable booths where you can choose whatt to watch on your own private television, plus individual recliners with excellent views of communal screens. You'll find 165 TVs in all. There's just something about sitting in a La-Z-Boy and having someone bring you beers and fried food. *Info: New York-New York - 3790 Las Vegas Blvd. S. at Tropicana. ESPN Zone* (Tel. 702/933-3776) is open from 11am-11pm daily.

Saturday should be your big night on the town. What better way to declare your presence than from the comfort of a **limousine**? Limos are everywhere in this town, and the law of supply and demand keeps prices low. You can rent one for as little as $35 an hour and pimp around the Strip. You'll feel like a player, avoid the hassles of driving or taxis, and be able to use it to your advantage with the ladies. We've got a full listing of limo services in Chapter 6.

Several places are excellent pre-game choices. **Jimmy Buffett's Margaritaville** has been a cornerstone in the Flamingo's attempt to draw in a younger crowd. It's been pretty successful too. Its mix of a festive patio, imaginative drinks, live music and a diverse fun-loving crowd makes this three-level complex a great choice. *Info: Flamingo Las Vegas - 3555 Las Vegas Blvd. S. at Flamingo. Jimmy Buffett's Margaritaville* (Tel. 702/733-3302) is open 11am-2am Sun-Thu, 2:30am Fri-Sat. No cover.

Strippers Only ... Strip!

Strippers are not prostitutes. They won't go home with you. They won't sleep with you. It's only your wallet she's interested in. **Prostitution is illegal in Las Vegas and the rest of Clark County**. Same goes for those "hot girls delivered to your hotel room" you'll see advertised on trucks and the R-rated flyers handed out by enterprising "porn slappers," as they're known. They're advertising strippers, not sex. If you really want to get a hooker, you'll have to head out to Pahrump, an hour's drive west. Just manage your expectations. Remember, if they were pretty they'd be dancing.

So not everybody likes Jimmy Buffett. In fact, lots of people kind of hate the guy. Fair enough. Head up the block to Treasure Island and **Kahunaville**. It sounds like a ripoff but it's actually more like an indoor Carnaval Court, with the same island party atmosphere. The draws include dueling pianos, flair bartenders, live entertainment and poolside dining. *Info: Treasure Island - 3300 Las Vegas Blvd. S. at Spring Mountain. Kahunaville* (Tel. 702/894-7390) is open 11am-3am. No cover.

If you want to party like a local, go a block east of the Strip to the unassuming **Ellis Island Brewery & Casino** on Koval Lane, where one of the city's most infamous karaoke lounges features

Avoid the Big Games

You might think Vegas would be a great place to be during the NCAA tournament or Super Bowl. And it can be, but at a price. Hotel rooms and table minimums skyrocket. Sports books and bars crowd up. The ESPN Zone insists on a $10 minimum purchase per hour, per person during these events. One more consideration especially for bachelor parties: Vegas turns into a citywide sausage party. Schedule accordingly.

affordable drunken debauchery and hilariously bad singing – it's one part comedy and two parts terror. It gets wild here just about every night. *Info: Ellis Island* – 4178 Koval Lane. Tel. 702/833-8901. Karaoke Lounge open from 9pm to 3am.

On your last day in town, try to make it **downtown**. By now your bankroll is probably mostly depleted, and the casinos here offer low limits, usually $3-5. But you can ruin more than just your wallet along Fremont Street. See the sidebar below!

LONG WEEKEND

Elsewhere, bachelor parties are one-night affairs. Here, they can be whole weekends. But sometimes two days just isn't enough. But can you really extend a bachelor party beyond 48 hours, without having to bury a hooker in the desert? Sure. If cigars are your thing, head over to the Paris Las Vegas and check out **Napoleon's**, a lounge featuring dueling pianos and a cigar humidor. At the new Palazzo, Jay-Z's **40/40 Club** is a high-end sports bar before transforming into a luxury nightclub. *Info: Paris Las Vegas* - 3655 Las Vegas

Deep-Fried WHAT?

With its tight payback, the downtown **Mermaids Slot Lounge**, 32 E. Fremont St., is a crummy place to play. But there is good news: it's also a crummy place to eat! Its snack bar offers Twinkies and Oreos – battered, deep fried and topped with chocolate sprinkles and powdered sugar. For 99 cents, you get your choice of these belly bombs. The Oreos are so sweet they're practically inedible; the Twinkies on the other hand are almost tasty.

Blvd. S., between Fla-
mingo and Harmon. Tel.
702/946-7000. *Napoleon's*
is open from 6pm-2am
Sun-Thu, 5pm-3am Fri-
Sat. *Palazzo* – 3325 Las Vegas Blvd S. at Sands. *40/40
Club* hours and cover not
available at press time.

Las Vegas is a great town for **golf** as well, with over 40 courses.
Two things to keep in mind: first, courses here are fairly expensive compared to elsewhere. Second, the weather! Temperatures
regularly top 110 degrees in the summer, which takes the fun out
of chasing errant drives. If you want to golf in the summer, you
need to get yourself a crack-of-dawn tee time, which necessitates
a quiet night and an early bedtime. Plan accordingly. If you're
staying at the Wynn or an MGM Mirage resort, you'll have access
to a private course – on-site in the case of the former or Shadow
Creek for the latter.

Still in town Monday night? Then there's no better place to go
than *JET* at the Mirage. Their unbelievably hot Monday night is
an "industry party," which means that the bitter waiter who spit
in your eggs will be there cutting loose, as will just about every
off-duty stripper in town. You want "beautiful babies ready to
party?" This is your spot. Same door rules and tips apply here as
anywhere else. *Info: Mirage* - 3400 Las Vegas Blvd. between
Flamingo and Spring Mountain. *JET* (Tel. 702/693-8300) is open
10:30pm-4:30am Fri, Sat, Mon. Admission is $30.

If you're still up for more adult entertainment, here are some
more suggestions, but bear this in mind: strip clubs in Vegas
serving alcohol are topless only. The dancers don't leave much to
the imagination, but some guys need to see everything. Never
fear, Vegas has you covered, and the strippers bare. In general,
the girls are hotter at the topless joints, but **Little Darlings** has its
share of winners, especially if you prefer your strippers under-
fed, unenhanced and nearly underage.

There is one exception to the nudes-or-booze rule: the **Palomino Club** in North Las Vegas. It was "grandfathered" in, and as the only place in town where you can have a drink surrounded by naked girls, they charge an arm and a leg. We'd sooner sneak a flask someplace nicer. *Info: Little Darlings* – 1514 Western Ave., 1/2 mi. west of the Strip between Sahara and Charleston. Tel. 702/366-0959. Open 11am-6am. Cover is $20 and includes unlimited non-alcoholic drinks. *Palomino Club* – 1848 Las Vegas Blvd. N., North Las Vegas. Tel. 702/642-2984. Open 5pm-5am daily. Cover is $30.

LADIES WEEKEND

Men aren't the only ones who get wild here. Historically, Las Vegas was built on testosterone, but that's changed quite a bit recently. **High-end and outlet shopping** beckon to the fairer sex, as do **luxurious spas**. Ladies can see skin at beefcake shows or even at several strip clubs catering to women. Hotels that make a particularly good choice for a ladies' weekend include **Rio** ($$$) or the **Palms** ($$$) for their phenomenal and diverse nightlife options, **Caesars Palace** ($$$$) for its opulent high-end shopping and dining, and **Flamingo** ($$) for its, uh, pinkness.

Ease into this city of excess with an **over-the-top meal**. If you're frustrated by your man's refusal to eat anything besides burgers and pizza, you'll swoon at the gourmet restaurants here. The head of the class is dominated by elegant French restaurants, combining impeccable service and rich, flavorful food. Don't worry about calories. This is Vegas. Nothing you eat here counts.

Alex at the Wynn is the newest jewel in the city's dining crown. Culinary impresario Alessandro Stratta infuses French dishes with Mediterranean accents at his eponymous AAA Five Star winner. Everything about this restaurant is gorgeous – from the décor of the fabulous room to the china to the food. *Info: Wynn Las Vegas* - 3131 Las

> ## Don't Miss ...
>
> • Fine dining at a **French restaurant**
> • **Las Vegas Premium Outlets**
> • **Via Bellagio** and the **Wynn Esplanade**
> • **Chippendales & Flirt** at the Rio

Vegas Blvd. S. at Spring Mountain. *Alex* (Tel. 702/770-3463) is open 6-10pm Tue-Sun.

Speaking of gorgeous, the **Eiffel Tower Restaurant**, 100 feet up, overlooks the Fountains of Bellagio. White linens juxtaposed with the tower's industrial girders provide a memorable setting for a classic French menu. Tasting menus, soufflés, dessertinis, and a bar menu are also available. *Info: Paris Las Vegas* - 3655 Las Vegas Blvd. S., between Flamingo and Harmon. *Eiffel Tower Restaurant* (Tel. 702/948-6937) serves dinner 5-10:30pm Sun-Thu, 5-11pm Fri-Sat. The bar and lounge open at 11am.

The Mandalay Bay's **Fleur de Lys** is a particularly unusual setting for a sumptuous meal. Instead of the chic and sleek postmodern décor of many fine restaurants in this town, the seafood-centric *prix fixe* menus here are served in a stone grotto, softened by fresh flowers. *Info: Mandalay Bay* – 3950 Las Vegas Blvd. S. at Russell Rd. *Fleur de Lys* (Tel. 702/632-9400) is open 5:30-10:30pm nightly.

Now get ready to objectify men as slabs of meat dance for your pleasure. **Thunder from Down Under** at the Excalibur features buff Australian men. If their abs don't make you swoon, their accents will. **Chippendales** at Rio is somewhat raunchier and more "themed," with musical numbers featuring men in uniform and other "fantasies" come to life. Both shows feature audience interaction and risqué, but tasteful stripteasing. *Info: Excalibur* – 3850 Las Vegas Blvd. S. at Tropicana. Tel. 702/597-7600. *Thunder* *from Down Under* shows at 9 nightly, with additional 11pm performances Fri-Sat. Admission is $39.95 and $49.95. *Rio* - 3700 W. Flamingo Rd., 3/4 mi. west of the Strip. *Chippendales* (Tel. 702/777-7776) shows at 8pm nightly Thu-Tue. Admission is $39.95-$49.95.

We like Chippendales, mostly because of the adjacent **Flirt Lounge**. With plush furniture bathed in warm purple neon, this place is an estrogen overload, except for the chivalrous servers dressed like Chippendales dancers. The music is exclusively female artists, and the drink menu includes lots of flavored liqueurs and fruit juices. How gynocentric is this place? They even put a "gossip pit" in the ladies' room. *Info: Flirt Lounge* opens to Chippendales ticketholders at 6:30pm and to the general public at 8:30pm Sun-Tue & Thu, 10:30pm Fri-Sat.

Las Vegas is a shopper's paradise. In addition to feature malls like the Forum Shops and the Grand Canal Shoppes, a few smaller shopping arcades feature the world's most renowned designers. **Wynn Esplanade** lets the ladies unleash their inner Carrie Bradshaw at the Manolo Blahnik shop. Other big names found here include Christian Dior, Louis Vuitton, Chanel and Cartier. **Via Bellagio** offers similarly exclusive shops, like Tiffany & Co., Hermes, Moschino, Gucci and Prada. Be prepared to moan softly and whimper longingly. *Info: Wynn Esplanade* - 3131 Las Vegas Blvd. S. at Sands. Tel. 702/770-7000. Open 10am-11pm Sun-Thu, 10am-midnight Fri-Sat. *Via Bellagio* – 3600 Las Vegas Blvd. S. at Flamingo. Tel. 702/693-7111. Open 10am-midnight daily.

It would be a shame to hit Vegas with your best girlfriends and  leave town without a **spa treatment**. Almost every hotel worth its salt has its own facility. Some that earn consistent raves include Caesars Palace, THEhotel (*photo at left*), Venetian, Bellagio, Four Seasons, Mirage, Paris

Las Vegas, Planet Hollywood, Westin Casuarina, JW Marriott, Red Rock and Green Valley Ranch. A spa visit is perfect refreshment before a big night out.

The nice thing about being with an all-girl group is that you'll have no problem getting into nightclubs, especially if you're a pack of foxes (you still have to dress to impress, meaning classy, slutty, or some combination thereof). Earn some good karma by befriending clueless guys in line so they can get in too. The Bellagio boasts one of the Strip's most spectacular clubs, the new **Bank**. The Bank opened on New Year's 2008, presenting an opulent space that's exceptionally intimate and dramatically cosmopolitan. *Info: Bellagio* - 3600 Las Vegas Blvd. S. at Flamingo. *The Bank* (Tel. 702/693-8300) is open 10am-4am Thu-Sun. Cover is $50.

Tryst at the Wynn is a similarly warm space, with red velvet walls and chocolate and vanilla colored furniture around a central dance floor. If that's not enough, the patio lounge wraps around a stunning lagoon fed by a 100-foot waterfall and surrounded by 200-year old trees. Bottle service is available, and for the well-heeled, opium beds. *Info: Wynn Las Vegas* - 3131 Las Vegas Blvd. S. at Spring Mountain. *Tryst* (Tel. 702/770-3375) is open 10pm-4am Thu-Sun. Cover is $30 for men, $20 for women.

The newest entry in the nightclub scene is *JET* at the Mirage, from the same Light Group responsible for The Bank. It's much different: contemporary and modern, but more accessible and less intimidating. It features state-of-the-art lighting and sound in three separate rooms featuring house, hip-hop and rock. It's also got a somewhat more relaxed door than its sister club, so expect a fun-loving everyman crowd instead of a room full of potential sugar daddies. *Info: Mirage* - 3400 Las Vegas Blvd. between Flamingo and Spring Mountain. *JET* (Tel. 702/693-8300) is open 10:30pm-4:30am Fri, Sat, Mon. Admission is $30.

All that high-end window shopping is the retail equivalent of the Chippendales show, nothing more than a tease. If you'd really like to score some affordable, quality threads, you're in luck. The greater Las Vegas area boasts three different outlet malls. Just off

I-15 close to downtown are the pleasant open-air **Las Vegas Premium Outlets,** with over 120 shops offering 25-65% savings on names like Kenneth Cole, A/X Armani Exchange, Dolce & Gabbana, French Connection, Liz Claiborne and Coach. *Info: Las Vegas Premium Outlets* – 875 Grand Central Pkwy., off I-15 exit 41B. Tel. 702/474-7500. Open 10am-9pm Mon-Sat, 10am-8pm Sun.

LONG WEEKEND

During the summer, Vegas overflows with pool parties. Besides the standard-bearer, **Rehab**, lots of other casinos offer daytime parties at poolside. See the barely dressed and beautiful at **Meditation Mondays** at the Venus Pool Club at Caesars Palace, with DJs, drink carts, high-end food and pampering services like Evian face spritzers and frozen towels. There's also **Ditch Fridays** at the new $40 million pool at the Palms. *Info: Caesars Palace* - 3570 Las Vegas Blvd. S. at Flamingo. Tel. 702/731-7110. *Palms* - 4321 W. Flamingo Rd., 1 mi. west of the Strip. Tel. 702/942-7777.

One of the hottest tickets in town, surprisingly enough, is for **Menopause: The Musical** at the Las Vegas Hilton. This hysterical ode to hot flashes has sold out literally every performance since opening, getting rave reviews from women who relate to its change-of-life content. Aimed at the same audience is the new **HATS! The Musical** at Harrah's. This uplifting musical captures the spirit of the Red Hat Society, a group of eccentric older women often found in bright red hats and purple dresses. *Info: Las Vegas Hilton* – 3000 Paradise Rd., between Desert Inn and Sahara, 3/4 mi. east of the Strip. *Menopause: The Musical* (Tel. 800/222-5361) performances are at 7pm Tue-Sat with matinees at 2pm Sun, Wed, Thu, 4pm Sat and 5pm Sun. Tickets are $49.50.

Enjoy a classic English high tea service at the ultraluxe Four Seasons. The **Verandah restaurant's tea service** includes scones with Devonshire cream and fruit preserves, cake and pastries, and an innovative variety of tea sandwiches. Champagne is available as well. *Info: Four Seasons* – 3960 Las Vegas Blvd. S. at Russell. Tel. 702/632-5000. *Verandah* serves afternoon tea from 3-4pm Mon-Thu. Afternoon tea is available for private parties on weekends, call for details. Cost is $30, $38 with champagne.

"YOU BROUGHT THE KIDS?!" WEEKEND

There was a period of about ten minutes in the '90s when Las Vegas attempted recasting itself as a family destination. Vegas sheepishly came to its senses when the MGM Grand's theme park closed and the Bellagio opened, banning out-right visitors under 18 who weren't hotel guests. And while bringing your kids to Vegas is not the best way to experience the city, nevertheless we'll show you how to have a great time in Vegas with your kids.

Picking a hotel for a family visit to Vegas can be tricky. The catacombs of the casino floors make it easy for kids to get lost. Non-gaming hotels are a viable option. Many offer comparable luxury without the chaos. Many of these hotels cater specifically to younger crowds with activity programs or amenities geared specifically to kids. Most of the **Station** and **Coast** hotels offer similar child care services to guests, allowing their adult customers to take in a show or dinner without the little rugrats in tow.

The best hotels for families are the **Luxor** ($$), **Orleans** ($$), **New York-New York** ($$), **Sunset Station** ($$) and **Four Seasons** ($$$$).

Don't Miss ...

Nighttime in Vegas is mostly just for grown-ups, but there are a few after-dark attractions for kids too. Tops is the **Fountains of Bellagio** (*see photo on page 31*). Everyone can appreciate the splendor of the dancing waters, although you

- **Fountains of Bellagio**
- **Siegfried & Roy's Secret Garden**
- **Fremont Street Experience**

might need to explain to your kids the significance of "Luck Be a Lady." *Info: Bellagio* - 3600 LasVegas Blvd. S. at Flamingo. Tel. 702/693-7111. Showtimes every half hour from 3pm-8pm Mon-Fri and 12pm-8pm Sat-Sun, with additional performances nightly every 15 minutes from 8pm-midnight. Free admission.

If the kids are still rambunctious, leave the Strip for the **Orleans** and some good old-fashioned bowling. Most Coast and Station casinos have outfitted their joints with bowling alleys and movie theaters. The Orleans' facility, voted the best in the city the past four years by the *Review-Journal*, has 70 lanes, a video arcade, snack bar, lounge for the grown-ups and a full array of services and accessories. *Info: Orleans* – 4500 W. Tropicana Ave., 1 1/2 mile west of the Strip. Tel. 702/365-7111. Open 24 hours, with open bowling before 5-5:30pm and after 9pm Mon-Fri and all day on weekends (availability subject to tournaments). Games are $2.90 for adults, $2 for seniors 55+ or kids under 16 during the week. Rates are $3.25 per person weekends and holidays.

On your first full day in town hit the **Adventuredome** at **Circus Circus**, an indoor theme park at the Strip's scariest casino. Taking

up 5 1/2 acres under a shimmering red glass dome, it's not just a kiddie park. It has serious thrill rides in its lineup, notably the Canyon Blaster roller coaster. The Sling Shot rockets riders 100 feet in the air at 4 Gs followed by a freefall. The Inverter and Chaos are midway-type spinners. The Rim Runner is a water ride culminating in a 60-foot drench drop. Tickets are available on a per-ride or full-day basis. Circus Circus also has a **carnival-style midway** where games of skill give kids and adults a chance to win goofy prizes, and circus acts perform every half hour. *Info: Circus Circus* – 2880 Las Vegas Blvd. S., between Convention Center and Sahara. Tel. 702/734-0410. *Adventuredome* (Tel. 702/794-3939) is open 10am-6pm Mon-Thu,

10am-midnight Fri-Sat, and 10am-9pm Sun. Rides are $4-7 each. All-day passes are $24.95 for adults, $14.95 for juniors.

Next to the MGM Grand, the Showcase Mall features **GameWorks**, an arcade on steroids. Its focal point is a 75-foot high climbing wall, but you'll also find the hottest, most technologically advanced games. There's a racing section with NASCAR, Waverunner and ATV games, as well as skiing, horseracing, and skateboarding sims. You'll also find a selection of old-school video games and pinball. *Info: GameWorks* – 3769 Las Vegas Blvd. at Tropicana. Tel. 702/432-4263. Open Sun-Thu 10am-midnight, 10am-1am Fri-Sat. Admission is free, game cards are available in denominations from $1 to $25.

There are a few show options suitable for a family audience. The most popular is the **Tournament of Kings** at the **Excalibur.** This Medieval Times knockoff embraces the Arthurian legend, with seven good kings and a dark knight, representing the evil Mordred. Guests cheer their "country" as jousting and fighting competitions bring us closer towards world domination,  or in this case, supper. The food is typical dinner-show assembly line crap: tomato soup, Cornish game hens, potatoes, broccoli, and dessert, all bland. Booze is available for an additional fee, and tends to help. *Info: Excalibur* – 3850 Las Vegas Blvd. S. at Tropicana. *Tournament of Kings* (Tel. 702/597-7600) is performed at 6 and 8:30pm Wed-Mon. Admission is $58.24 per person.

Magic shows tend to be family-friendly as well, and the pick of the litter here is the charming, natural **Lance Burton**, performing at a custom-built $27 million theater at the Monte Carlo. Burton keeps things moving along at a brisk pace in a show that includes a juggler, six attractive female assistants, more birds than a Hitchcock outtake, and in the grand finale, a levitating Corvette. *Info: Monte Carlo* – 3770 Las Vegas Blvd. S. between Tropicana and

Best Kiddie Food!

There are plenty of fun themed restaurants inoffensive to your kids' palates, and maybe even to yours. Consider the **Hard Rock Café** (4475 Paradise Rd.), **Planet Hollywood** (Forum Shops), **Rainforest Café** (Forum Shops), **NASCAR Café** (Sahara) and the **ESPN Zone** (New York-New York). Casino coffee shops will work, and buffets are also good options, but stick to the budget-priced ones, gourmet items will be lost on your children.

Harmon. *Lance Burton: Master Magician* (Tel. 702/730-7160) performs Tue-Sat at 7pm, with additional 10pm performances on Tue and Sat. Tickets are $66.50-$72.55.

Downtown, the **Fremont Street Experience** is another nighttime option suitable for kids. While the soundtrack, which includes the likes of the Doors, Led Zeppelin and Blue Oyster Cult, might as well be Greek to your kids, they will be mesmerized by the bright colors and action unfolding on the LED screen above. Live bands frequently perform on the street stages, adding to the fun, as do special events like Party Gras or various cruises and car shows. *Info: Fremont Street Experience* - E. Fremont St. between Main St. and Las Vegas Blvd. Tel. 702/678-5600. Shows every hour on the hour between 7pm and midnight.

Bear in mind that unlike the Strip, the casinos downtown offer pay-parking garages. Don't fret though, they're free with validation. You can get your parking ticket validated, usually at the main cage, without having to make a bet or purchase. Like anywhere else in town, nobody under 21 is allowed to loiter on the casino floor.

Back on the Strip, few things catch eyes like the **Roller Coaster at New York-New York**, taking that first terrifying drop along Tropicana Avenue amid a backdrop of faux skyscrapers. The New York-New York is still one of the more family-friendly options in town, thanks in no small part to the 32,000 sq. ft. Coney Island Emporium midway/arcade. *Info: New York-New York -*

3790 Las Vegas Blvd. S. at Tropicana. Tel. 702/740-6969. *Roller Coaster* open 11am-11 pm Sun-Thu, 10:30am-midnight Fri-Sat. Riders must be 54" tall.

Take Flamingo east about 15 minutes from the Strip to the Boulder Highway for Sam's Town, a bustling, cowboy-heavy locals' casino. Its lovely Mystic Falls Park, a live forest atrium, hosts a nightly water, laser and light show called **Sunset Stampede.** It's set to a custom score recorded by the Indianapolis Philharmonic Orchestra. It's free to everyone, and can be more enjoyable than Bellagio's fountains. *Info: Sam's Town* – 5111 Boulder Hwy. Tel. 702/456-7777. *Sunset Stampede* shows at 2, 6, 8 and 10pm nightly. Free admission.

If your kids are big animal-lovers, don't leave town without seeing **Siegfried & Roy's Secret Garden**. Nestled in the tropical rain forest atmosphere of the Mirage is this habitat for exotic animals, with a particular focus on cats: **snow white tigers**, striped white tigers, white lions, heterozygous lions and tigers, and a ceremonial Thai elephant. The centerpiece, however, is the 2.5 million gallon habitat to a family of **Atlantic bottlenose dolphins** – most of which were actually born here. It contains four connected pools, an artificial coral reef, and a sandy bottom. *Info: Siegfried & Roy's Secret Garden* is open from 10am-7pm daily during summer  hours; 11am-5:30pm weekdays and 10am-5:30pm weekends during winter hours. Admission is $15 for adults, $10 for kids 4-12, and free for kids 3 and under. Remember, the volcano erupts at the top of every hour from 7pm to midnight. Free admission.

LONG WEEKEND
Like the Circus Circus and the Excalibur, the **Luxor** offers a strong array of activities and attractions for kids of all ages like a 280-seat

IMAX theater and three "ridefilms," themed motion simulators that take you to cyberspace, subterranean Egypt, or Transylvania. There's also a "4-D" movie and the fascinating King Tut Museum. The Atrium Level also includes the Games of the Gods arcade, several shops and dining/drinking options. The Super Passport includes one IMAX movie, one ridefilms, a pass to the Museum and entry into Shark Reef next door at Mandalay Bay. *Info: Luxor* – 3900 Las Vegas Blvd. S. between Tropicana and Russell. Tel. 702/262-4102. Atrium Level is open 10am-11pm daily. Super Passport is $34 per adult, $29 for kids.

Mac King's comedy magic show at Harrah's gets consistent props for his appeal to kids and adults alike thanks to a disarming personality and winning illusions. Another daytime show worth your family's consideration is **Ronn Lucas**, a most enthusiastic and amusing ventriloquist. Lucas has earned critical acclaim from all corners of the globe for his lifelike and funny show at the Luxor. *Info: Harrah's Las Vegas* – 3475 Las Vegas Blvd S. between Flamingo and Sands. Tel. 702/369-5222. *Mac King* tickets are $24.95. Shows are at 1 and 3pm Tue-Sat. *Ronn Lucas* (Tel. 702/262-4400) performs Sat-Thu at 3pm. Tickets are $29.95 and $39.95.

Consider a day trip to **Buffalo Bill's**, 35 miles southwest of Vegas just inside the California border. This family-friendly casino resort boasts the wicked **Desperado roller coaster**. It's brilliantly integrated into the hotel, with the track penetrating the roof of the casino and passing through the porte cochère. Other attractions include the Vault 3-D simulator ride, the Turbo Drop freefall ride and the Adventure Canyon Log Flume. *Info: Buffalo Bill's* – 31900 Las Vegas Blvd. S., Primm. Tel. 702/386-7867. Attractions are open 12pm-6pm Mon & Thu, 11am-midnight Fri, 10am-midnight

Sat and 10am-7pm Sun. Admission ranges from $3-7 per ride. Wristbands offering unlimited rides for the day are $30, $12 for kids under 48". Desperado riders must be 48" tall.

VINTAGE VEGAS WEEKEND

In Las Vegas, the only constant is change. They build casinos with an eye towards eventually blowing them up. It's best not to get too attached. The Vegas of old is nearly extinct from the Strip, but it is still there for those who know where to look. We'll point you in the right direction for a weekend of **retro fun.**

Caesars Palace ($$$$) was the city's first megaresort, opening in 1966 and pretty much never looking back. Caesars will always be steeped in history. We'd be shocked to live long enough to see it imploded. **Bally's** ($$) strives to recapture that lost Vegas vibe as well. Beyond that, the quality of nostalgic Strip choices takes a big step down.

Real vintage Vegas, however, lives **downtown** (see map on the next page). The **Golden Nugget** ($$$) provides four-star service, class and luxury. The **Main Street Station** ($$) and the remodeled **Las Vegas Club** ($) are particularly good values for basic accommodations. All of the casinos along or adjacent to the Fremont Street Experience offer rooms that are cheap, clean, and generally satisfactory. But I wouldn't venture further east than the utilitarian **El Cortez** ($) at night.

Downtown is a magnet for serious poker aficionados. Here are the best places to play:

• With 18 tables including $1/$2 and $2/$4 no-limit and hold'em games up to $10/$20, **Binion's** is pushing its reputation as a top poker joint into the 21st century, while paying homage to its past. Check out the Poker Hall of Fame photo gallery on the east wall of the casino. *Info:* 128 S. Fremont St. Tel. 702/382-1600.

• The **Golden Nugget's** $200 million remodel included an intimate new poker room with ten non-smoking tables. Plenty of options for low-limit players here too. *Info:* 129 S. Fremont St. Tel. 702/385-7111.

• The **Plaza** offers a good variety and gets high marks for the management of the games. *Info:* 1 S. Main St. Tel. 702/386-2110.

While you're downtown, stop by the **Golden Gate**. This tiny casino, which opened in 1906, is best known for its shrimp cocktail, a gluttonous pile of shrimp in a tulip glass, served with cocktail sauce and lemon. The price? 99 cents. *Info: Golden Gate –* 1 Fremont St. Tel. 702/385-1906.

While the focus on nightlife these days is on mash-ups, progressive house and hip-hop, there are alternatives. Mandalay Bay's **House of Blues** hosts Flashback Fridays, with DJ-spun 70s and 80s dance music along with retro 80s hits performed by the Spazmatics. On Saturdays the Boogie Knights play disco music there. Downtown's retro hipster hangout, the **Beauty Bar** is the place to be on Saturday nights for Rawkerz, a party playing post-punk, Britpop and electro for an irresistible mix of gloom and glee. The first Friday of every month is the Get Back, a funky soul party. *Info: Mandalay Bay –* 3950 Las Vegas Blvd. S. at Russell Rd. Tel. 702/632-7777. *House of Blues* (Tel. 702/632-7600) - Doors open at 11pm. Admission is free for women, $10 for men Fri; $10 for women, $15 for men Sat. *Beauty Bar –* 517 S. Fremont St. Tel. 702/598-1965. Admission is $5 Fri-Sat.

One option combining the nostalgic and contemporary is **Studio 54** at the MGM Grand. Celebrities' photos remain on the walls, and Steve Rubell's iconic moon and spoon are accounted for. The shimmering disco music synonymous with Studio 54 plays early on in the evening, mixed with new wave and old-school hip-hop. Later they add techno and house to the mix. Revelers gape at dancers, acrobats, and other assorted freaks entertaining the

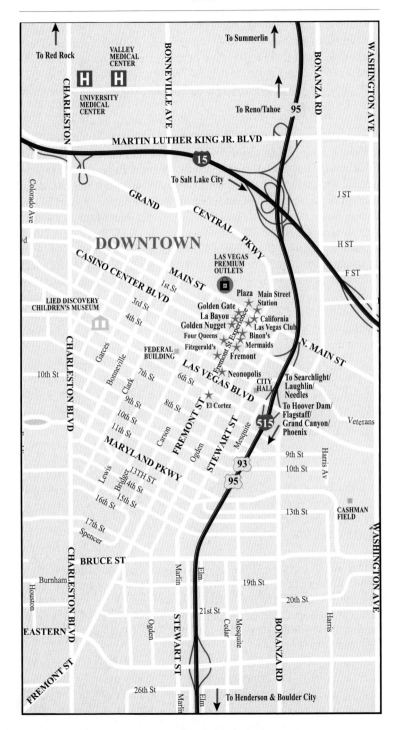

crowd from above. The crowd tends to be more diverse and laid back (read: older) than at some of the glitzier places. *Info: MGM Grand* - 3799 Las Vegas Blvd. S. at Tropicana. *Studio 54* (Tel. 702/ 891-7254) opens at 10pm Tue-Sat. Cover is $10-20 for women and $20-30 for men.

A few restaurants in Las Vegas also seem like time-warps. There are the classic Vegas gourmet rooms like **Michael's** at the South Point and **Hugo's Cellar** at the Four Queens. **Peppermill**, next to the Riviera, offers better-than-average coffee shop fare in a 70s atmosphere. There's also the elegant and masculine **Lawry's The Prime Rib**, which has been serving up its succulent namesake specialty ever since 1938. *Info: South Point* – 9777 Las Vegas Blvd. S., at Silverado Ranch. Tel. 702/796-7111. *Michael's* offers two seatings nightly, at 6 or 6:30 and 9 or 9:30pm. *Four Queens* – 202 Fremont St. Tel. 702/385-4011. *Hugo's Cellar* is open 5:30-11pm nightly. *Peppermill* – 2985 Las Vegas Blvd. S., at Convention Center. Tel. 702/735-4177. Open 24 hours. *Lawry's The Prime Rib* – 4043 Howard Hughes Pkwy. Tel. 702/893-2223. Open 5pm-10pm Sun-Thu, 5pm-11pm Fri-Sat.

Lounge acts in Las Vegas are great fun. You can relax with a martini and enjoy live entertainment for free. While they vary from one place to the next and one week to the next, there are a few dependable options.

• The Bellagio offers live entertainment at the Baccarat Bar, Petrossian Bar and the Fontana Lounge. The pick of the litter here is **Dian Diaz**, whose exotic beauty, poise and voice exude star quality. She performs at the remodeled Fontana. Showtimes were not available at the time of writing. *Info:* 3600 Las Vegas Blvd. S. Tel. 702/693-7111.

• The Rocks Lounge at the new Red Rock casino features **Zowie Bowie**, an energetic duo with the versatility to cover everyone from Sinatra to 50 Cent and the chemistry to banter comfortably à la Sonny and Cher. They perform 10pm-12:30am Thu, 11pm-3am Fri, and 8:30pm-3am Sat. *Info:* 10973 W. Charleston Blvd. Tel. 702/797-7777.

• Although it doesn't have a long-term resident holding court, the Sahara's **Casbar Lounge** is usually a lot of fun, with a laid-back, down-to-earth crowd and a broad variety of musical acts: everything from lounge, jazz and standards to R&B, Motown and rock. Performance times vary, call for details. *Info:* 2535 Las Vegas Blvd. S. Tel. 702/737-2111.

Another quintessential Vegas experience is the topless production show, and the best-reviewed in town is **Donn Arden's Jubilee!**, which recently celebrated its 25th anniversary. Its showgirls are perennially named the city's best, but the spectacle doesn't end on these rhinestone-studded stunners. The show at Bally's is such a paean to excess, they sink the Titanic on stage. *Info: Bally's* – 3645 Las Vegas Blvd. S. at Flamingo. *Donn Arden's Jubilee!* (Tel. 800/237-SHOW) is performed at 7:30 and 10:30pm Sat-Thu. Tickets are $48-110.

Downtown's **Neon Museum** is another place to take in long-gone Vegas. In addition to lovingly restored casino icons, you'll find stylized signs dating all the way back

Best Places to See Elvis

Elvis is everywhere here. You may randomly encounter an Elvis on the Strip making timeshare appointments, or a pair of Elvi on Fremont Street posing for photos in exchange for tips. But here are a couple of surefire places to catch one:

• The **Dealertainer black-jack pit** at the Imperial Palace.
• **Legends in Concert** at the Imperial Palace.
• **American Superstars** at the Stratosphere.
• Trent Carlini stars in **The Musical History of the King** at Sahara.
• At the **Graceland Wedding Chapel**.
• In statue form **just inside the main entrance** of the Las Vegas Hilton.
• On his own 25-cent progressive-jackpot slot machine in many casinos.

to the 1940s. They certainly don't make 'em like this anymore. The non-profit museum also maintains a 3-acre Boneyard open by appointment. *Info: Neon Museum* – 702/387-NEON. Open 24 hours. *Boneyard* – tours available by appointment 11am-5pm Tue-Fri. Free admission to Museum, Boneyard tours require minimum $15 donation per person. Tours start at noon and 2pm Tue-Fri.

LONG WEEKEND

Unfortunately, one of the must-see acts of the Vegas lounge scene doesn't do weekends. He's **Pete Vallee,** playing Big Elvis at Bill's (the former Barbary Coast). He's been impersonating the King since he was 13, and judging from his 500-pound girth, eating fried peanut butter and banana sandwiches for about as long. There won't be much gyration of the hips, but oh my, that voice. *Info: Bill's Gamblin' Hall & Saloon* - 3595 Las Vegas Blvd. S., at Flamingo Road. Tel. 702/737-2100. *Pete Vallee* performs at 1, 3 and 4:30pm Mon and 3, 5 and 6:30 Tue-Fri in Bill's Lounge. No cover.

If you want to take a serious trip in the Wayback Machine, visit the 115-acre **Bonnie Springs Ranch,** which dates back to the 1840s as a wagon train stop, but in its current incarnation recreates an 1880s mining town. On weekends the "posse" show lets guests help the sheriff track down a mustachioed bad guy. All the western archetypes are here: the boot hill cemetery, saloon confrontation, the high noon gunfight, the tumbleweed, and the public hanging. It's a little hokey, but fun for the right kind of mind. *Info: Bonnie Springs Ranch* – 1 Gunslinger Way, Blue Diamond. Tel. 702/875-4191. Open from 10:30am-6pm during the summer, 10:30am-5pm in the winter. Admission is $20 per carload. Melodrama shows and hangings are each performed three times daily.

We have to mention **Wayne Newton**. While Mr. Las Vegas has in recent years descended into sad self-parody, seeing the tuxedo-clad crooner perform is a fairly definitive experience. In addition to singing Newton plays at various points the fiddle, banjo, piano and guitar. Audiences still seem to love him. Health issues forced him to cancel the last chunk of his run at Harrah's after appearing on "Dancing With the Stars", but hopefully he'll be back on his feet again soon.

The **Liberace Museum** pays tribute to "Mr. Showmanship," who at first blush seems irrelevant to modern music, until you look deeper and realize that the man was a quarter century ahead of his time. You want to talk pimped rides? The cars on display here include a pair of unique Rolls Royce specimens: one hand-painted in

Best Vegas Blogs

Our personal favorite is Two Way Hard Three (*www.ratevegas.com/blog*), where gregarious blogger Hunter examines the business side of gaming, the customer's perspective, news, interviews and other stuff. **The Movable Buffet,** the LA Times' Vegas blog, *vegasblog.latimes.com*, is good but less personal. And **Robin Leach** gets all the good gossip out on *vegaspopular.com*.

red, white and blue; the second covered in mirrored tile and etched with a design of galloping horses. You want to talk bling-bling? The collection's Liberace stage jewelry and costumes include a rhinestone-encrusted black diamond mink cape, his trademark candelabra ring, a yellow gold piano-shaped ring comprised of over 250 diamonds, and a piano-shaped watch glittering with diamonds, rubies, sapphires and emeralds. *Info: Liberace Museum* – 1775 E. Tropicana Ave, 2 1/2 mi. east of the Strip. Tel. 702/798-5595. Open 10am-5pm Tue-Sat, noon-4pm Sun. Admission is $12.50, $8.50 for seniors and students.

Video gamers get nostalgic too. The **Pinball Hall of Fame Museum** is a true labor of love paying homage to this dying breed. Much as the reel slot machine fades away in favor of high-tech video slots, increasingly advanced video games are pushing pinball into extinction. This non-profit entity has collected hundreds of classic pinball games – from 1948's Rondevoo to 1999's South Park, all lovingly refurbished and maintained by volunteers. If you grew

up punching quarters into these games, this place will smoke any slot machine in town. And while blowing Junior's college tuition trying to hit Megabucks can leave you green around the gills, you can feel good about your coin-in here. All proceeds are donated to the Salvation Army. *Info: Pinball Hall of Fame Museum* – 3330 E. Tropicana Ave., 3 mi. east of the Strip. Open 11am-11pm Sun-Thu, 'til midnight on Fri-Sat. Free admission.

"COMEDY TONIGHT" WEEKEND

Comedy has long been a mainstay of the Vegas experience. Legends such as George Burns and Don Rickles were mainstays back in the day. Today, the city's comedy headliners are a mix of B-list residents and A-list touring acts. Since **almost all the comedy acts in Vegas perform after dark,** you're probably going to want to spend your days inside the casinos, by the pool, or cherry-picking options from some of our other plans. Of course, we'll mention the few daytime comedy options.

Stand-up comedians are everywhere in this town. A few of them pack showrooms every night for long-term engagements:

• The soft-spoken **Rita Rudner** took Clint Holmes' spot at Harrah's after a successful five-year run at New York-New York. RJ readers followed her up the street to name her the city's best comedian for the sixth time. *Info:* Tickets are $54. Shows at 8pm Tue-Sat. 3475 Las Vegas Blvd. S. Tel. 702/369-5222.

• One unique thing about Las Vegas is that it provides a lucrative base for niche acts who might struggle to fill seats elsewhere. Surprisingly, **Luxor's Carrot Top** is actually hysterically funny on stage, with a trunk full of props and a surprisingly smart routine that takes aim at everything and everyone: from notorious celebrities to Vegas cheese. *Info:* Performances are at 8pm Sun-Mon, Wed-Fri and at 9pm on Sat. Tickets cost $54.95-65.95. 3900 Las Vegas Blvd. S. Tel. 702/262-4000.

• **George Wallace** has been keeping Flamingo crowds in stitches with audience razzing, observational humor, celebrity skewering and of course, the "yo' mama" jokes for which he is famous. This well-connected comedian is known to incorporate surprise guests and co-stars like David Brenner, Chris Tucker and Jerry Seinfeld. *Info:* Wallace performs at 10pm Tue-Sat. Tickets are $59.95 and $75. 3555 Las Vegas Blvd. S. Tel. 702/733-3333.

• Fat, fifty-something **Louie Anderson** shares theater space with the Thunder from Down Under male revue at the Excalibur. He's probably acutely aware of the irony, as self-deprecating fat jokes have been his trademark for decades. Comedy Central named him one of the top 100 stand-ups of all time. *Info:* He performs at 7pm Sat-Thu. Tickets are $54 and $79. 3850 Las Vegas Blvd. S. Tel. 702/597-7600.

The intersection of comedy and magic is well-populated in Vegas, and best exemplified by **Penn & Teller**. As fans of their Showtime series already know, there is no sacred cow this duo won't grind into hamburger. Magic is no exception, as they pull the curtain back on their tricks without detracting from the amazement. The loquacious Penn Gillette lays out the secrets of their tricks in detail before performing while the diminutive, mute, and mildly creepy Teller does the heavy lifting. The dynamic has served them well for 25 years. *Info: Rio* - 3700 W. Flamingo Rd., 3/4 mi. west of the Strip. *Penn & Teller* (Tel. 702/777-7776) performances at 9pm Sat-thu. Tickets are $75 and $85.

The **Amazing Johnathan** may be the world's most inept magician, but he's quite possibly the most hilarious. His demented, obscenity-laden act at the Sahara leaves no one intact. Not the audience at large, who are caught on camera with humiliating and hilarious captions. Not the audience volunteer who he tortures for the better part of a half hour. And certainly not his long-suffering stage crew. The act includes gay-baiting, retard-bashing, simulated drug use, and other unsavory elements, rather than any real "magic," so caveat emptor. *Info: Sahara* – 2535 Las Vegas Blvd. S. *The Amazing Johnathan* (Tel. 800/634-6787) performs at 10pm Fri-Tue. Tickets are $49.95 and $54.95.

Best Daytime Comedy

The best afternoon comedy options in Las Vegas include:

- **Ronn Lucas' ventriloquist act** at Luxor.
- **Mac King's Comedy Magic** show at Harrah's.
- The long-running variety show **Viva Las Vegas** at the Plaza.
- The Hilton's **Menopause: The Musical.**

Another recent Strip trend has been the import of Broadway musicals. Some, like Mamma Mia, have done very well. Others, like Avenue Q, are lost on the Vegas audience. One excellent fit for Las Vegas is **Monty Python's Spamalot** at the Wynn. Winner of the 2005 Tony for best musical, Spamalot was "lovingly ripped off" from the 1975 classic, *Monty Python and the Holy Grail* by Eric Idle and Mike Nichols. Trimmed down to 90 minutes, it keeps the silly bits coming at a fast and furious pace. *Info: Wynn Las Vegas* - 3131 Las Vegas Blvd. S. at Spring Mountain. Tel. 702/693-7111.

Improv is one of the most unpredictable and enjoyable genres of comedy, and **Second City** helped put it on the map, with alumni like John Candy, Bill Murray and Mike Myers. You never know which of today's ensemble players will be tomorrow's superstar. The 75-minute show combines satire, music, and impressions based on ideas from the audience. *Info: Flamingo Las Vegas* - 3555 Las Vegas Blvd. S. at Flamingo. *Second City* (Tel. 702/733-3333) performances at 8pm Thu-Tue, with additional 10:30pm shows Thu, Sat, Sun. Tickets are $39.95.

Combine the unpredictability of improve and the triple-threat star power of a Las Vegas headliner and what do you get? He's **Wayne Brady**, b*tch! This multi-talented performer is a permanent headliner at the intimate Venetian Showroom. His show, called Makin' %@it Up, is a classic Vegas variety show with song, dance and the backing of a three-piece band. A pure showman, Brady is a natural for this kind of act. *Info: Venetian* – 3355 Las Vegas Blvd. S. at Sands. Tel. 702/414-9000. *Wayne Brady* performs at 9pm Thu-Mon. Tickets are $49-149.

LONG WEEKEND
One lesser-known comic who gets riotous laughs is Boston-based
Vinnie Favorito, who works the showroom at O'Sheas, next to
Flamingo. He tortures his audience like Don Rickles' heir apparent, needling them for their appearance, hometown, profession
or whatever else. These improvisational riffs are not for the easily
offended, or for those under 18. *Info: O'Sheas* - 3555 Las Vegas
Blvd. S. at Flamingo. Tel. 702/733-3333. *Vinnie Favorito* performs
at 7:30 and 9:30pm Tue-Sat. Tickets are $39.95 and $49.95.

Hypnosis shows can be fun but it takes something really special
to stand out. **Anthony Cools** pushes the envelope. Any hypnotist
can inspire silliness, but it takes real *cojones* to convince a volunteer to make dirty-talking phone calls, fake a porno audition, or
believe that their genitalia are talking to them. Some men in
Cools' audience are hypnotized into thinking theirs are growing
out of their forehead. He closes his show by hypnotizing volunteers into spontaneous orgasm. Not a bad talent. Cools' show is
filthy, juvenile, evil, and utterly outrageous. *Info: Paris Las Vegas*
- 3655 Las Vegas Blvd. S. between Flamingo and Tropicana. Tel.
877/374-7469. Performances are at 9pm Thu-Tue. Tickets are
$52.75 and $75.75.

Another show that's amassed quite a following is **Menopause:
The Musical** at the Las Vegas Hilton. While it's clearly more
resonant to women, men who've had to live with their significant
other's "change" will certainly relate as well. Buy your tickets in
advance, this show sells out. *Info: Las Vegas Hilton* – 3000 Paradise
Rd., between Desert Inn and Sahara, 3/4 mi. east of the Strip.
Menopause: The Musical (Tel. 800/222-5361) performances are at
7pm daily with matinees at 2pm Wed and 4pm Sat-Sun. Tickets
are $49.50.

Here are some more top choices for your long weekend. These
places specialize in standup, with rotating and touring lineups
featuring comedians of varied stature and quality. They include:

• **The Improv** at Harrah's (Tel. 888/392-9002, ext. 5222. Shows at
8:30 and 10:30pm Tue-Sun, $29.05), a Vegas fixture for 25 years,
voted the best comedy club in Vegas by the RJ the past four;

• **Comedy Stop** at the Tropicana (Tel. 800/829-9034. Shows at 8 and 10:30pm nightly, $19.95 including one drink), the *What's On* choice as the city's best;

• **Riviera Comedy Club** at the Riviera (Tel. 702/794-9433. Shows at 8:30 and 10:30pm nightly, $19.95); and

• **LA Comedy Club** at Palace Station (Tel. 866/264-1818. Shows at 7pm and 9pm nightly, $27.95 and $38.50, includes buffet dinner or two drinks).

FEEL THE MUSIC WEEKEND

Vegas is a refuge for big stars past their prime, but at the same time has enough **hot venues** and flush money to draw just about every **touring act**, offering something for every taste.

The discussion has to start with one of the most anticipated additions to the Las Vegas show scene: **LOVE**, a new Cirque du Soleil show set to the music of the Beatles. LOVE features a

soundtrack cobbled together from Abbey Road master tapes by Sir George Martin and Giles Martin. The cast of 60 performs on a theater-in-the-round. The show's content is derived from the lyrics of the songs and transcends the line between real and imaginary. It's quite an evolution for Cirque. *Info: Mirage -* 3400 Las Vegas Blvd. S. between Flamingo and Spring Mountain. *LOVE* – Tel. 702/792-7777. Performances are at 7pm and 10pm Thu-Mon. Tickets range from $69 to $150.

The Beatles are also represented

in Vegas by a talented quartet of tribute artists at the Sahara Theater in the **Fab Four Mania** show. This note-perfect tribute is delivered with keen attention to detail at the site of the Beatles' first Vegas visit. No key changes, no sequencers, no backing tracks, no studio tricks – just four guys playing the songs of the lads of Liverpool. *Info: Sahara* – 2535 S. Las Vegas Blvd at Sahara. Tel. 702/737-2515. *Fab Four Mania* performs at 7pm Mon-Sat. Tickets are $60.90-$93.90 for adults, $31.20-$41.20 for kids.

Another British invader is **Elton John**, whose acclaimed Red Piano show alternates with Bette Midler at the Colosseum. The 95-minute performance showcases music spanning his whole career, surrounding the music with David LaChapelle's sometimes nostalgic, sometimes risqué imagery. Sir Elton remains a consummate performer, demonstrating a strong command of the low notes, adding a richness and depth to songs that sounded flimsy before. *Info: Caesars Palace* - 3570 Las Vegas Blvd. S. at Flamingo. *Elton John: The Red Piano* (Tel. 888/4-ELTON-J) performances are

Best Tribute Shows

• **Legends in Concert** at the Imperial Palace; the longest running impersonation show and by far the best. Admission is $49.95 for adults, $34.95 for kids. 3535 Las Vegas Blvd. S. Tel. 888/777-7664

• **American Superstars** at the Stratosphere; contemporary artists, readily available coupons. Tickets are $39.25. 2000 Las Vegas Blvd S. Tel. 800/99-TOWER.

• **Purple Reign** pays tribute to Prince at 10pm Wed at the Monte Carlo Brewpub, at 10pm Sun at the House of Blues, and at the South Point at 10:30 pm Fri. Free.

• **A Neil Diamond Tribute Starring Jay White**; heartily endorsed by the real thing. At the Riviera at 7pm Sun-Thu. Tickets are $49.95. 2901 Las Vegas Blvd. S. Tel. 877/892-7469.

• **A Musical Tribute to Liberace**, at the Liberace Museum. 1pm Tue, Wed, and Sat. Included with museum admission, $12.50. 1775 E. Tropicana Ave, 2 1/2 mi. east of the Strip. Tel. 702/798-5595.

at 7:30pm for several weeks out of the year. Call or check online for current dates. Tickets range from $100 to $250.

Toni Braxton's, residency in the Flamingo Showroom keeps getting held over by popular demand. The sexy R&B diva's show, "Revealed," promises to be an intimate, high-fashion retrospective of her 15-year career. She is initially contracted to perform through March 2006. *Info: Flamingo Las Vegas* - 3555 Las Vegas Blvd. S., at Flamingo Rd. *Toni Braxton* (Tel. 702/733-3333) performs at 7:30pm Tue-Sat. Tickets are $65-100.

So far, **Mamma Mia!** has been the most successful Broadway import, running since 2003 at Mandalay Bay. It's slated to close around mid-year. Another show that could potentially put together a lengthy run is the upcoming **Jersey Boys**, the story of Frankie Valli and the Four Seasons, coming to the **Palazzo** starting in April. *Info: Mandalay Bay* – 3950 Las Vegas Blvd. S. at Russell Rd. *Mamma Mia!* (Tel. 877/632-7400) performances are 7:30pm Sun-Thu, 6 and 10pm Sat. Tickets are $45, $75 and $100. *Palazzo* – 3325 Las Vegas Blvd. S. at Sands. *Jersey Boys* (Tel. 702/414-4300) tickets are $65-220 and performances are at 7pm Thu-Tue.

Yet another addition to the Vegas theatre scene is **Phantom: The Las Vegas Spectacular**, Andrew Lloyd Webber's mid-80s masterpiece, which recently surpassed *Cats* as the longest-running show in Broadway history. The music is gorgeous, but the book is underwhelming – which makes the revamped 95-minute production a much better-paced affair. The show is performed in a custom-built $40 million theater, with all-new special effects. The splendor and excess of *Phantom* mesh perfectly with the opulent cheese of the Venetian. *Info: Venetian* – 3355 Las Vegas Blvd. S. at Sands. *Phantom* (Tel. 866/641-7469) performances are Mon-Sat at 7pm, with additional 9:30pm performances on Mon, Sat. Tickets are $75.90, $108.90, $132, and $158.

The **Empire Ballroom** is a well-regarded independent club with a diverse mix of live music and DJ entertainment. Various nights feature 80s retro, hair metal, rock, Latin and progressive, with occasional headliners. Empire also doubles as a popular after-hours club on weekends. *Info: Empire Ballroom* – 3765 Las Vegas Blvd. S. between Tropicana and Harmon. Tel. 702/737-7376. Open at 10pm nightly, with after-hours starting at 1am Fri and Sat. Admission is $20, higher for special events.

LONG WEEKEND
There are great places to hear music without all the hype. One of them is the **Sand Dollar Blues Lounge**, named one of AOL Cityguide's 12 best bars in the US. It's the only exclusive blues room in town, and has been for the last 16 years. It combines neighborhood bar vibe with soul-soothing live music almost every night, just a stone's throw from the Strip. *Info: Sand Dollar Blues Lounge* – 3355 Spring Mountain Rd. at Polaris, 3/4 mi. west of the Strip. Tel. 702/871-6651. Open 24 hours, live music and $10 cover start at 10pm.

While not exactly a music-related attraction, an honorable mention goes to **Madame Tussaud's Wax Museum** at the Venetian. The London-based museum's trademark lifelike figurines are arranged in interactive ways perfectly suited for photo-ops with you. Celebrate thug life with Tupac, shake your hips with Elvis, get molested by Michael Jackson and live out all your other twisted stalker fantasies. *Info: Madame Tussaud's Wax Museum* – 3377 Las Vegas Blvd. S. between Sands and Flamingo. Tel. 702/ 862-7800. Open daily 10am-10pm. Admission is $24 for adults, $18 for seniors and students, $14 for kids 6-12.

BACK TO NATURE WEEKEND

It's a shame most visitors to Las Vegas never make it past the Strip, because the valley that surrounds it is an inspiringly beautiful piece of nature. With a trio of **enormous public recreation areas within an easy drive**, it's not hard. If you prefer your nature a little more pre-fab, there are several worthwhile attractions on the Strip itself.

Several hotels make good use of their surroundings and afford fantastic views of the mountain ranges that surround the city.

They are all fairly remote from the action of the Strip, but many of them boast amenities that don't make you miss it at all. These include the brand new **Red Rock** ($$$) and the two ultraluxe hotels on Lake Las Vegas, the **Loews** ($$$$) and **Ritz-Carlton** ($$$$). Out in Summerlin, the **JW Marriott** ($$$$) and the **Suncoast** ($$) offer Strip views from one side of the hotel and mountain vistas from the other.

If you're a hiker, visit **Red Rock National Conservation Area**, aka Red Rock Canyon. The Federal Bureau of Land Management  operates this gorgeous parkland less than a half-hour drive west of the Strip. Carved by water and wind erosion, its beautiful red sandstone and gray limestone formations and cliff outcroppings change colors throughout the day based on how the sunlight hits them. Be sure to visit the Visitors Center for trail guides and maps. There's a wide variety of hiking trails of varying lengths and difficulties, many of which offer unmatched views. For the less adventurous, the 13-mile scenic loop road provides unforgettable eyefuls on its own. Camping is allowed with a permit. *Info: Red Rock National Conservation Area* – Off W. Charleston Dr., about 25 minutes west of the Strip. Tel. 702/363-1921. The Conservation Area is open from dusk til dawn daily. Scenic drive is open at 6am daily, closes between 5pm-8pm, depending on season. Visitors Center is open from 8am-4:30pm daily, except Thanksgiving and Christmas. Admission is $5 per car.

Valley of Fire is a Nevada state park offering similar hiking and camping opportunities. Red sandstone juts out in all directions, creating a picture-perfect desert landscape. Look for bighorn sheep, burros, desert tortoise, wild horses and other southwestern animals. In addition, visitors can see prehistoric petroglyphs, carved by the Basketmaker people who predated the ancestral

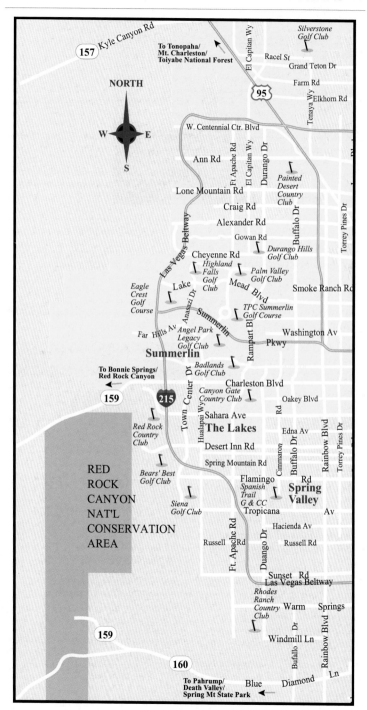

Puebloans of the southwest. The best petroglyphs are reached by a somewhat strenuous metal staircase that ascends Atlatl Rock. Most of the important formations in the Valley of Fire are alongside the road or reached by relatively short and easy trails. *Info: Valley of Fire State Park* – Tel. 702/397-2088. Park is open for day visits between dawn and dusk. The visitor center is open daily (except Christmas) from 8:30am until 4:30pm. Admission is $5 per vehicle.

If wetsuits are more your thing than dry heat, visit **Siegfried and Roy's Secret Garden** at the Mirage. In addition to lush faux rainforests where rare lions and tigers reside, the Atlantic bottlenose dolphin habitat conducts guided tours and research daily. The Secret Garden also offers the *Trainer for a Day* program, putting guests waist-deep in the water, side-by-side with these fascinating creatures. *Info: Mirage* - 3400 Las Vegas Blvd. S. between Flamingo and Spring Mountain. *Siegfried & Roy's Secret Garden* (Tel. 702/791-7889) is open from 10am-7pm daily during summer hours; 11am-5:30pm weekdays and 10am-5:30pm weekends during winter hours. Admission is $15 for adults, $10 for kids 4-12, and free for kids 3 and under. *Trainer for a*

Hiking Tips

• **Bring plenty of water** if you'll be walking the trails. Count on four liters per day per person.
• During the summer months, take your hike first thing in the morning.
• If you take an afternoon hike, be sure to give yourself enough time to find your way back before it gets dark. Otherwise you could be wandering til morning.
• **Stay on the trails** and watch your footing.
• Watch for snakes.
• Don't forget your camera.

Day program runs from 9:45am-3:15pm and costs $500 per person.

The Mirage has an impressive aquarium behind the front desk, but it's nothing compared to what you'll see down the block at Mandalay Bay's **Shark Reef**. This accredited, themed aquarium features over 1,200 species, including 15 different kinds of shark, sea turtles, and the only golden crocodiles left in the Western hemisphere. Towards the end of the exhibit is a "touch pool" where guests can pet rays, sharks and crabs. *Info: Mandalay Bay* – 3950 Las Vegas Blvd. S. at Russell Rd. Tel. 702/632-7777. *Shark Reef* is open 10am-11pm daily. Admission is $15.95 for adults, $10.95 for children 5-12.

The newest slice of nature in Las Vegas is the **Springs Preserve**, which includes historic museum galleries, the "green" Desert Living Center, 1.8 miles of trails through eight acres of botanical gardens, and the upcoming Nevada State Museum. *Info: Springs Preserve* – 333 S. Valley View Blvd. at US 95 & Alta. Tel. 702/822-7700. Admission is free to the trails and gardens. Tickets provide entry to the rest of the complex and cost $18.95 for adults, $17.05 for seniors and students, and $10.95 for kids ages 5-17.

LONG WEEKEND

The **Las Vegas Zoo**, aka the Southern Nevada Zoological-Botanical Park, doesn't stack up to those in places like San Diego, Washington or the Bronx, measuring only three acres. But it does offer a look at the flora and fauna that make the desert ecosystem unlike any other. Over 200 species are represented, including truly rare creatures, like the last family of Barbary apes in America and endangered cats. They also offer half- and full-day eco-tours that include the ghost town of Delamar, Area 51, and gemstone beds. *Info: Las Vegas Zoo* – 1775 N. Rancho Dr. Tel. 702/647-4685. Open daily 9am-5pm. Admission is $7 for adults, $5 for kids under 12 and seniors over 62. Ecotours range from $109 to $179 and include a year's membership to the zoo.

Just east of the Las Vegas Valley is the massive **Lake Mead National Recreation Area**. As the result of downstream Hoover Dam, Lake Mead is the largest man-made lake in the Western

Hemisphere, providing 550 miles of shoreline, six marinas and 247 square miles of watersports, boating and fishing. The lake contains largemouth and striped bass, catfish, crappie, trout and bluegill. *Info: Lake Mead National Recreation Area* – 601 Nevada Way, Boulder City. Tel. 702/293-8990. Open 24 hours. Visitor center open 8:30am-4:30pm every day but Thanksgiving, Christmas and New Year's. Fee of $5 per car or $3 per individual for five days' access. Annual passes are $20. Additional fees for boating, camping, etc.

Lake Mead Cruises offers very pleasant scenic rides on paddle-wheeler *The Desert Princess*. The boat departs from the Hemenway Harbor, which is the first right off of Lakeshore Scenic Drive after Lake Mead Visitor Center. The 300-passenger vessel takes passengers onto the deep blue waters of Lake Mead, surrounded by the red sandstone cliffs, turning around as it gets near the rear of Hoover Dam. *Info: Lake Mead Cruises* - Tel. 702/293-6180. Excursion cruises leave at 10am, noon, 2pm and 4pm (only at noon and 2pm November through March). Fare is $22 for adults and $10 for children. Reservations are recommended. Breakfast, dinner, dinner dance and pizza party cruises are also available.

Rental boats are also available at the Las Vegas Boat Harbor adjacent to Hemenway Harbor. Just up Lakeshore Drive is **Boulder Beach**, a popular spot for swimming and diving. River rafting is another option. Auto tours through the area also work. Take Lakeshore Drive (NV 166) to Lake Mead Parkway (NV 146) and then return to I-515. A longer tour via Northshore Road leads about 42 miles up Lake Mead and the Overton Arm to near the town of Overton at NV 169. Be sure to stop on your way to or from Hoover Dam at the beautiful **Lake Mead Overlook,** about a quarter mile off of US 93. *Info: Alan Bible Visitor Center* - US 93 at

Lakeshore Drive. Tel. 702/293-8906. Visitor center hours are daily from 8:30am until 4:30pm except for New Year's Day, Thanksgiving and Christmas.

XTREME VEGAS!!! WEEKEND

Adrenaline junkies and **aficionados of the bizarre** will find themselves right at home in Las Vegas. Beyond the rush of a hot hand at the craps table, there are countless other ways to get your blood flowing.

For pure thrill value it's hard to beat skydiving. **Skydive Las Vegas** is perfect for first-time jumpers, offering ground training several times a day. You'll jump out of a Cessna from 1-3 miles up, where you can see the Strip, Hoover Dam, Lake Mead, Mt. Charleston, the Colorado River, Red Rock and Valley of Fire. Instructor tandem jumps are recommended for virgins. For a 3-mile dive, you can expect about 60 seconds of freefall before your instructor pulls the rip cord, then you'll coast for 5 to 7 minutes before you land back where you started, at the Boulder City Airport. A 1-mile dive only gives you about 5 seconds of freefall. Shuttle transportation from the Strip is available, departing at 8 and 11am. *Info: Skydive Las Vegas* - 1608 Foothill Dr., Boulder City. Tel. 702/SKY-DIVE. Price is $199 for a 1-mile dive, $249 for a 3-mile dive. Repeat dives are discounted. Reservations recommended. You must be 18 or older to jump.

If you're not trying to jump out of a plane, you can't get higher in Vegas than on the **Stratosphere Tower** (*photo at right*), the tallest building west of the Mississippi. On its 100-story perch are three rides: the tame

Big Shot rockets riders up to the 1,081 foot height – 4 Gs upwards, negative Gs down. A big step up is **X Scream,** a seesaw-like ride that pushes you 27 feet off the edge of the tower, facing straight down. Take on the granddaddy of them all, **Insanity: The Ride.** This 64-foot arm dangles riders over the Strip and then spins them at 3 Gs and 70 degrees, over the edge, facing straight down at the city of lights, a hundred stories below. *Info: Stratosphere* – 2000 Las Vegas Blvd. S. at Baltimore. Tel. 702/380-7777. *Tower* – admission is $10.95, $7 for hotel guests, locals, seniors and children 4-12. Tower admission plus one ride is $16.95; plus two rides is $20.95; plus three rides is $24.95. Rides are $9 each purchased individually. The Xtreme All Day Unlimited package is $30.95.

There are other forms of extreme in Vegas. Perhaps the best example thereof is the **Amazing Johnathan**, a shock comic with the pretense of being a magician. His best-known trick involves knifing gruesomely through his forearm. His current act at the Sahara includes all sorts of unsavory bits, as he scarfs down cleaning products, subjects his audience to a simulated acid trip, and ensures that you'll never think of the Blue Man Group the same. *Info: Sahara* – 2535 Las Vegas Blvd. S. *The Amazing Johnathan* (Tel. 800/634-6787) performs at 10pm Fri-Tue. Tickets are $49.95 and $54.95.

LONG WEEKEND

Take a day to check out some roller coasters in and around Vegas – there's quite a few worth your attention. The city's only indoor coaster is the **Canyon Blaster** at Circus Circus' Adventuredome. It features a double loop but other than that is relatively tame.

We've mentioned the **Roller Coaster at New York-New York** before – this impressive stomach-churner's taxi-like cars go through a nearly mile-long series of barrel rolls, loops, and a tight spiral series at the very end, plus a pair of big drops. You can tell from the street that the Sahara's **Speed: The Ride** is nasty. Driven by linear induction motors, the coaster goes from 0 to 70 in four seconds, through a loop, and then straight up 224 feet in the air, before doing the whole thing in reverse. It's only 45 seconds long, but that's more than enough time for you to refund your purchases from the NASCAR Café.

The biggest, baddest coaster in town is actually about 30 miles from the Strip,the **Desperado** at Buffalo Bill's in Primm. It nearly hits the 90mph mark. It's also ungodly long: nearly three minutes, and well over a mile. Astronauts lifting off don't experience the 4 G's you'll feel here.

Info: Circus Circus – 2880 Las Vegas Blvd. S., between Convention Center and Sahara. Tel. 702/734-0410. *Canyon Blaster* is open 11am-6pm Mon-Thu, 9am-midnight Fri-Sat, and 10am-9pm Sun. Admission is $6. Riders must be 48" tall. *New York-New York* - 3790 Las Vegas Blvd. S. at Tropicana. Tel. 702/740-6969. *Roller Coaster* is open 11am-11 pm Sun-Thu, 10:30am-midnight Fri-Sat. Tickets are $14 for the first ride, $7 for re-rides, $25 for an all-day pass. Riders must be 54" tall. *Sahara* – 2535 Las Vegas Blvd. S. Tel. 702/737-2111. *Speed* is open 11am-10pm Sun-Thu and 11am-midnight Fri-Sat. Tickets are $10. Riders must be 54" tall. *Buffalo Bill's* – 31900 Las Vegas Blvd. S., Primm. Tel. 702/386-7867. *Desperado* is open 12pm-6pm Mon & Thu, 11am-midnight Fri, 10am-midnight Sat and 10am-7pm Sun. Admission is $7. Riders must be 48" tall.

Nightlife exists beyond the superclub and the ultralounge. Just like stellar ethnic food is often found in holes-in-the-wall, it's hard to find a more raucous night out than at a good old-fashioned dive bar. Vegas' finest dive, bar none, is the **Double Down Saloon**, whose clientele is a diverse mix of every kind of freak, geek, drunk and punk imaginable. These are some seriously screwed up people and you'll love every minute here. *Info: Double Down Saloon* – 4640 Paradise Rd. Tel. 702/791-5775. Open 24 hours. No cover.

To experience the sensation of skydiving without any actual sky, visit **Flyaway Indoor Skydiving**, located just off the Strip. This facility consists of a DC-3 propeller inside a 12-foot high, 22-foot wide wind tunnel, sending a blast of air upon which you will float, fall, and fly, but no worries, there's netting in between you and the prop. Instructors train the basics and then set you loose, making sure you stay aloft without careening into the padded walls. *Info: Flyaway Indoor Skydiving* – 200 Convention Center Dr. Tel. 877/545-8093. Open from 10am-9pm daily. Single flights are

$75, additional same-day flights are $40. Five flights are $200. A private 15 minute block party for five is $325. Height and weight restrictions apply.

YOU MIGHT BE A REDNECK... WEEKEND

This town has cowboy roots,the iconic Vegas Vic towering over Fremont Street is proof. Or, the **National Finals Rodeo** that fills the town with cowboys every December, selling out every hotel months in advance. There's plenty year-round for visitors who like both kinds of music: country and western.

A few hotels really get down with the cowboy vibe, both on the Strip and off. On the Strip, there's **Harrah's** ($$) and the **Sahara** ($), with an old-school Vegas casino and NASCAR, while **Hooters** ($$) and the **Las Vegas Hilton** ($$) are just off the Strip.

One casino defines the cowboy experience in Las Vegas: **Sam's Town** ($$). It's located on Boulder Highway. Its Old West décor is complemented by a **Shepler's Western Wear** department store. There's also **South Point** ($$), four miles south of the Mandalay Bay. Its equestrian center and diverse musical entertainment make it a year-round draw. Nearby the **Silverton** ($$) is a locals' casino with an attractive park lodge feel.

Our recommend for a night of line dancing is **Dylan's** on the Boulder Highway. Walk through the saloon doors to find a beer tub, a mechanical bull and an expansive dance floor where weekends see crowds dressed the part, line dancing to remixes of country hits. Free dance lessons are offered from 7:30 ro 9pm. *Info: Dylan's* – 4660 Boulder Highway. Tel. 702/451-4006. Open from 7pm-6am Thu-Sat. No cover.

It may not make a lot of sense, but the **Sahara** is ground zero in Vegas for stock car fans. Besides the Speed roller coaster, there's also a NASCAR Café, a racing-themed midway, and the **Las Vegas Cyber Speedway**, a simulator pitting you against seven other drivers in 7/8 scale stock cars at simulated speeds of 220mph. *Info: Sahara* – 2535 Las Vegas Blvd. S. *Las Vegas Cyber Speedway* (Tel. 702/737-2750) is open 11am-8pm Sun-Thu, 11am-10pm Fri-Sat. Admission is $10. All-day passes to this and Speed are $21.95.

There's plenty of redneck-friendly dining in Vegas. The most recent addition to the scene is **Toby Keith's I Love This Bar & Grill**. Located at Harrah's, this lively eatery includes a concert stage, a guitar-shaped bar, TK memorabilia and the Dixie Chicks in manacles. There's nightly entertainment and a Southern-influenced menu including a fried bologna sandwich.

At the Sahara, the **NASCAR Café** features a variety of down-home food, stock cars, assorted memorabilia and the Carzilla Bar. If you prefer two wheels to four, there's a large **Harley-Davidson Café** with 15 custom hogs on display. The 32-foot replica of the classic Heritage Softail bike at the front façade has real curb appeal.

Info: Harrah's Las Vegas – 3475 Las Vegas Blvd. S., between Flamingo and Sands. *Toby Keith's I Love This Bar & Grill* (Tel. 702/697-2880) opens at 11:30 am weekdays and 10 am weekends, with food served until 11pm Sun-Thu and midnight Fri-Sat, with live music until 2am. *Sahara* –2535 Las Vegas Blvd. S. at Sahara. Tel. 702/737-2111. *NASCAR Café* (Tel. 702/734-7223) is open 11am-10pm Mon-Thu, 11am-11pm Fri, 10am-midnight Sat, and 9am-10pm Sun. *Harley-Davidson Café* – 3725 Las Vegas Blvd. S. at Harmon. Tel. 702/740-4555. Open 11am-11pm Sun-Thu, 11am-midnight Fri-Sat.

Near the South Point is one of the city's most boisterous country-western bars, **Stoney's Rockin' Country**. Along with a huge hardwood

NASCAR Weekend Tip

Avoid the Sahara during NASCAR weekend, usually in early March. Crowds here are massive. This is a busy and bustling time all over town, with a 300-mile Busch series race on Saturday and a 400-mile NEXTEL Cup race on Sunday taking place at the Las Vegas Motor Speedway.

dance floor and a mechanical bull, the club has bowling, cowboy arcade and pool tables – plus an attractive $20 all-you-can-drink draft beer. On weekends, bikini bull riding and go-go dancers make for a wild time. *Info: Stoney's Rockin' Country* – 9151 Las Vegas Blvd S. between Serene and Pebble. Tel. 702/435-BULL.

More in the mood for PG entertainment? One of the more wholesome acts in town is that of the **Scintas** in **LOL – Laugh Out Loud** at the Las Vegas Hilton's Shimmer Cabaret. This family combines music, comedy, and impressions in a light-hearted fashion, with a strong focus on God and country. Brooks & Dunn perform regularly at the Hilton, which has turned out to be a surprisingly country-friendly venue. Reba McEntire recently completed an extended run there. Other acts coming through include Big & Rich, Trace Adkins and Vince Gill. *Info: Las Vegas Hilton* - 3000 Paradise Rd., between Desert Inn and Sahara, 3/4 mi. east of the Strip. Tel. 702/732-5111. *The Scintas* shows at 7pm Tue-Sat. Tickets are $59.95.

LONG WEEKEND
The attractions at Sahara may get you jonesing to drive a race car for real. The Las Vegas Motor Speedway hosts two attractions that capture the thrill of the checkered flag. The **Richard Petty Driving Experience** lets you feel the rush of speeding along the oval in a stock car at 165mph, either as driver or passenger. The **Mario Andretti Racing School** is a similar concept, only with custom-built Indy-style cars that hit 180mph.

Info: Richard Petty Experience – 6975 Speedway Blvd., Unit D-106. Tel. 800/BE-PETTY. Ride-alongs are $159. Driving experiences range from $399 to $2999. Reservations are required, hours vary by program. *Mario Andretti Racing School* – 6925 Speedway Blvd., Suite C-106. Tel. 702/315-6300. Ride-alongs are $75-319. Driving experiences are $399-$3999. Reservations are required, call for dates of sessions.

KEEP IT GAY WEEKEND

They don't call it "Fabulous" Las Vegas for nothing. As one of America's most gay-friendly cities, Sin City gets plenty of this affluent demographic's travel dollars. While many of Vegas' mainstream entertainment options appeal to gays, there's also a strong local LGBT scene, with a respectable circuit of bars and even a gay resort, the **Blue Moon** ($$$), a boutique hotel whose amenities include a clothing-optional pool and a Jacuzzi grotto. Other hotels in close proximity to the circuit are the **Hard Rock** ($$$), **Terrible's** ($) and **Atrium Suites** ($$). For up to date event information, check out *Q Vegas* magazine.

Perhaps nothing signifies the tolerant ethos of Las Vegas like the presence of drag shows. The grand dame of them all, so to speak, is Riviera's **An Evening at La Cage**. As Joan Rivers, acclaimed impersonator Frank Marino leads the festivities. Performers play icons like Madonna, Cher, Whitney Houston, Britney Spears, Jennifer Lopez and... Michael Jackson? *Info: Riviera* – 2901 Las Vegas Blvd. S. between Sahara and Convention Center. Tel. 702/ 734-5110. *An Evening at La Cage* (Tel. 702/794-9433) shows at 7:30pm Wed-Mon. Tickets are $55.

Also of interest is **Fashionistas**, a critically acclaimed erotic (but not topless) show at the Harmon Theater, aka **Krave**, the alternative nightclub at Miracle Mile. There's a distinct fetish element to this show, combining a boy-meets-girl story with a titillating girl-meets-girl subplot, setting the "story," such as it was, to the music of the Prodigy, Crystal Method, Madonna and Evanescence, with modern dance and an occasional bit of Cirque-style aerialism. This show, interestingly, was adapted from the porn movie of the same name by director John Stagliano. Its choreography was voted the city's best by the *Review-Journal*. Fashionistas can be legitimately described as a sleeper hit. Along similar lines, **Zumanity**, the adult Cirque du Soleil show at the New York-New York has something for everybody, with a transvestite emcee as well as bisexual and gay segments. *Info: Harmon Theater* – 3663

Las Vegas Blvd. S. at Harmon St. Tel. 702/836-0833. *Fashionistas* shows at 9pm Tue-Sun. Tickets are $49.95-79.95. *New York-New York* - 3790 Las Vegas Blvd. S. at Tropicana. *Zumanity* (702/740-6815) showtimes are 7:30 and 10:30pm Tue, Wed, Fri-Sun. Tickets are $69, $79 and $99. Duo Sofas are $129 per person.

Las Vegas has a thriving art and antique district near the intersection of Charleston and Main just south of downtown, with dozens of small galleries, shops, and co-ops where virtually any type of curio or creation can be found. **The Attic** is a renowned and popular spot for vintage and vintage-style clothing, while the **Arts Factory** houses a diverse collective. The **Funk House** is a colorful can't-miss shop credited as the genesis for the Gateway Arts District's renaissance, including the popular First Fridays event. *Info: The Attic* – 1018 S. Main St. Tel. 702/388-4088. Open 9am-5pm Mon-Sat. *Arts Factory* – 101-109 E. Charleston Blvd. Tel. 702/676-1111. Individual gallery hours vary, but usually include Mon-Fri noon-4pm and weekends by appointment. *Funk House* – 1228 Casino Center Blvd. Tel. 702/678-6278. Open 10am-5pm.

The newest diva on the Strip has pretty big shoes to fill, as **Bette Midler** took the stage of The Colosseum at Caesars Palace in February, replacing the most successful Vegas headline stint in history, Celine Dion's A New Day. Midler's show will be tacky and bawdy compared to her predecessor, and the Divine Miss M wouldn't have it any other way. *Info: Caesars Palace* - 3570 Las Vegas Blvd. S. at Flamingo. *Bette Midler* (Tel. 877/7-BETTE-M) performs Tue-Wed and Fri-Sun at 7:30pm. Tickets are $95-$250.

Las Vegas has a decent bar circuit as well, although most of it lies off the Strip. **Krave** is the only alternative club on the Strip, with themed parties (including drag shows) almost every night of the week. Friday nights bring out black-clad breeders for Sanctuary, a goth party. *Info: Krave* – 3663 Las Vegas Blvd. S. at Harmon St. Tel. 702/836-0833. Open at 11pm nightly, 10pm Sun. Admission varies.

Located at the heart of the so-called "Fruit Loop," **Gipsy** is a popular dance clubs in town, especially among the younger set, owing to a casual, down-to-earth vibe and relaxed dress code. Entertainment here includes go-go boys, balloon drops, cabaret and drag shows, depending on the night. Right across Paradise are Get Booked, a gay bookstore, the low-key **Buffalo**, a neighborhood bar with slots and pool tables; the **Suede Lounge,** an ultralounge style piano bar featuring karaoke and movie nights; and **FreeZone**, a multi-faceted nightclub featuring karaoke, beer busts, a martini social on Fridays, and drag shows every weekend.

Info: Gipsy – 4605 Paradise Rd. at Naples, between Flamingo and Tropicana. Tel. 702/731-1919. Open 9pm nightly, cover varies, free before 10pm. *The Buffalo* – 4640 Paradise Rd. at Naples, between Flamingo and Tropicana. Tel. 702/733-8355. Open 24 hours, no cover. *Suede Lounge* - 4640 Paradise Rd. Suite 4 at Naples, between Flamingo and Tropicana. Tel. 702/364-1167. Open Tue-Sun 6pm-9am. Cover varies. *FreeZone* – 610 E. Naples Dr. at Paradise. Tel. 702/733-6701. Open 24 hours, no cover.

LONG WEEKEND
Consider a trip to **Lake Mead National Recreation Area,** which boasts a gay nude beach. Take Lake Mead Blvd. east past Hollywood Blvd. to the stop sign. Turn left towards Overton and Calville Bay, then 4 3/4 mi. later turn right on 8.0 Road. Take every left fork in the road and park in the lot overlooking the lake. It's about a five minute walk north of the lot.

A mile east of the Strip is Commercial Center, another gay epicenter. It's located between Sahara and Karen, east of Paradise. Nightlife options here include the **Las Vegas Lounge**, a transsexual bar; the **Spotlight Lounge**, with 24-hour slots and pool; **Ramrod**, a cruise bar with a storied history and slots, darts, pool and a dance floor; and the **Badlands Saloon**, a country-western bar for your inner Brokeback. *Info: Las Vegas Lounge* – 900 E. Karen. Tel. 702/737-9350. *Spotlight Lounge* – 957 E. Sahara. Tel. 702/696-0202. *Ramrod* – 900 E. Karen, #H-102. Tel. 702/735-0885. *Badlands Saloon* – 953 E. Sahara #22. Tel. 702/792-9262. All are open 24 hours, with no cover.

Though drag shows used to be bigger on the Strip, their popularity has faded in recent years. The self-described "drag queen capital of the world," **Lucky Cheng's** bucks the trend at Krave. This imported East Village cabaret is entirely staffed by transvestites, both fabulous and campy. Audience participation, comedy and music highlight meals. Seatings are open all night long and include a prix fixe three-course pan-Asian meal prepared by chef Jean David Daudet, formerly of Drai's. *Info: Lucky Cheng's* – 3663 Las Vegas Blvd. S. Tel. 702/836-0836. Admission, including three-course meal, is $69.95.

VEGAS CULTURE & HISTORY WEEKEND

Even though Las Vegas celebrated its centennial recently, it's often derided as a town without history. It's understandably difficult for a town in such a constant state of flux. But that's not to say that this is a city of barbarians with no appreciation for the finer things, or that there's no historical perspective to be found. You just have to look.

Perhaps the city's most popular cultural event, **First Fridays** draws as many as 100,000 locals to the **Gateway Arts District** on the first Friday of every month, as dozens of small galleries around Commerce, Main and Charleston open their doors to the exceptionally diverse crowd. The streets are blocked off and a festive party atmosphere pervades, with live musicians performing on just about every block, playing everything imaginable; entertainers like tarot readers, breakdancers and fire breathers; and full bars under the night sky. *Info: First Fridays* – Gateway Arts District, near Charleston & Main. Tel. 702/384-0092. Held from 6pm-10pm on the first Friday of the month, though individual gallery hours may vary. Free admission.

While Vegas doesn't have the same kind of art scene as cities like New York or Washington, it does a respectable job. There are two notable galleries on the Strip, the **Guggenheim Hermitage Museum** at the Venetian and the **Bellagio Gallery of Fine Art**. The exhibition on display at press time featured modern masters including Cezanne, Picasso, Manet, Chagall and van Gogh. The Bellagio gallery recently featured Picasso's ceramics and Ansel Adams' photography. *Info: Venetian* – 3355 Las Vegas Blvd. S. between Sands and Flamingo. *Guggenheim Hermitage Museum* (Tel. 702/414-2440) is open 9:30am-8:30pm daily. Admission is $15 for adults, $12 for seniors and Nevada residents, $10 for students with ID and free for children under 12. Annual passes are available. *Bellagio* - 3600 Las Vegas Blvd. S. at Flamingo. *Bellagio Gallery of Fine Art* (702/693-7871) is open 9am-10pm. Admission is $17, $14 for students, seniors and Nevada residents. Annual passes are available.

The city's premier gallery is the Smithsonian-affiliated **Las Vegas Art Museum**, with over 50 years of history 10 miles from the Strip. It rotates a varied mix of ambitious exhibitions. The museum also sponsors many art competitions and community outreach programs. *Info: Las Vegas Art Museum* – 9600 W. Sahara. Tel. 702/360-8000. Open 10am-5pm Tue-Sat, 1-5pm Sun. Admission is $6, $5 for seniors, $3 for students with ID, free for kids under 12.

Downtown is the hub for Vegas history, with two interesting stops: the **Neon Museum**, which features about a dozen lovingly restored vintage neon signs; and the **Lost Vegas Gambling Museum**, which walks visitors through the hundred year history of the shining jewel of the desert with an impressive collection of photos and assorted memorabilia including slot machines, matchbooks, postcards, chips and cards. One section pays homage to luminaries who called this city home, people like Howard Hughes, Frank Sinatra, and of course the King. *Info: Neon Museum* – 702/387-NEON. Open 24 hours, free admission. Guided tours are a suggested $15 donation per person. *Lost Vegas Gambling Museum* – 450 Fremont St. Tel. 702/385-1883. Open 10am-8pm daily. Admission is $2.50 for adults, $1.25 for seniors.

Of course, any discussion of Nevada history must include the Eighth Wonder of the World, the **Hoover Dam.** About 35 miles from the Strip, it draws about a million visitors each year who marvel at this 725-foot high behemoth, which sustains Las Vegas with both its water supply and its electricity. A highly informa-

tive guided tour is available, lasting about two hours if you partake in each of the sections. You can pick and choose which parts of the tour to take. To get here, take I-215 or I-515 to US 93 south. *Info: Hoover Dam –* US 93, Boulder City. Tel. 702/494-2517. Tours available from 9am-6pm daily. Admission is $11, $9 for seniors and military, $6 for kids 7-16. Parking is $7.

Henderson's **Clark County Heritage Museum** traces the area's history from the Paleolithic era to the present. Its highlight is Heritage Street, a tree-lined boulevard with eight historic buildings, transplanted and restored. They include the 1932 Boulder City Depot, complete with Union Pacific steam engine and a turn-of-the-century newspaper print shop. *Info: Clark County Heritage Museum –* 1820 S. Boulder Hwy., Henderson. Tel. 702/455-7955. Open 9am-4:30pm. Admission is $1.50, $1 for children under 15 and seniors.

LONG WEEKEND
In nearby Overton, the **Lost City Museum of Archaeology** showcases Anasazi Indian artifacts that were excavated from Pueblo Grande de Nevada, a thousand year old city along the Virgin and Muddy River valleys. To get here, take I-15 north to exit 93, turn right on Moapa Valley Blvd., and continue 11 miles. *Info: Lost City Museum of Archaeology –* 721 S. Moapa Valley Blvd., Overton. Tel. 702/397-2193. Open 8:30am-4:30pm daily. Admission is $3, $2 for seniors, free for children.

Located on the campus of UNLV, the **Marjorie Barrick Museum of Natural History** features living desert wildlife as well as a permanent exhibition spotlighting the Navajo, Hopi and Paiute Indian tribes. Art and artifacts are also on display. It's fascinating and free. *Info: Marjorie Barrick Museum of Natural History –* 4505 S. Maryland Pkwy., near Harmon on the UNLV campus. Open 8am-4:45pm Mon-Fri, 10am-2pm Sat. Admission is free.

Bonnie Springs Ranch is a recreated 19th-century Old West mining town, with restored and recreated buildings including a bank, opera house, sheriff's office, schoolhouse, and even a wax museum. For something less sanitized, visit the **Pioneer Saloon** in Goodsprings, an honest-to-goodness ghost town. During its boomtown mining days, this was a popular hangout for silver miners who worked nearby. Just take I-15 south to the Jean/Goodsprings exit, head west on Highway 161 for 7 miles to W. Spring St. *Info: Bonnie Springs Ranch* – 1 Gunslinger Way, Blue Diamond. Tel. 702/875-4191. Open from 10:30am-6pm during the summer, 10:30am-5pm in the winter. Admission is $20 per carload. *Pioneer Saloon* – W. Spring St., Goodsprings. Tel. 702/874-9362. Free admission.

One of Nevada's most interesting bits of history is its role in the development of the A-bomb at the Nevada Test Site, home of nearly 1,000 nuclear tests. The stark 8,000 sq. ft. **Atomic Testing Museum** features Geiger counters and other measurement devices, photographs, pop culture items and interactive exhibits including "manipulators," the mechanical arms used to handle radioactive materials, and a simulated bunker from which you can view an above-ground detonation. *Info: Atomic Testing Museum* – 755 E. Flamingo Rd., east of Paradise. Tel. 702/794-5161. Open 9am-5pm Mon-Sat, 1pm-5pm Sun. Admission is $12, $9 for seniors, students, children 7-17 and military.

THE HIGH ROLLER WEEKEND

If money is no object, you'll have access to some of the most spectacular meals, entertainment, and accommodations anywhere on the planet. If you're planning on gambling and don't have an existing relationship with a casino, **consider putting your bankroll on deposit** prior to your visit. This way **a casino host**, the all-important connection who can hook you up with comps, **will know your level of play** right off the bat and can treat you accordingly from the moment you arrive. When you're ready to gamble, simply withdraw the money from the casino cage.

Best High-End Hotels

- **Wynn Las Vegas**
(especially the Tower Suites)
- **Caesars Palace**
(particularly the new
Augustus Tower)
- **Four Seasons**
- **Red Rock**
- **Bellagio**

Even for non-gamblers, ultraluxe high-end accommodations are available. The hotel-within-a-hotel concept is gaining momentum, offering premium accommodations and attentive service. Perhaps the most luxurious and stylish are the 51 **Skylofts at MGM Grand**, two-story suites featuring modern urban design and cutting-edge amenities, including plasma TVs, infinity bathtubs and in-mirror LCD televisions. Personalized service features include complimentary airport transfers in a Maybach 62, in-loft check-in and 24 hour butler service, which includes complimentary packing, unpacking and bath spa amenities. These AAA Five Diamond accommodations start at $800 a night.

The **Fantasy Suites** at the **Palms** have ridiculous amenities like a half basketball court in the Hardwood Suite, two bowling lanes in the Kingpin Suite and a DJ booth in the Crib Suite. Located on the 25th and 26th floors, they all boast impressive Strip views through the floor-to-ceiling glass windows. These start at $2,500 a night. The **Fairway Villas** at the **Wynn**, spotlight their own secluded private entrance and check-in, expansive marble entryways, audiophile sound systems, a massage room, his and hers master bathrooms, mirrored ceilings, a private pool (shared by villa guests, but exclusively theirs), and lovely balconies or patios. These start around $1,000.

Cirque du Soleil is everywhere on the Strip, and their MGM Grand installation, **KÀ**, breaks new technological ground in its presentation. It includes Cirque's most intricate lighting rig, its biggest projection system, plus innovative uses of puppetry and pyrotechnics. It also introduces several disciplines of performance new to Cirque stages, so the "seen one, seen 'em all" attitude that some people have about Cirque doesn't apply. *Info: MGM Grand* - 3799 Las Vegas Blvd. S. at Tropicana. *KÀ* (Tel. 702/796-9999) shows at 7 and 9:30pm Tue-Sat. Tickets are $69-150.

Later on in the evening, visit the new hot spot in town: **Seamless**. This $20 million hotspot starts off as a strip club, and then later in the evening turns into a bona fide after hours ultralounge. Its bathrooms are intense, with morphing colors, LCD lighting effects, and water effects. The club actually transforms furniture, lighting, music from one use to the other. The catwalk rises off the wooden dance floor, and the grooving commences. VIP membership provides perks aplenty, including a complimentary bottle on every visit. *Info: Seamless* – 4740 Arville St., north of Tropicana, about 1 1/2 mi. east of the Strip. Tel. 702/227-5200. Open 24 hours. Cover is $30.

While the mountains surrounding the Las Vegas valley are majestic, they are nothing compared to the awe-inspiring Grand Canyon. And while it's a manageable day trip of a drive, you can do it in half the time with twice the style via helicopter. Try **Maverick's** 3 1/2 hour Wind Dancer tour, which takes you past the extinct volcano Fortification Hill and deep into the Grand Canyon, landing on the floor for a champagne toast, then flying back through the neon canyon of the Strip. *Info: Maverick Helicopter Tours* – 6075 Las Vegas Blvd. S. Tel. 702/261-0007. Wind Dancer tours are $447-477 per person and run approximately 4 hours. Hours by appointment/reservation.

Or, for a more whimsical flight, charter a hot air balloon. **Adventure Balloons** flies its balloons over the Strip and Red Rock Canyon at dawn. Though prevailing winds blow out of the south-

Comps for Whales

VIP goes by another name here: **RFB**. This stands for Room, Food and Beverage and denotes a guest whose expenses are **comped**, that is, picked up by the house. Usually this red carpet treatment is given to high rollers (AKA whales), with the expectation that they will give the casino a certain amount of action over the course of their visit. For an average casino, to get RFB you must make $10,000-$20,000 in total bets (not necessarily gamble that amount of your own money) over the course of a weekend. If you want a high roller suite, **try betting $10,000 a hand!**

west, it's a crapshoot on any given day. Upon successful landing, the chase crew brings you cake and champagne. Be aware that hot temperatures and strong winds scrub flights. *Info: Adventure Balloons* – Tel. 702/247-6905. Flights at dawn daily. Reservations required. Flights are $175-200 per person, depending on season.

Las Vegas is home to some of the most extravagant restaurants in America. Perhaps the most opulent of the bunch is **Joël Robuchon**, at the Mansion at MGM Grand. For $360 a head, you'll get the "chef of the century" making a heavenly 16-course *menu dégustation* that changes daily based on season and market. French artisanal cheeses and a dessert cart round out the evening at the only Michelin Three Star restaurant in Vegas. *Info: MGM Grand* - 3799 Las Vegas Blvd. S. at Tropicana. *Joël Robuchon* (Tel. 702/891-7925) is open 5:30-10pm Sun-Thu, til 10:30pm on Fri-Sat. Reservations required.

Another world-renowned French chef has opened up his first stateside venture on the Las Vegas Strip. Located at Caesars Palace, Michelin Two Star winner **Restaurant Guy Savoy** features the all of Savoy's inspired signature dishes and breathtaking presentation in a recreation of his landmark Paris dining room. Three full time sommeliers include one just for champagne. *Info: Caesars Palace* - 3570 Las Vegas Blvd. S. at Flamingo. *Restaurant Guy Savoy* (Tel. 877/346-4642) is open 5:30-10:30pm Wed-Sun.

When night falls, you'll want to check out one of the other top shows in town – **Danny Gans** has been selling out his showroom at the Mirage for years, performing his schizophrenic repertoire of over 300 nuanced, strikingly accurate impressions. Gans is a versatile and enchanting performer who can sing Macy Gray and Billy Joel, and impersonate George Burns or George Bush. *Info: Mirage* - 3400 Las Vegas Blvd. S. between Flamingo and Spring Mountain. Tel. 702/791-7111. *Danny Gans* (Tel. 702/792-7777) performs at 8pm Tue, Wed, Fri, Sat. Tickets are $100.

The Bellagio's Cirque du Soleil installation, '**O**,' is a wonder to behold. Concept here is the infinite and the elements, most notably water. *Eau* is the French word for it, making the title a clever homonym. Unlike other Cirque shows, a good portion of this one is in and under the water of this 1.5 million gallon pool. so divers and synchronized swimmers join the usual repertoire of dancers, acrobats, and other performers. This show is quite different than the aforementioned KÀ, and generally better reviewed. If you're into the whole Cirque thing, there's no reason you wouldn't enjoy either or both. *Info: Bellagio* - 3600 Las Vegas Blvd. S. at Flamingo. 'O' (Tel. 888-488-7111) shows at 7:30 and 10:30pm Wed-Sun. Tickets are $99-$150.

On Sunday mornings, the place to be is Bally's, where you'll find the **Sterling Brunch**, a classically indulgent spread where the sushi is made to order, the Perrier-Jouet champagne flows like wine, and an array of remarkable desserts may just inspire a bulimic episode just to make room. Other featured menu items include exotic delicacies like venison, rack of lamb, horseradish-crusted lobster tail, and breast of pheasant. The waitstaff will actually fetch your food of choice and bring it to your table, eliminating buffet-style queues. *Info: Bally's Las Vegas* – 3645 Las Vegas Blvd. S. at Flamingo. Tel. 702/739-4111. *Sterling Brunch* starts at 9:30am, last seating is at 1:30pm. Cost is $65 per person plus tax and tip.

Papmering yourself with a spa day offers the chance to decompress and rejuvenate from the hustle and bustle of a Vegas vacation. One of the newest spas in town is also the oldest: the **Qua Baths & Spa** at Caesars Palace. This facility harkens back to the days of the Empire itself, offering Roman baths (warm, hot and cold) designed to invigorate. It also boasts a Laconium room, tea sommeliers and the Arctice Ice room, where snow falls from

Other Great Spas

The spa is the new must-have amenity for any Vegas hotel worth its salt. But the high-end places are truly decadent. Besides the ones we've already mentioned, we really like:

- **Planet Hollywood Spa by Mandara** (Planet Hollywood)
- **Spa Bellagio**
- **Spa Vita di Lago** (Ritz-Carlton Lake Las Vegas)
- **Hibiscus Spa** (Westin Casuarina)
- **Paris Spa by Mandara** (Paris Las Vegas)

from the ceiling. *Info: Caesars Palace* - 3570 Las Vegas Blvd. S. at Flamingo. *Qua Baths & Spa* (Tel. 866/782-0655) day passes are $35.

Out in Summerlin, the stately JW Marriott's **Aquae Sulis** spa is quite attractive, with ultramodern facilities overlooking the  resort's water features, plus Zen-friendly décor with music and scents practically relaxing you into a trance. The decadent, refreshing treatments make this place a favorite among locals and visitors alike. We highly recommend their signature treatment, the Fire and Ice Massage, combining traditional Swedish techniques with hot basalt and cold marble stones. Aquae Sulis also features extensive hydrotherapy facilities. *Info: JW Marriott Las Vegas Resort & Spa* – 21 N. Rampart Blvd., off Summerlin Pkwy, Tel. 702/869-7807 or 877/869-8777.

LONG WEEKEND

There are so many great restaurants in this town that a weekend is practically just an appetizer. Take, for example, the Bellagio, one of the few places in the world with two Five Diamond restaurants under the same roof. Julian Serrano's **Picasso** offers Mediterranean cuisine served in seasonal four- or five-course prix fixe showcases, available with wine pairings. The walls are adorned with an extensive collection of original Pablo Picasso paintings. **Le Cirque** is one of the best-reviewed French restaurants around, eschewing the heavy, super-rich dishes that tend to define this cuisine in favor of more rustic fare, while at the same time including elegant ingredients and superlative preparations. *Info: Bellagio* - 3600 Las Vegas Blvd. S. at Flamingo. Tel. 702/693-7111. *Picasso* is open 6-9:30pm Wed-Mon. *Le Cirque* is open 5:30-10pm nightly. Reservations for both can be made by calling 877/234-6358. Reservations and jackets are necessary for each.

Consider taking advantage of **bottle service** at one of the city's top nightspots. Bottle service gets you the liquor of your choice, mixers and glasses enough for four people, plus your own private booth or table. It's one of the ultimate status symbols in this town. One of the newest hotspots is **Cherry** at Red Rock. Once you walk through the most blatantly suggestive entryway ever, you'll discover a plush club whose décor and features mimic the natural beauty of Red Rock Canyon. We also like the tables on the patio at **Tryst**. White linen affords some semblance of privacy while you gaze out at the waterfall that serves as the club's visual focus. *Info: Red Rock* – 11011 W. Charleston Blvd. at the 215 freeway. Tel. 702/797-7777. *Cherry* is open Wed-Sun from 10pm-4am. No cover. *Wynn Las Vegas* - 3131 Las Vegas Blvd. S. at Spring Mountain. *Tryst* (Tel. 702/770-3375) is open 10pm-4am Thu-Sun. Cover is $30 for men, $20 for women.

Right now though, the crème de la crème of the ever-changing Vegas club scene is **PURE** at Caesars Palace. It's a favored haunt of all the Paris and Britneys of the world. Here you'll find the most beautiful party people in Vegas, and more silicone than you'll find in a half dozen strip clubs. DJ AM reportedly gets paid $100,000 a week for his Friday night residency here, so that should give you an idea of the kind of money that gets thrown around by the patrons of this always-in-demand hotspot. *Info: Caesars Palace* - 3570 Las Vegas Blvd. S. at Flamingo. Tel. 702/731-7110. *PURE* is open 8pm-4am Tue-Sat. Cover is $20.

Scores now inhabits the elaborate building that used to house the Jaguars club. This place would fit right in at Caesars Palace, with Corinthian columns and opulent luxury everywhere. The club even includes its own steakhouse, wine cellar and cigar humidor. *Info: Scores* – 3355 Procyon St., at Desert Inn, 1 mi. west of the Strip. Tel. 702/367-6040. Open from 8pm-5am. Cover is $30.

Art lovers can take home plenty of home décor from Las Vegas. Many of the premium shopping malls on the Strip feature numerous galleries showcasing diverse artists. These small galleries can be a great place to browse or buy. For starters, check out Peter Max and the Elysium Gallery at the **Forum Shops**, Kush Fine Art and Oh My Godard Gallery at Planet Hollywood's **Miracle Mile**, or the Bernard K. Passman and Regis galleries at the **Venetian's Grand Canal Shoppes**.

For a really indulgent meal, the most expensive in town can be found at **Fleur de Lys** at Mandalay Bay. The FleurBurger 5000, so named for its mind-boggling $5,000 price, is made with Kobe beef, black truffles and foie gras on a truffle brioche. It comes with a bottle of 1990 Chateau Petrus and imported glassware that you keep. *Info: Mandalay Bay* – 3950 Las Vegas Blvd. S. at Russell Rd. Tel. 702/632-7777. *Fleur de Lys* open 5:30-10:30pm.

5. ONE TO TWO WEEKS

If you've got a week or two in Las Vegas, that should give you enough time to experience quite a bit of what it has to offer. There's time aplenty, so you can do it all: shows, great restaurants, a few buffets, strip clubs, nightclubs, whatever turns you on. This chapter features our tips for making the most out of longer trips to Vegas.

SIN CITY "RELAXCITEMENT!"

In this first one-week plan, we're going to give you some basic tips on how to pace yourself at the tables, ideas on where to stay and eat, and getting that perfect mix of relaxation and excitement that Las Vegas is all about!

Bankroll yourself properly

Pace yourself while gambling. Divide your total budget by the number of days to get your daily bankroll, and stick to it. There are few worse feelings than running out of money early. Don't "chase" your losses. It's certainly preferable to end a night down than to dig yourself a hole. Don't miss out on the fun because you blew your budget at the roulette wheel.

Consider splitting your week between two or three different properties

There are several advantages to this. If you have sufficient play history at several casinos, you may be able to get your entire week comped, two nights here, three there. Also, you can save money by spending weeknights at the nicer places and weekends in more budget digs.

Rent a car

For longer trips, taxis become tiresome and really start to add up. Las Vegas has some of the cheapest car rental rates in the country, so this winds up being a more cost-effective alternative for longer stays.

Join slot/players clubs

Though we recommend this for all visits regardless of length, it's particularly important for longer trips, because you'll likely put in enough play to get at least a few comps or a little cashback for your action, plus hotel room offers for your next trip.

Since a trip of this length doesn't need quite the regimented approach of a quick weekend, we've broken this trip into suggestions by category.

Hotels
Stay at a **casino hotel** for most of the trip. Otherwise it's just too much hassle to get back and forth, enjoy a midday siesta, take a swim, or do all other kinds of things. Most non-gaming hotels are fairly limited-service, so you'll wind up spending most of your trip elsewhere. You'd think that non-gaming hotels would be generally cheaper than casino hotels of equivalent quality, but that doesn't really hold true. The casinos have all kinds of other ways to get your money besides your room: dining, entertainment and of course the slots and tables. Non-gaming hotels only have the one revenue stream, so you actually tend to get better value at gaming hotels.

Also, consider staying at one of the **locals' casinos** for part of your trip. They offer expansive casino floors, better return on your slot/ video poker investment than the Strip, and generous comps. Many of Station Casinos' properties are excellent choices in this respect. **Sunset Station** ($$) and **Santa Fe Station** ($$), while somewhat remote from the Strip and downtown, feature excellent rooms for the price. **The Orleans** ($$), **Gold Coast** ($$) and **Terrible's** ($) combine value accommodations and easy Strip access.

Dining
One week in Vegas means twenty-one chances to stuff your face. You're not going to want to do the fancy gourmet thing every night, so we're going to break down some other options for you as well.

Vegas does have some of America's best fine dining, so do take advantage. Try **Nobu,** the brainchild of Nobu Matsuhisa and Iron Chef Masaharu Morimoto, at the Hard Rock for exquisite Japanese cuisine in a modern yet warm and inviting Eastern environment. They import their fish daily from Tokyo. Charlie Palmer's **Aureole** at Mandalay Bay and **Bradley Ogden** at Caesars Palace provide innovative and inspired new American cuisine, thoughtful wine pairings, spectacular desserts and engaged, supremely competent service.

For Italian fare, **Café Martorano** serves ballsy South Philly favorites in a party environment. You want wiseguy cred? Chef Steve Martorano catered every Sopranos wrap party. Of course, that can't compare to **Rao's** at Caesars Palace – East Harlem's "Dorsia" of Neapolitan cuisine – this restaurant's hundred-year history includes mob hits, Prohibition bootlegging and legendary lemon chicken.. Meanwhile, Food Network star Mario Batali holds court at his Palazzo steakhouse, **Carnevino**, and next door at Venetian's **B&B Ristorante**.

Info: *Nobu* (Tel. 702/693-5090) is open 6-11pm nightly. *Caesars Palace* - 3570 Las Vegas Blvd. S. at Flamingo. *Bradley Ogden* (Tel. 702/731-7413) and *Rao's* (Tel. 877/346-4642) are open from 5-11pm nightly. *Mandalay Bay* – 3950 Las Vegas Blvd. S. at Russell Rd. *Aureole* (Tel. 702/632-7401) is open 5:30-10pm nightly. *Rio* - 3700 W. Flamingo Rd., 3/4 mi. west of the Strip. *Café Martorano* (Tel. 702/221-8279) is open from 5:30pm to 2am nightly. *Palazzo* – 3265 Las Vegas Blvd S. at Sands. *Carnevino* (Tel. 702.789-4141) hours not available at press time. *Venetian* – 3355 Las Vegas Blvd. S. between Sands and Flamingo. *B&B Ristorante* (Tel. 702/266-9977) is open from 5pm-11pm.

Casual dining options abound here besides the ubiquitous casino coffee shops. But even many of these are special. Among the best is the **Grand Lux Café** at the Venetian, an offshoot of the Cheesecake Factory sharing its parent company's pan-everything menu

scope and generous portions. Another excellent choice is **Planet Dailies** at Planet Hollywood, with over 200 items to choose from and 48 high-def screens to feast your eyes on. **Firefly on Paradise** features killer mojitos and an enormous menu of hot and cold tapas in a bustling environment off the Strip. Great for groups or finicky eaters – the extensive menu features diverse exotic and comfortable dishes, perfect for sharing. Reservations are a must! **Casa di Amore** is a great time-warp Italian joint with great food, old-Vegas atmosphere and live entertainment nightly.

Info: *Venetian* – 3355 Las Vegas Blvd. S. between Sands and Flamingo. *Grand Lux Café* (Tel. 702/414-3888) is open 24 hours. *Planet Hollywood* – 3667 Las Vegas Blvd. S. at Harmon. Tel. 702/785-5555. *Planet Dailies* is open 24 hours. *Firefly on Paradise* (3900 Paradise Rd. between Flamingo and Sands, Tel. 702/369-3971) is open from 11:30am-2am, until 3am on weekends. *Casa di Amore* (2850 E. Tropicana Ave., 3 mi. east of the Strip, Tel. 702/433-4967) is open from 4pm-8am nightly, all day and night on Sundays.

Posh suburban Green Valley seems an unlikely place for an incredible soul food restaurant, but **Kathy's Southern Cooking** is just that: a Zagat-rated hole in the wall with long lines of regulars who swear by its made-to-order fried chicken, smothered steak, catfish and chitlins.

Downtown, Main Street Station's **Triple 7 Restaurant & Brewery** offers its own line of microbrews, which are quite good. A more expansive beer menu can be found at **Crown & Anchor**, a British pub right next to UNLV. They've got about 30 different beers on tap and traditional English dishes.

Info: *Kathy's Southern Cooking* – 6407 Mountain Vista St., Henderson. Tel. 702/433-1005. Open 11am-8:30pm Tue-Thu, 11am-9:30pm Fri-Sat, 1-7:30pm Sun. *Main Street Station* - 200 N. Main St. *Triple 7 Restaurant & Brewery* is open 11am-7am. *Crown & Anchor* – 1350 E. Tropicana at Maryland, 2 mi. east of the Strip. Tel. 702/739-8676. Open 24 hours.

We're told that breakfast is the most important meal of the day, and it certainly gets the proper respect here. Check out **The Egg & I** on Sahara, a favorite early-AM hangout for the celebrity crowd. Hearty eaters devour the chorizo frittata or the Cincy omelet. The unusual **Hash House A Go Go** touts its "twisted farm food," including egg hashes topped with grilled chicken, corned beef, mushrooms and artichokes, meatloaf or even salmon. The **Original Pancake House** is another favorite, using premium ingredients to whip up its signature dishes, like the apple pancake and the Dutch baby. The OPH has four locations across the Las Vegas Valley.

Info: *The Egg & I* (4533 W. Sahara, 2 1/2 mi. west of the Strip. Tel. 702/364-9686) is open 6am-3pm Sun-Tue, 6am-10pm Wed-Sat. *Hash House A Go Go* (6800 W. Sahara, 4 mi. west of the Strip, Tel. 702/804-4646) is open 7:30am-2:30pm daily for breakfast/lunch, dinner is also served from 5-10pm Mon-Sat. *Original Pancake House* – locations include Green Valley Ranch (2300 Paseo Verde Pkwy., Henderson) – Tel. 702/614-7200, open 6am-8pm; and 4833 W. Charleston Blvd. at Decatur – Tel. 702/259-7755, open 7am-3pm.

Of course, we must mention the buffets in Vegas. These spectacular smorgasbords make cruise ship spreads look like college cafeterias. On the high end of the scale, The **Buffet at Bellagio** has exotic and ambitious fare like wild boar ribs, salmon sausage, and venison. The **Buffet at Wynn** has a striking, bright and airy dining room and an especially impressive seafood-laden breakfast, with cooking stations whipping up everything from omelets to congee.

Info: *Bellagio* - 3600 Las Vegas Blvd. S. at Flamingo. *Buffet* (Tel. 702/693-7223) serves breakfast 8-10:30am Mon-Fri ($14.95), brunch 8am-3:30pm Sat-Sun ($28.95 with champagne, $23.95 without), lunch 11am-3pm Mon-Thu, til 3:30pm Fri ($19.95) and dinner 4-10pm nightly, starts at 4:30 Fri-Sun ($27.95, $34.95 Fri-Sat). *Wynn Las Vegas* - 3131 Las Vegas Blvd. S. at Spring Mountain. *The Buffet* (Tel. 702/770-3463) serves breakfast 8-10:30am Mon-Fri ($17.95), brunch 8am-3:30pm Sat-Sun ($34.95 with champagne, $28.95 without), lunch from 11am-3:30 pm Mon-Fri ($21.95) and dinner 4-10pm Sun-Thu ($33.95) and 4:30-10:30pm Fri-Sat ($37.95).

Outperforming its price tag, Rio's **Carnival World Buffet** wins accolades as the city's best year after year, with over 300 dishes including teppanyaki, freshly carved prime rib and over 70 different desserts. Also worth a taste is the **Spice Market Buffet** at Planet Hollywood, which boasts succulent desserts, much-coveted crab legs and an extensive selection of Middle Eastern cuisine.

Info: *Rio* - 3700 W. Flamingo Rd., 3/4 mi. west of the Strip. Tel. 702/777-7777. *Carnival World Buffet* serves breakfast 7-11am Mon-

Fri, 7:30-10:30am Sat-Sun ($14.99), brunch 10:30am-3:30pm Sat-Sun ($23.99), lunch 11am-3:30pm Mon-Fri ($16.99) and dinner 3:30-10pm ($23.99). *Planet Hollywood* – 3667 Las Vegas Blvd. S. at Harmon. Tel. 702/785-5555. *Spice Market Buffet* (Tel. 702/785-9005) serves breakfast 8-10:30am Mon-Fri ($13.99), brunch 8:30am-2:30pm Sat-Sun ($23.99 with champagne, $20.99 without), lunch 11am-2:30pm Mon-Fri ($16.99) and dinner 4-9:30pm ($24.99).

The best buffets on the more affordable side of the spectrum include the **Feast Buffets** at Station Casino properties. The ones at Green Valley Ranch and Red Rock are the best of the bunch. These are an even better value for Boarding Pass cardholders, who get discounts from $1 to 75% off the price.

Info: *Green Valley Ranch* – 2300 Paseo Verde Pkwy., Henderson. Tel. 702/797-7777. *Red Rock* – 11011 W. Charleston Blvd. Tel. 702/617-7777. *Sunset Station* – 1301 W. Sunset Rd., Henderson. Tel. 702/547-7777. GVR and Red Rock *Feast Buffets* serve breakfast from 8-11:30am Mon-Fri ($8.99), brunch 8am-3:30pm Sat-Sun ($18.99), lunch 11:30am-3pm Mon-Fri ($10.99) and dinner 4-10pm ($17.99 Mon-Thu, $18.99 Fri-Sat).

Shows

Shows are a big part of the Vegas experience, and you'll have time for a few. Big production extravaganzas like the Cirque du Soleils are king, with five excellent options, and one derivative worth checking out: **Le Rêve** at Wynn. With its vivid, evocative dreamscape performances, it's like the dark side of Cirque. Steve Wynn plans on integrating new technological elements into the show after press time. *Info*: *Wynn Las Vegas* - 3131 Las Vegas Blvd. S. at Sands. *Le Rêve* (Tel. 702/293-SHOW) is performed at 7:30 and 10:30pm Sat-Wed. Tickets are $80-100.

One of our favorite shows in town is **Legends in Concert** at the Imperial Palace. It's played to over 5 million people during its run, featuring an ever-changing cast of talented impersonators. At the Sahara, Elvis impersonator **Trent Carlini** performs in *The Dream King*, a retrospective that covers the King's entire career. *Info*: *Imperial Palace* - 3535 Las Vegas Blvd. S. between Flamingo and Sands. Tel. 702/731-3311. *Legends in Concert* (Tel. 888/777-7664) has 7:30 and 10pm shows Mon-Sat. Tickets are $49.95-59.95 adults, $34.95-44.95 kids. *Sahara* – 2535 Las Vegas Blvd. S. at Sahara. *The Dream King* (Tel. 702/737-2515) performances at 9pm Mon-Sat. Tickets are $71.90 for adults, $23.50 for kids 5-12.

Many headliners in Vegas are also worth seeing – their performances are often more relaxed and polished because they don't have to deal with the rigors of touring. Our recommendations:

• **Elton John** has an amazing stage show at Caesars Palace's Colosseum you'd never get to see anywhere else.

• **Barry Manilow**'s still got "it" at his ripe old age, making women of all ages (and more than a few men) swoon at the Hilton.

• If you'd prefer comedians, **Carrot Top** is funnier than you'd ever expect, and **Vinnie Favorito** is absolutely hilarious and raunchy.

• **Lance Burton** and **Penn & Teller** are the best-known magicians in the city, while the **Amazing Johnathan** is the most hysterical.

Nightlife
Some of the best parties in town are "industry nights," locals-oriented parties geared towards service industry employees. Since they happen during the week, most visitors are unaware of their existence, so these fun nights aren't overrun with tourists. The most popular service industry nights are Spoil U Rotten (ladies drink free) at **rumjungle** and **JET** Mondays, **Moon's** Tuesday night party, IT Wednesdays at **Tabu** and Worship Thursdays at **Tao**.

Info: *Mandalay Bay* – 3950 Las Vegas Blvd. S. at Russell Rd. Tel. 702/632-7777. *rumjungle* Spoil U Rotten party is 11pm-2am Mon, cover is $20. *Mirage* - 3400 Las Vegas Blvd. between Flamingo and Spring Mountain. Tel. 702/791-7111. *JET* service industry party is 10:30pm-4:30am Mon. Admission is $30. *Palms* - 4321 W. Flamingo Rd., 1 mi. west of the Strip. *Moon* (Tel. 702/942-6832) opens at 10:30pm. Admission is $20. *MGM Grand* - 3799 Las Vegas Blvd. S. at Tropicana. Tel. 702/891-1111. *Tabu's* IT party starts at 10pm Wed. Admission is $20. *Venetian* – 3355 Las Vegas Blvd. S. between Sands and Flamingo. *Tao* Worship is open 10:30pm-5:30am Thu. Admission is $20.

Free attractions
Of course, you'll want to visit some of the free attractions that Las Vegas has to offer, likethe **Fountains of Bellagio**, the **Volcano** at Mirage, and the **Wildlife Habitat** at Flamingo, Rio's **Masquerade in the Sky,** and Sam's Town's nightly light show, **Sunset Stampede,** in its atrium.

ROAD TRIP

Many of the striking sights of the great southwest are easily accessible by car from Las Vegas. Plus, there are out-of-the-way options where you can enjoy everything that the Strip has to offer at a fraction of the price with crowds to match.

Hoover Dam is the easiest excursion from Las Vegas. it's so close, in fact, that it barely even qualifies as a road trip. But it's a must-see, and you'll pass it on your way to or from the Grand Canyon on US 93, so why not check it out? The self-paced Discovery Tour offers six guided segments, and while it'll only take you two hours, lines form early. A highlight of the tour is the elevator ride down to the base where the force of the water rotates the huge turbines that generate the electric power. *Info*: *Hoover Dam* – US 93, Boulder City. Tel. 702/494-2517. Tours available from 9am-6pm daily. Admission is $11, $9 for kids, seniors and military. Parking is $7.

About 250 miles past Hoover Dam in Arizona is the **Grand Canyon**. This is a fairly exhausting day trip, so consider staying overnight. You can choose to visit either the North Rim or the South Rim, but not both unless you allocate several days. The canyon runs 277 miles in length, is a mile deep and almost 20 miles across at its widest point. The South Rim is the more heavily visited portion of the park although many experienced travelers will tell you that the lightly traveled North Rim may even be more spectacular.

Getting there is quite simple. For the South Rim take US 93 south to I-40 at Kingman, Arizona, and then take I-40 eastbound to AZ 64 north into the park. For the North Rim, take I-15 north to UT 9 east (north of St. George) to US 89 at Mount Carmel. Go south to the AZ 67 turnoff and follow it to the end. Keep in mind that

accommodations at the North Rim are extremely limited. *Info*: *Grand Canyon* – Grand Canyon, AZ. Tel. 928/638-7888. Admission is $25 per vehicle.

You can also see the Grand Canyon by air, a much quicker trip. Tours depart from a number of places in the area, mostly the North Las Vegas Airport. In addition to flying over either one or both rims, these flights usually pass Lake Mead and Hoover Dam. Flights are no longer allowed to go into the canyon for safety and environmental reasons. Therefore, you should enhance the overall experience with a package that includes some time on the ground at the Grand Canyon. These trips aren't cheap. Prices start at about $90 for air only and around $135 for air/bus tours. Helicopter tours cost even more.

Airplane tour operators include:
• **Air Vegas Airlines**, Tel. 702/736-3599 or 800/255-7474
• **Lake Mead Air**, Tel. 702/293-1848
• **Scenic Airlines**, Tel. 702/638-3300 or 800/634-6801

The Other Grand Canyon

Grand Canyon West is located on the Hualapai Indian Reservation about 120 miles from Las Vegas. At this theme-park like attraction, visitors can walk out over the canyon on a specially designed glass platform and look straight down into the canyon – for $75! Helicopter rides, horseback riding and river floats are also options. *Info:* To get to Grand Canyon West take US 93 south to the cutoff for Dolan Springs and then follow signs. For more information, call 877/716-WEST.

Helicopter tour operators include:
• **Grand Canyon Tours**, Tel. 702/655-6060 or 800/512-0075. This company also offers plane and bus tours.
• **Heli USA Airways**, Tel. 702/736-8787 or 800/359-8727
• **Maverick Helicopters**, Tel. 702/261-0007 or 888/261-4414
• **Papillon Grand Canyon Helicopters**, Tel. 702/736-7243 or 888/635-7272
• **Sundance Helicopters**, Tel. 702/597-5525 or 800/653-1881

You'll also want to pay a visit to **Valley of Fire**. Red sandstone juts out in all directions, creating a picture-perfect desert landscape of rock formations like Mouse's Tank, Seven Sisters and Elephant Rock. *Info: Valley of Fire State Park* - The park is open for day visits between dawn and dusk. The visitor center is open daily (except Christmas) from 8:30am until 4:30pm. There is a $6 vehicle entry charge. Tel. 702/397-2088.

If you prefer your excursions to lead you to the great indoors, consider a jaunt down I-15 south to **Primm**, inside the California state line. It's on the way in or out of Vegas if you're coming from Southern California. Primm isn't really a town but a group of three casino hotels, a golf course and a factory outlet mall straddling I-15. The three Primm casinos are **Whiskey Pete's, Primm Valley Resort** and **Buffalo Bill's**. They're connected by shuttle bus, monorail or miniature train ride but you can even walk. Buffalo Bill's has some wild rides - a log flume and one of the world's highest and fastest roller coasters, *Desperado*. The casinos have the usual amenities found in Las Vegas. Name entertainment appears in the Star of the West Arena.

The shopping mall, **Fashion Outlets Las Vegas** has 100 stores representing many recognizable names in fashion. We wouldn't make the trip to Primm just for this. However, if you're coming here for a few hours or the day to see the casinos or are just passing by, then it's a good stop. Take I-15 south to the Primm exit (#1). It's a distance of about 40 miles from the Strip and should take well under 45 minutes. *Info*: *Primm Valley Resorts* – 31900 Las Vegas Blvd. S., Primm. Tel. 702/386-7867. *Fashion Outlets Las Vegas* – 32100 Las Vegas Blvd. S., Primm. Tel. 702/874-1400. Open daily 10am-8pm.

Laughlin's Best Hotels

Many budget-minded visitors appreciate the cheap rooms in Laughlin, starting in the $19-29 range during the week. These are the best choices:

- **Harrah's**, Tel. 702/298-4600 or 800/447-8700 (best high-end choice)
- **Golden Nugget**, Tel. 702/298-7111 or 800/237-1739 (best moderate choice)
- **Edgewater**, Tel. 702/298-2453 or 800/67-RIVER(best budget choice)

Ninety miles from the Strip on the picturesque Colorado River, **Laughlin** is another option for casino fun. The river provides boating, fishing, and even a couple of white sand beaches. Lots of tour operators offer free transportation to and from, but only in full-day excursions, so if you get out there and decide you don't like it, you're screwed. But there's no reason someone who likes Vegas wouldn't like Laughlin too.

Laughlin has more than 10,000 hotel rooms in nine major properties. Many of them are Vegas off-shoots like Golden Nugget, Harrah's, and the Aquarius, formerly the Flamingo. Just about all of the casinos in Laughlin are along a mile-long stretch of Casino Drive, which parallels the river. The **River Walk** is a promenade connecting most of the hotels on the water side. Hoofing it is easy via either the River Walk or Casino Drive. The most remote hotel, also the nicest, is Harrah's. Their free shuttle bus service connects to the main casino center. River taxis that stop at most of the hotels and cross the river to Bullhead City. *Info:* To get to Laughlin take US 93/95 south to the split before Boulder City. Follow US 95 south for about 1 1/2 hours to NV 163 east. The last part of the trip descends steeply and is quite scenic.

The fascination with **Area 51** has spawned a mini-tourism boom in an area to the north of Las Vegas. This trip is more than 300 miles round trip and there isn't particularly much to see when you get there. The trip up US 93 offers nice mountain views as you cross the **Pahranagat National Wildlife Refuge**. NV 375, which connects US 93 and US 6 has been officially designated as the **Extra-Terrestrial Highway**, complete with drawings of flying saucers on the road sign. At the small town of **Rachel**, you can purchase alien burgers and other souvenirs, or sleep at the **Little Al'E'Inn**. The whole thing's quite campy. Area 51 is located about 30 miles off Highway 375 just west of the Hancock Summit. From Las Vegas take I-15 north to the exit for US 93 north. Then go 85 miles to Crystal Springs, where NV 375 begins. *Info: Little Al'E'Inn* – Tel. 775/729-2515.

Southern Nevada also has a few ghost towns : deserted. short-lived silver, lead or zinc boomtowns built to support the mining industry. The main ghost town we recommend (most of the other ghost towns have little or nothing to show for themselves) is **Goodsprings**, 35 miles southwest of Vegas. Goodsprings had several thousand residents until a 1918 flu epidemic, soon followed by the collapse of metal and mineral prices. About 100 people now live here. The big attraction is the old **Pioneer Saloon**. To get here, take I-15 south to Jean, go west on NV 161 for seven miles.

Mesquite's Best Hotels

Mesquite has casino hotels offering buffets, restaurants and entertainment options – not at the same level of quality as what you'll find on the Las Vegas Strip, but they aren't at Strip prices either!

- **CasaBlanca Casino Hotel Resort**, Tel. 800/459-PLAY
- **Eureka Casino Hotel**, Tel. 800/346-4611
- **Oasis Resort Hotel Casino**, Tel. 800/621-0187
- **Virgin River Hotel Casino**, Tel. 800/346-7721

For those taking Utah excursions or traveling to Las Vegas on I-15 from the north, you'll pass **Mesquite** near the Arizona state line. Many Las Vegans come here for the inexpensive hotels and abundance of golf. It's 80 miles from the Strip and can be reached in just over an hour via I-15. There are several casino-hotels, including some very attractive ones. Most of the casino properties offer perfectly acceptable rooms for under $35 on weeknights.

Death Valley's highlights can be done in a single day, but you'll have to leave early and return late to make it worth the drive. For a more leisurely pace, accommodations are available within Death Valley and in the town of **Beatty**. Avoid Death Valley between late May and mid-September. On the other hand, wintertime in Death Valley is delightful and spring and fall are definitely manageable. **Death Valley National Park** is a natural wonderland with tons of beautiful scenery. The diversity comes as a surprise to people who figure it's just a barren wasteland. Besides stopping at **Badwater**, the lowest point in the United States, visitors should take a ride on **Artist's Drive**, an easy one-way loop road; and drive up to the incredible **Dante's View** where the panorama of mountains and valley is spread out before you. **Zabriskie Point** has gold colored rocks and makes you feel like you're on another planet. Services within Death Valley are mostly concentrated at **Furnace Creek**.

The quickest way to get there is to take I-15 south to Blue Diamond Road and then head west on NV 160. Just north of Pahrump turn left on NV 210, heading into California. At Death Valley Junction take CA 190 into the heart of the national park. To see more of Death Valley, when you hit Pahrump follow NV 372 to CA 178 through Shoshone and into the southern entrance of the park. *Info: Death Valley National Park* – Death Valley, CA. Tel. 760/786-3200. Admission is $20 per car.

6. BEST SLEEPS & EATS

Las Vegas has more hotel rooms than just about any city in the world. It also boasts **nine of the world's ten largest hotels**. Vegas hotels now boast some the highest occupancy rates around, well over 90% and far closer to 100% on weekends. Many Strip hotels are quite nice, mostly in the three-to-five star range.

Las Vegas has become **one of the best cities in the world for dining**, often mentioned in the same breath as New York and Paris. That's not surprising considering how many of their best chefs have been lured here. And plenty of good eats can be found without breaking the bank. Buffets in particular are great deals, featuring fresh food, innovative preparations and custom cooking.

NORTH STRIP

Hotel Price Key

$ starting below $50
$$ starting at $50-$100
$$$ tarting at $100-150
$$$$ starting above $150

BEST SLEEPS
The Palazzo $$$$
The Strip's newest casino, a part of the gargantuan 7,128-room complex that also includes the Venetian and the Sands Expo Center, opened as this book was going to press. Expectations were high for the resort, which like its sister property, is an all-suite destination with a dazzling array of dining, retail and entertainment – think **Charlie Trotter, Wolfgang Puck, Mario Batali, Jay-Z,** Barney's of New York and the Tony Award-winning musical, *Jersey Boys.* The hotel has **warm, attractive spaces, much sleeker and classier** than the gaudy nouveau-riche Venetian, but there's a rub. The casino is tiny for a hotel of this size – and its sister property's overcrowded public areas make this a big question mark at this point. The rooms, actually more like mini-suites, are spectacular enough to roll the dice on the Palazzo. *Info:* www.palazzolasvegas.com. Tel. 702/414-1000 or 877/263-3001. 3325 Las Vegas Blvd. S. at Sands. 3,068 rooms.

The Venetian $$$$
A **$100 million room renovation** underway should bring the spacious Venetian guestrooms up to snuff with a warmer, more modern style than what had been seen here in further years. With over 4,000 rooms, this resort sometimes seems too big for its own good, and the Palazzo's impact is still TBD. However, there's no denying the **quality of the dining and entertainment** options here – not with names like Wayne

Brady, Mario Batali, the Phantom of the Opera, Emeril Lagasse, David Burke and the Blue Man Group. AAA awarded the Venetian Five Diamonds. *Info:* www.venetian.com. Tel. 702/414-1000 or 877/883-6423. 3355 Las Vegas Blvd. S. between Sands and Flamingo. 4,027 rooms.

Wynn Las Vegas $$$$
Steve Wynn's Five Diamond, Five Star namesake is an obvious evolution from Bellagio and a triumph on almost every count.

The spacious rooms are **technologically advanced and sleekly stunning**, simultaneously modern and soft. Bedding is luxuriant, and bathrooms are opulent. The **Tower Suites** are even better. The casino floor is navigable, intimate and bathed in natural light. **Botanical gardens and Picasso paintings** grace the lobby. Eighteen restaurants include the Five Diamond winning Alex. Nightspots include Tryst and Blush, a so-called "Boutique Nightclub." The 18-hole golf course on the site of the old Desert Inn course is reserved for hotel guests, as is the spa. The Wynn also boasts exclusive shopping, a Ferrari Maserati dealership and two showrooms. Coming in 2009 is an all-suite sister property called Encore. *Info:* www.wynnlasvegas.com. Tel. 702/770-7100 or 888/320-9966. 3131 Las Vegas Blvd. S. at Spring Mountain. 2,716 rooms.

Mirage $$$
The first modern mega-resort remains one of Steve Wynn's finest creations. An ambitious refurbishment has recently added several new restaurants and one of **the city's hottest nightclubs**, JET. Standard rooms are not huge, but quite luxurious. **Mirage's pool** is one of the nicest in town, with the same waterfalls and lush tropical vegetation as out front, plus a topless pool, appropriately called Bare. **Attention to detail** is a hallmark of this beautiful luxury hotel boasting eleven restaurants, a spa, a salon by TV

stylist Kim Vo, two show-
rooms and an elegant ca-
sino. There's also a botanical garden and a beautiful
aquarium in the atrium.
Info: www.mirage.com.
Tel. 702/791-7111 or 800/
374-9000. 3400 Las Vegas
Blvd. S., between Flamingo
and Spring Mountain.
3,044 rooms.

North
Strip

ti - Treasure Island $$$
Mirage's sister hotel was recently stripped of its "pirate" theme,
in favor of something more universal: sex. Evidence includes the
Tangerine burlesque nightclub, the *Sirens of TI* show and the
unique, oversized **50-person TI Party Tub Jacuzzi**. The rooms
have been significantly upgraded both in décor and amenities.
Treasure Island feels intimate and accessible. Soft earth tones,
woodworking, traditional furnishings and fine European fabrics
are now standard. Its sushi bar, Social House, is a popular
celebrity hangout. *Mystère*, **Vegas' first permanent Cirque show**,
is performed here. *Info:* www.treasureisland.com. Tel. 702/894-
7111 or 800/288-7206. 3300 Las Vegas Blvd. S. at Spring Mountain. 2,885 rooms.

Stratosphere $
The Strat has overcome a troubled opening and a terrible location, carving a niche as one of the **strongest budget-priced
options** on the Strip. Its casino is boisterous, with strong video
poker and low limit tables. There's quite a few restaurants.
Accommodations range from roomy and comfortable to somewhat small (the original Regency tower has the smallest) but
they're all serviceable. For what we've paid, we have no com-
plaints. The $5 "resort fee" that they charge actually includes
some value-added amenities including free afternoon admission
to its 109-story tower, free tickets to the American Superstars
show and more. You'll probably want to rent a car, there's
nothing worth walking to, unless you're into head shops and
Asian massage. *Info:* www.stratospherehotel.com Tel. 702/380-

7777 or 800/998-6937. 2000 Las Vegas Blvd. S. between Baltimore and Main Streets. 2,442 rooms.

BEST EATS

Alex $$$$

AAA awarded Alessandro Strata's French-Mediterranean-Continental restaurant **Five Diamonds** right off the bat. Its view of the Wynn's pools is spectacular, and the décor is rich with crystal and mahogany. Dining options include a $120 four-course dinner or a $150 tasting menu. Chef's table seatings are also available.. *Info:* Wynn Las Vegas - 3131 Las Vegas Blvd. S. Tel. 702/770-3300. Closed Mondays. Reservations suggested. Jackets required.

CarneVino $$$$

Mario Batali's second Vegas restaurant, barely open for business at this writing, has garnered early attention for its appealing combination of traditional steakhouse fare, aged in-house and dry-rubbed with sea salt, black pepper and rosemary. The menu also includes Italian fare made from artisinal ingredients. *Info:* Palazzo Las Vegas - 3325 Las Vegas Blvd. S. at Sands. Tel. 702/ 789-4141. Lunch and dinner.

Daniel Boulud Brassiere $$$

Boulud, a James Beard winner, produces magnificent new French cuisine at another Wynn restaurant, taking full advantage of the resort's water features. It's all quite **innovative and robust**, but though there are nods to tradition, it's **not a butter-and-cream dominated menu**. *Info:* Wynn Las Vegas - 3131 Las Vegas Blvd. S. Tel. 702/770-9966. Lunch and dinner. Reservations suggested.

Delmonico Steakhouse $$$

Have some "Bam!" with your beef at Emeril's successful New Orleans/Creole steakhouse at the Venetian. Succulent hand-cut beef is prepared perfectly and served with flair. The **French onion soup here is a standout,** with an English muffin crouton. The wine list earns similar raves. *Info:* Venetian – 3355 Las Vegas Blvd. S.

Restaurant Price Key

$	under $25 per person
$$	$25-50 per person
$$$	$50-100 per person
$$$$	over $100 per person

Tel. 702/414-3737. Lunch and dinner. Reservations optional. Dress code at dinner.

SW Steakhouse $$$
The signature steakhouse at the Wynn features the masterwork of Eric Klein, one of *Food & Wine* magazine's 10 Best Chefs of 2004. It's one of the most intimate and romantic steakhouses in town, featuring **more diversity** than most. The view of the Lake of Dreams only add to the ambiance. *Info:* Wynn Las Vegas - 3131 Las Vegas Blvd. S. Tel. 702/770-3320. Dinner nightly. Reservations suggested.

STACK $$
At first glance, STACK seems a post-modern steakhouse. But it's much more than that. Imagine **upscale comfort food** in a contemporary, classy atmosphere. Pigs in blankets. Cheesy tater tots. Crab cakes. Dining to soothe your inner child. Then there's beef. Choose from cowboy steaks, Brooklyn filets, center-cut rib eyes, and NYC sirloin. Drinks and desserts also seem to be stuck in arrested development, with s'mores available in traditional form and as an alcoholic beverage.

Best Buffets, North Strip

North Strip

• **The Buffet** ($$) – Wynn. Excellent food in a gorgeous, open and airy atmosphere. You'll be astounded at the amount of seafood on the breakfast buffet alone. Desserts are kind of disappointing. Bellagio just beats it out as the best in town.
• **The Buffet at TI** ($$) – Treasure Island. More comfort food and a warmer atmosphere than you'll find next door, although this buffet in the same niche, right down to the cutesy name.
• **Cravings** ($$) – Mirage. Its recent renovation ushered in the era of "action station cooking," and while preparation is fresh, the selection isn't on a par with others. Sushi and other seafood items are, however, in steady supply.
• **Courtyard Buffet** ($) – Stratosphere. Great appetizers and sides, not so hot on the main dishes. Acceptable for the price.

Top of the World $$
The menu at the Stratosphere's top restaurant is somewhat pedestrian albeit well-executed, offering new American and new

Best 24-Hour Cafes

On the Strip, these are the best cafes:

- **Grand Lux Café** – Venetian & Palazzo
- **Planet Dailies** – Planet Hollywood
- **Monte Carlo Café** – Monte Carlo
- **Augustus Café** – Caesars Palace
- **Raffles** – Mandalay Bay

French twists on the usual array of steaks, fresh fish and seafood. The reason to come here, however, is **the view**. At 108 stories above the Strip, the restaurant rotates once per hour, giving diners impressive vistas as day turns into night. *Info:* Stratosphere – 2000 Las Vegas Blvd. S. Tel. 702/380-7711. Lunch and dinner served daily. Business casual.

Café Ba Ba Reeba! $
We love a good tapas. It's got all the variety of a buffet, without the cattle-herd mentality and the indignities of underutilized sneezeguards. The small plates are perfect for sharing, enabling fun social meals taking the awkward sting out of a first date. They offer **al fresco seating** on one patio with Strip views and another with live entertainment. The potent sangria and heavenly paellas complement the small plates. Even if you've had tapas before, some of the menu items here still surprise. *Info:* Fashion Show Mall – 3200 Las Vegas Blvd. S. Tel. 702/258-1211. Lunch and dinner daily. Reservations optional.

Grand Lux Café $
From the people behind the Cheesecake Factory is this recognizably derivative concept. A bit more upscale, the Grand Lux is open 24 hours and features many of the features that made Cheesecake so successful, like the **huge portions** and the phone book of a menu. The décor is more elaborate and fancy, but the place is still decidedly casual. The ambitious globe-trotting menu includes a bacon cheeseburger topped with short ribs, Jamaican pork tenderloin with black pepper sauce and mango salsa and Austrian style wiener schnitzel. Think ahead and order **baked-to-order desserts** like molten chocolate cake and New Orleans beignets. *Info:* Two locations: Venetian - 3355 Las Vegas Blvd. S. and Palazzo – 3325 Las Vegas Blvd. S. Tel. 702/414-3888. Breakfast, lunch and dinner served daily.

Peppermill $
This Las Vegas legend, featured in the movie *Casino*, remains one of the most popular and timeless eateries in town, having barely changed in 25 years. It may seem like a diner, but it's very well done, with massive portions, familiar, friendly service and **old-school Vegas atmosphere**. The menu's actually broader than most diners, and most diners don't offer a place like the Fireside Lounge, **custom designed for snuggling and smooching**. *Info:* 2985 Las Vegas Blvd. S. Tel. 702/735-7635. Open 24 hours. Reservations optional.

North
Strip

Center
Strip

CENTER STRIP

BEST SLEEPS
Bellagio $$$$
As **the only AAA Five Diamond casino hotel on the Strip**, Bellagio offers every imaginable luxury and extravagance. It's one of the top hotels in the world, an **aesthetic wonder** inside and out. Its rooms are among the city's most posh, especially the new Spa Tower. Standard rooms are a generous 510 sq. ft. with marble floors,  separate tub and stall shower, fine fabrics and wall coverings, and a **complete entertainment system**. Comfortable chairs and desks give plenty of working room. The pool is lovely. **Restaurants are out of this world**, including two Five Diamond joints, but even the casual bites cost a ton. The pricey buffet offers extremely exotic food. **Bars and clubs are superb** here, with live entertainment at Fontana, Caramel and the Petrossian. The Bellagio's nightclub is the new, ostentatiously upscale Bank. *Info:* www.bellagio.com. Tel. 702/693-7111 or 888/987-6667. 3600 Las Vegas Blvd. S. at Flamingo. 3,933 rooms.

Caesars Palace $$$$
Caesars Palace (*see photo on page 128*) celebrated its 40th anni-

versary in 2006, and remains one of the most **well-maintained and cutting-edge** hotels on the Strip thanks to constant improvements. Choose a lavish suite in the 26-story **Augustus Tower** or the freshly renovated ForumTower. The over-the-top opulence of the public areas is echoed in the amenities of these tasteful rooms, with amenities like whirlpool tubs and flat-screen TVs. The Palace Tower is also top-notch and fairly new. Some more unique offerings include its array of restaurants, focusing on **renowned chefs with limited geographic reach**, like Bobby Flay and Guy Savoy; and the new Qua Baths & Spa, which harkens back to the public baths of ancient Rome. For nightlife, the Shadow Bar, Cleopatra's Barge and PURE make a formidable trio. *Info:* www.caesarspalace.com. Tel. 702/731-7110 or 877/ 427-7243. 3570 Las Vegas Blvd. S. at Flamingo. 3,410 rooms.

Paris Las Vegas $$$

The elegance and style of this cheerful hotel are among the city's best. Its casino is particularly welcoming, as are well-appointed rooms with pleasant touches like custom furnishings, crown moldings, French fabrics and ornate armoires. You can **swim in the shadows of the Eiffel Tower** or relax in the Mandara Spa. Napoleon's and Le Cabaret are **excellent bars with live entertainment**, although Risqué is B-list. Restaurants abound here, featuring varied French regional cuisine at Le Village Buffet and pan-Asian fare at Ah Sin. Of course, there's also the Eiffel Tower Experience, with a restaurant 100 feet up. *Info:* www.parislasvegas.com. Tel. 702/967-3836 or 877/ 796-2096. 3655 Las Vegas Blvd. S., between Flamingo and Harmon. 2,914 rooms.

Bally's $$

She doesn't look like much from the outside, but Bally's is like a **time capsule of old-Vegas charm**. Though this is one of the Strip's older hotels, you'd never know it from the **frequently**

remodeled rooms. Bally's restaurants are good with affordable prices. The casino floor is tasteful, as is Donn Arden's Jubilee!, a topless show with 25 years of history. Another popular show is the **interactive afternoon Price Is Right Live show**, giving guests the opportunity to play classic games for cash and prizes. This hotel is often one of the better bargains on Center Strip. *Info:* www.ballyslasvegas.com. Tel. 702/739-4111 or 888/742-9248. 3645 Las Vegas Blvd. S. at Flamingo. 2,818 rooms.

Flamingo $$

One of the Strip's most legendary names, Flamingo has freshened itself up for a younger demographic, adding **Toni Braxton** and psychic medium **John Edward** to the entertainment lineup – and a Vince Neil tattoo parlor at the adjacent O'Sheas. We can't deny the drawing power of Jimmy Buffett's Margaritaville. The casino floor is **bathed in natural light**, a welcome rarity. Ask for a Go Room – recently upgraded and critically acclaimed for its retro-chic design and ultra-modern amenities. The centerpiece of the resort is its **beautiful 15-acre pool and wildlife preserve**. Somehow Flamingo achieves intimacy while boasting all the

amenities of a first-class hotel. The rooms are decorated in an island motif, with rattan furniture and soft colors. *Info:* www.flamingolasvegas.com. Tel. 702/733-3111 or 888/308-8899. 3555 Las Vegas Blvd. S. at Flamingo. 3,642 rooms.

Imperial Palace $$

The 1960s-vintage Imperial Palace is especially rollicking in the champagne pit and the "Dealertainers" pit, with **celebrity im-**

personators who throw blackjack in between on stage performances. On a recent visit, we saw Elvis, Neil Diamond, and an
uncannily convincing Gwen Stefani and Alice Cooper. This whets
your appetite for the highly recommended Legends in Concert
show. The spacious rooms here are plain and do show their age,
although they're certainly acceptable. The Strip-side Rockhouse
is an unassuming nightspot with dive-bar excitement and
ultralounge location. The Imperial Palace is a moderately priced
Strip hotel with a **loyal fan base and a fun environment**, sadly,
a dying breed. *Info:* www.imperialpalace.com. Tel. 702/731-3311
or 800/634-6441. 3535 Las Vegas Blvd. S., between Flamingo and
Sands.

BEST EATS
Le Cirque $$$$
This AAA Five Diamond gem is decorated in festive colors and
plush, overstuffed chairs for more of a **homelike, childish
whimsy**. As for the food, it's **sublime** New French and Continental. Add a knowledgeable sommelier and fountain views and you
have yourself a winner, provided you're ready to shell out $100
for five courses or $125 for seven. *Info:* Bellagio – 3600 Las Vegas
Blvd. S. Tel. 702/693-7223. Reservations suggested.

Picasso $$$$
Anyone can do china and silver and crystal. But **original Picasso
paintings** on the wall? That's extravagant. Julian Serrano's cuisine at Bellagio's premier restaurant reflects the region that
influenced the impressionist painter, with French and Spanish
dishes like poached oysters, shrimp and scallops, grilled lamb on
noisettes and roasted veal chop. Desserts are simply fantastic.
Zagat named Picasso the best service and décor in town. Prix fixe
menus range from $70 to $90. *Info:* Bellagio – 3600 Las Vegas Blvd.
S. Tel. 702/693-7223. Dinner served Wed-Mon. Reservations
suggested. Dress code.

Restaurant Guy Savoy $$$$
This Michelin two-star restaurant showcases the cuisine of the
Legion of Honor winning French epicurean. Spend an indulgent
evening in the Jean Wilmotte designed dining room with the 16-
course degustation menu or a quick indulgence of Champagne

and small plates at the Bubble Bar. Either way, don't miss his signature artichoke and black truffle soup. There's even a bar menu of small plates for those who want to experience Savoy's cuisine without the commitment of a whole evening or a belly full of Francais. *Info:* Caesars Palace – 3570 Las Vegas Blvd. S. Tel. 877/346-4642. Dinner served Wed-Sun. Reservations suggested.

Andre's $$$

The newer outpost of the award-winning downtown French, the intimate Renaissance-style dining room creates an **intimate environment** to consume one of over 12,000 bottles of wine along with your meal. **Haute cuisine** on the menu is rich as can be, with butter and cream sauces anchoring dishes of Dover sole, 2 lb. Maine lobster, Muscovy duck and rack of lamb. It's decadence as only the French can do it. *Info:* Monte Carlo – 3770 Las Vegas Blvd. S. Tel. 702/730-7955. Dinner nightly. Reservations optional.

Best Buffets, Center Strip

Center Strip

• **The Buffet ($$)** – Bellagio. The be-all, end-all of Vegas buffets, with truly exotic and well-prepared fare including wild boar ribs and salmon sausage.
• **Le Village Buffet ($$)** – Paris. Could it be? The world's first theme buffet? The live-action cooking stations here each represent different provincial cuisines of France. Desserts are out of this world.
• **Paradise Garden Buffet ($$)** – Flamingo. The atmosphere, overlooking beautiful waterfalls and lush landscaping, is unbeatable. The food service area is spacious.
• **Monte Carlo Buffet ($$)** – Monte Carlo. Good value for the money, and at least it lacks that cavernous mess-hall feel you'll find at other buffets at hotels this size.

Bradley Ogden $$$

The James Beard Foundation named this America's best new restaurant in 2003, and we're inclined to agree: A meal here is **absolutely heart-rending**, with artistic presentations, skillful contrasts of flavors and a creative flair executed with grace by the universally enthusiastic and talented staff. The menu changes based on seasonal availability, as **freshness of ingredients** is a key to its success. This is one of our favorite meals in all of Las Vegas, and we recommend it about as strongly as anything. *Info:* Caesars Palace – 3570 Las Vegas Blvd. S. Tel. 702/731-7731. Dinner nightly, lunch during the week. Reservations suggested.

808 $$

Hawaiian ingredients meet French sensibilities at this innovative seafood-focused spot. The signature dish, featured prominently on posters around Caesars, is the **deconstructed Ahi roll**: tartare stacked upon avocado salad, crab ceviche and white truffle vinaigrette. Many entrées have varying Eurasian influences, making this one of the more diverse and palatable menus in town. The service can be hit or miss but when it's a hit, more often than not it's for extra bases. Tasting menus are available. *Info:* Caesars Palace – 3570 Las Vegas Blvd. S. Tel. 702/731-7731. Dinner served Wed-Sun. Reservations suggested.

Mesa Grill $$

There's no denying the talent of brash, controversial New Yorker Bobby Flay. His piquant Southwestern cuisine has made him a superstar in Manhattan, and the Michelin-starred Caesars location is his first venture outside there. Fans of his television shows know that his emphasis is on **well-spiced grilled meats**. Coffee spice rubbed tenderloin is a signature dish, and his duck-stuffed blue corn pancake is the stuff of legend. They also offer an **innovative and ambitious brunch**. *Info:* Caesars Palace – 3570 Las Vegas Blvd. S. Tel. 702/731-7731. Dinner served nightly, lunch on weekdays, brunch on Sat-Sun. Reservations suggested.

Mon Ami Gabi $$

Like Ah Sin, this is an al fresco casual dining restaurant with a **great view of the Bellagio fountains**. It actually echoes the Parisian theme of the hotel, with semi-Americanized French dishes. The steak frites are wonderful and the steaks are good for the price. The atmosphere at streetside is fantastic. In the shadows of the Eiffel Tower, you've got the fountains across the street, and you're perfectly situated to watch the crowd go by. *Info:* Paris Las Vegas – 3655 Las Vegas Blvd. S. Tel. 702/944-4224. Lunch and dinner served daily. Reservations suggested.

Payard Patisserie & Bistro $$
Known as one of the world's finest chocolatiers, Francois Payard now sells his wares at Caesars. Try the pain perdu French toast for breakfast or the sublime, rustic croquet-monsieur for lunch. Sweet teeth will appreciate the dessert tasting menu, as well as the retail counter serving decadent pastries and chocolates. *Info:* Caesars Palace – 3570 Las Vegas Blvd. S. Tel. 702/731-7731. Breakfast, lunch and dinner served daily.

Center
Strip

South
Strip

SOUTH STRIP

BEST SLEEPS
Four Seasons $$$$
Four Seasons is right in the middle of the action on the top five floors of the Mandalay Bay tower. The hallmark is **gracious, anticipatory, high-level service** attending to its guests' every whim and desire. That includes its littlest guests. Kids under 12 get a gift on arrival, infants and toddlers get in-room cribs. a basket of essentials and automatic childproofing, older kids get M&M goodies, child-sized bathrobes, kids menus and in-room entertainment options. Older guests can enjoy service **chilled towels, spritzers and fruit poolside**, twice-daily housekeeping service, nightly turndown, cold water and chilled towels for joggers, in-room coffeemaker, one-hour pressing: the list goes on for days. *Travel & Leisure* readers named this hotel #2 in the world for service. Other knock-em-dead features include Charlie Palmer Steak, named the best steakhouse in Vegas by *Review-Journal* readers just four months after opening, and a **spa rated four stars by Mobil** every year. The Four Seasons also holds the distinction of being the **first hotel ever to win AAA's Five Diamond rating in its first year** of operation. *Info:* www.fourseasons.com/lasvegas. Tel. 702/632-5195 or 800/819-5053. 3960 Las Vegas Blvd. S., at Russell. 424 rooms.

THEhotel at Mandalay Bay $$$$
While the Four Seasons is a hotel-within-a-hotel, THEhotel is more like an annex. Even though the separate, L-shaped tower looks similar to Mandalay Bay's colossus, THEhotel has its own **distinct style**. It's much more masculine and serious looking, with cherry woods and dark colors throughout. **Standard rooms are mini-suites** measuring 750 sq. ft., loaded with 42" plasma screen TVs and elegant marble baths. Mix Restaurant and Lounge are more subdued than what you'll find next door, but highly recommended. THEhotel also has its own spa, THEbathhouse and a 24-hour spot called THEcafe. Service here aims for boutique hotel ambiance but misses as often as it hits, it's hard to truly provide boutique service to over a thousand rooms. THEhotel guests can access to the main Mandalay Bay hotel, pool and casino. *Info:* www.thehotelatmandalaybay.com. 3950 Las Vegas Blvd. S. at Russell Rd. Tel. 877/632-7800. 1,120 rooms.

Mandalay Bay $$$
One of our favorite Strip hotels, the 60-acre Mandalay Bay has some of the most attractive public areas in Las Vegas, with tropical South Seas décor never descending into kitsch. The hotel's centerpiece is its pool, Mandalay Beach, a **gargantuan complex with six-foot waves,** a lazy river and white sand. The rooms are generous, bright and cheery with robes and slippers, large screen TVs twin vanities and **oversized stone-floored bathrooms with irresistible soaking baths**. The restaurants here number over a dozen, and some are quite good. Charlie Palmer's showcase Aureole is a celebration on the plate, while rumjungle and Border Grill are also excellent choices. Three nightclubs, several bars and a production of Mamma Mia round out the offerings. *Info:* www.mandalaybay.com. Tel. 702/632-7777 or 877/632-7800. 3950 Las Vegas Blvd. S. between Tropicana and Russell. 3,268 rooms.

MGM Grand $$$
MGM Grand has
steadily improved
with extensive
room remodeling
and exciting new
restaurant offer-
ings, earning the
AAA Four Dia-
mond for the first
time this year. The

South
Strip

world's largest hotel divides its rooms into four 30-story emerald
green towers. The oldest, the West Wing, was recently remodeled
with a **sexy contemporary flair**. The rooms are smaller than
elsewhere, but the vibrant décor makes up for it, as do **tech
amenities** like Bose Wave radios, bathroom TVs, and flat-screens
and DVDs in the bedroom. Bathrooms have retained the art deco
look, with black and white marble. The downside of size is that
the hotel's difficult to navigate. At the restaurants, celebrity is the
keyword. Emeril and Wolfgang have namesake joints here.
Michael Mina's Nobhill offers California-influenced continental.
And French "chef of the century" Joël Robuchon has two. *Info:*
www.mgmgrand.com. Tel. 702/891-1111 or 877/880-0880. 3799
Las Vegas Blvd. S. at Tropicana. 5,034 rooms.

Luxor $$
Nice rooms at a mid-price point can be found in both the original
31-story pyramid and in two adjacent towers at this hotel which
is trading its ancient Egyptian theming for hipper-than-thou
cachet, with LAX, the nightclub-of-the-moment, various stylish
bars and several chic new restaurants. The open corridors provide striking views of the world's largest atrium, big enough to
fit a jetliner. This is a very good choice for families, with a decent
arcade and midway plus several IMAX movies and simulator
rides. Carrot Top and the sexy Fantasy revue are the entertainment options. All in all, a better-than-average, middle-of-the-
road choice. *Info:* www.luxor.com. Tel. 702/262-4000 or 888/777-
0188. 3900 Las Vegas Blvd. S. at Reno. 4,476 rooms.

Monte Carlo $$
Monte Carlo is inches away from greatness, which makes its

blandness that much more disappointing. Perhaps they were going for clean and uncluttered, but it just doesn't excite. That being said, the rooms are **excellent for the price**. The marble, granite and brass bathrooms are tasteful and the cherry wood furniture is nice as well. There are **two highly recommended food choices here**, the sublime French restaurant Andre's and the Brewpub, which sadly no longer makes its own beer in-house. Magician Lance Burton just marked his tenth year in residence. *Info:* www.montecarlo.com. Tel. 702/730-7777 or 888/ 529-4828. 3770 Las Vegas Blvd. S., between Tropicana and Harmon. 3,014 rooms.

Planet Hollywood $$
The recent renovations at former Aladdin have made this formerly frustrating resort one of the best choices on the Strip. **Rooms include movie tie-ins and theming** with pleasant décor and plenty of space. The Spice Market Buffet and Planet Dailies, the resort's café, are **ambitious**. Planet Hollywood has **more entertainment to offer than most**, with a legendary performing arts center, a new showroom, and the Prive nightclub from Miami Beach heavyweights Opium Group. At the Miracle Mile shops, the V Theater, Steve Wyrick complex and Krave Nightclub add to the lineup. *Info:* www.planethollywoodresort.com. Tel. 702/785-5555 or 877/333-9474. 3667 Las Vegas Blvd. S. at Harmon.

BEST EATS
Aureole $$$$
Let's start the discussion where everyone starts when discussing Charlie Palmer's post-modern gourmet room – the **wine tower**. Leather-clad "wine angels" rappel up and down the futuristic four-story vertical wine cellar, fetching bottles that go for as much as $40,000. The food is plated in similarly spectacular fashion, although the taste isn't quite up to the presentation. Service here is enthusiastic, attentive and perfectly timed. The tasting menu here is an experience. *Info:* Mandalay Bay – 3950 Las Vegas Blvd. S. Tel. 702/632-7401. Dinner nightly. Reservations suggested.

L'Atelier du Joël Robuchon $$$$
You can enjoy the three-time Michelin three-star chef's cuisine without having to buy the most expensive meal in town. The

atmosphere is completely different at L'Atelier. Diners sit at a bar fronting an open kitchen and watch their meals' creation. The Asian and Spanish influenced menu includes tasting options, à la carte entrées and tapas perfect for sharing. While the price is significantly lower, the restaurant still offers magnificent décor and exquisite service. *Info:* MGM Grand – 3799 Las Vegas Blvd. S. Tel. 702/891-7358. Dinner nightly. Reservations suggested.

South Strip

miX $$$$
Alain Ducasse earned two Michelin three-star designations in Europe, and looks to continue that tradition of excellence with a menu blending **American, French and eclectic flavors** in both classic and contemporary ways. Some of the most spectacular views in Vegas can be had here, and especially from the miX Lounge, which wraps around three sides of the building. *Info:* THEhotel at Mandalay Bay – 3950 Las Vegas Blvd. S. Tel. 702/ 632-9500.

Charlie Palmer Steak $$$
Palmer's second restaurant in the tower is perhaps even more acclaimed than the first. The *Review-Journal* named it the best steakhouse in Vegas only four months after opening. The focus is on **three-week artisan-aged beef**. The pepper-seared hanger steak is out of this world, as is the stuffed Maine lobster. Charlie Palmer is also known for his **signature potato sides**, like truffle baked potato and three cheese potatoes au gratin, and for innovative desserts. *Info:* Four Seasons – 3960 Las Vegas Blvd. S. Tel. 702/632-5123. Dinner nightly. Reservations suggested.

Fleur de Lys $$$
Hubert Keller infuses his signature French Alsatian style with delicate hints of other ethnic styles, offering three, four and five course tasting menus plus caviar and artisanal French cheeses. The unusual décor eschews the typical post-modern hip

Best Buffets, South Strip

• **Spice Market Buffet ($)** – Planet Hollywood: Some say it's the best in Vegas; it's certainly the most diverse. We're big fans of the Middle Eastern selection, including hummus, falafel, and tandoori chicken.

• **Bayside Buffet ($$)** – Mandalay Bay: What it lacks in variety, it makes up in atmosphere, overlooking the 11-acre lagoon. Everything is fresh and well-prepared.

• **Todai ($)** – Miracle Mile: see review below.

• **More ($$)** – Luxor: Fascinating atmosphere and family friendly, which means the food isn't incredible – but a good choice if you're with the kids.

style for a more intimate look that uses **strata of stone and fresh flowers.** *Info:* Mandalay Bay – 3950 Las Vegas Blvd. S. Tel. 702/632-9400. Dinner nightly. Reservations suggested.

Koi $$$
One of the new restaurants at Planet Hollywood, Koi fuses Japanese cuisine with California accents in an environment inspired by feng shui, the Eastern art of arrangement. Eye-catching dishes include chamomile smoked salmon, crispy rice topped with raw tuna, Kobe-style filets and sirloins, and roasted duck breast with shishito peppers. *Info:* Planet Hollywood. Tel. 702/754-4555. 3667 Las Vegas Blvd. S. at Harmon. Dinner nightly. Reservations suggested.

Todai $
Part of a small chain of excellent, affordable sushi buffets. It's so popular that nothing stays out long enough to get stale. The quality and selection are both excellent. Hot food, soups, salads and sides are also served. *Info:* Miracle Mile at Planet Hollywood – 3663 Las Vegas Blvd. S. Tel. 702/892-0021. Lunch and dinner daily.

EAST STRIP VICINITY

BEST SLEEPS
Hard Rock Hotel $$$$
A reported $1 billion in changes are afoot here – including a new

poker room, 1,000 guestrooms and suites, a new live music venue, a new nightspot and new dining – plus additional space for one of the city's smallest casino floors. Of course, it's more of a place to see and be seen than to gamble. The Joint is **one of the best live music spots** in town, and Body English is an incredibly popular nightclub that hosts some of the world's best DJs. The Circle Bar is perpetually bustling. The Hard Rock hits a **dining home run** with the famed Japanese gourmet, Nobu and Robert DeNiro's Italian **AGO**. Sixty tequilas and Mexican food are featured at the Pink Taco. The **Beach Club** is a big draw, hosting the must-see summertime pool parties Rehab on Sundays and Relax on Mondays. If you can't bounce a quarter off your abs, you'll likely feel out of place. *Info:* www.hardrockhotel.com. Tel. 702/693-5000 or 800/473-7625. 4455 Paradise Rd. at Flamingo, 3/4 mi. east of the Strip.

East Strip Vicinity

Platinum $$$
Located just one block off the Strip, Platinum is an attractive boutique hotel with a smartly appointed spa, an indoor-outdoor pool on the fifth floor and a decent restaurant with a view of the Strip. Every room is a suite – and not the mini-suites found at Rio, Venetian, THEhotel and Palazzo – these are the real deal, 900 square feet and up, including full kitchens, plasma screen TVs, Bose radios, whirlpool tubs and balconies – the latter of which is a true rarity in this town (too many jumpers?). *Info:* www.theplatinumhotel.com. Tel. 702/365-5000 or 877/211-9211. 211 E. Flamingo, 1/4 mi. east of the Strip.

Renaissance $$$
Renaissance offers upscale accommodations for business travelers. It's the biggest non-gaming hotel in the entire state. Its guestrooms are **noteworthy in terms of their size and design.** The layout oozes feng shui, with amenities like LCD televisions, data ports, work desks and a wet bar. The monorail station at the Convention Center makes the Strip easily accessible. Its steakhouse, Envy, is on a par with top gourmet rooms on the Strip. *Info:* www.renaissancelasvegas.com. Tel. 702/733-6533 or 866/352-3434. 3400 Paradise Rd. at Desert Inn, 1/2 mi. east of the Strip.

Westin Casuarina $$$

The tiny casino almost seems like an afterthought at the former Maxim, an **attractive, upscale** hotel just off the heart of the Strip. The colorful exterior belies a **subdued, calming room décor** and modern amenities like infinity shower rods. Suede is an excellent 24-hour coffeeshop. Its spa is more relaxing and less flashy than some of the big-name places in town. *Info:* www.starwoodhotels.com/westin/lasvegas. Tel. 702/836-9775 or 866/837-4215. 160 E. Flamingo Rd. at Koval, 1/2 mi. east of the Strip.

BEST EATS

Nobu $$$$

The legendary neo-Japanese restaurant founded by Nobu Matsuhisa and Iron Chef Masaharu Morimoto matches its hype, serving incredible, innovative dishes: primarily seafood, but the Kobe beef carpaccio is so tender you can cut it with chopsticks. You can't go wrong with any of the sushi offerings either. The setting is romantic, hip and sleek at the same time. If you appreciate good sake, Nobu is a must. *Info:* Hard Rock Hotel – 4455 Paradise Rd. Tel. 702/693-5090. Dinner nightly. Reservations suggested.

The Tillerman $$$

Fresh seafood is discriminatingly selected at this family-owned, 20-year Vegas landmark renowned for a wine list that includes well-known and boutique wineries. Their happy hour offers half price bottles. *Info:* 2245 E. Flamingo Rd. Tel. 702/731-4036. Dinner nightly. Reservations optional.

AJ's Steakhouse $$

Somehow the hip, modern, edgy Hard Rock Hotel boasts this totally retro flashback steakhouse. A live piano player, killer martinis and superb steaks and chops put AJ's among the top Las Vegas steakhouses, especially in terms of atmosphere. *Info:* Hard Rock Hotel – 4455 Paradise Rd. Tel. 702/693-5500. Dinner nightly. Reservations suggested.

Roy's $$

Roy Yamaguchi is famous for his Hawaiian fusion cuisine, preparing fresh seafood with Pacific Rim and French touches. Black Ahi and macadamia-crusted mahi mahi are delicious, although everything has its charm, including the "aloha" service provided by the attentive, informed staff. *Info:* 620 E. Flamingo Rd. Tel. 702/691-2053. Dinner nightly. Reservations suggested.

Bahama Breeze $
One of our favorite casual dine-and-drinks, Bahama Breeze features Americanized Caribbean cuisine in gigantic portions. Live music and a fire pit enhance dining outside, while indoors an open kitchen and colorful décor set the mood. We've yet to have anything we haven't liked, and the appetizers, particularly the goat cheese and coconut-breaded onion rings, are favorites. Wild and potent tropical drinks are prominently featured. *Info:* 375 Hughes Center Dr. Tel. 702/731-3252. Lunch and dinner daily.

Bougainvillea Café $
It may seem ironic, but the café at Terrible's is anything but. The servers are consistently quick and affable, serving a wide array of dirt-cheap dishes including pages of Chinese and Mexican dishes. They have some of the best steak, rotisserie and breakfast specials in town. *Info:* Terrible's – 4100 Paradise Rd. Tel. 702/733-7000. Breakfast, lunch and dinner daily.

Casa di Amore $
This is a relative newcomer, but you'd never know it from the distinct throwback vibe, familiar service and classic Italian dishes: copious plates of pasta, pizza that's practically deep dish and retro appetizers like chicken pastina soup, baked clams and scungili salad. It's got an unmistakably Vegas charm all its own. Open 24 hours. *Info:* 2850 E. Tropicana Ave. Tel. 702/433-4967. Lunch and dinner daily.

Firefly on Paradise $
For tourists, this is a hidden gem off the Strip – but it's far from a well-kept secret, as tables are hard to come by all night long at this excellent tapas restaurant. It's hard to know where to begin with so many mouth-watering choices, but here's a few recommendations: the decadent mushroom tart, smothered in boursin; the melt-in-your-mouth artichoke toasts; and a craveworthy

Best Buffets, Strip Vicinity

• **Carnival World Buffet** ($$) – Rio : One of two buffets at Rio, Carnival World single-handedly transformed the Vegas buffet to the gourmet experience.
• **French Market Buffet** ($) – Orleans : Don't be fooled by the low price. The French Market serves up high-quality buffet fare in a festive, pleasant environment.
• **Village Seafood Buffet** ($$)– Rio : All-you-can-eat crab legs, lobster, and freshly prepared sushi. It's a little pricey, but coupons are readily available.
• **Seasons** ($) – Silverton: Located on Blue Diamond, southwest of Mandalay Bay, the newly renovated Seasons is a great choice for breakfast or brunch.

mac-and-cheese made with manchego, a Spanish sheep's milk cheese and the filet mignon sliders, topped with crispy onions, cabrales cheese and Serrano ham. The service is frustratingly hit-or-miss, so be sure you have enough of the delicious sangrias or mojitos that you don't care when it misses. *Info:* 3900 Paradise Rd., Suite C. Tel. 702/369-3971. Lunch and dinner served daily.

Hofbräuhaus $

This is an authentic, licensed recreation of the famous original Hofbräuhaus beer hall in Munich, Germany: an exact copy, inside and out. Three types of beer imported directly from Munich are served in large steins, accompanied by hearty and delicious German cuisine. Diners can eat in the Schwemme (beer hall) or the faux outdoor Biergarten. The beer hall features live entertainment and communal seating for eight to 16. If you're looking for an intimate, romantic, quiet night out, this is not that night. *Info:* 4510 Paradise Rd. Tel. 702/853-2337. Lunch and dinner served daily. Reservations optional.

Lotus of Siam $

The city's best Thai restaurant, like most truly great ethnic restaurants, is a hole in the wall. But the food is spectacular. In fact, *Gourmet* magazine called it the best Thai food on the entire continent. There's a Northern menu featuring chili dips and milder dishes, plus a wide array of traditional, powerfully flavorful dishes. Their pad thai is a superb take on a classic dish, while options like Issan sausage (a hearty street food) or the nam kao tod (crisped rice with ham, red and green onion, ginger, peanut, cilantro, dried chiles and lime) are things we've never even seen another Thai restaurant offer. Best of all, it's dirt cheap. Perhaps Mario Batali said it best: "Long before I wanted to go to any celebrity restaurant in Las Vegas, I wanted to go to Lotus of Siam. It's world-class." Well played, sir. *Info:* 953 E. Sahara Ave. Tel. 702/735-3033. Lunch served weekdays, dinner nightly. Reservations recommended for dinner – don't dare show up without them on weekends.

East Strip Vicinity

West Strip Vicinity

WEST STRIP VICINITY

BEST SLEEPS
Palms $$
Owner George Maloof has one-upped the Vegas ethos: "Whatever happens at the Palms never happened." The home of *Real World Las Vegas*, this star-studded hotel is a prime place to get into trouble. Its recently remodeled $40 million pool is a **jumping party spot**. Palms offers **excellent slot and video poker payback**, creating a diverse mix between bluehairs and A-list celebrities.

The new **Fantasy Tower** includes the **Playboy Club** and additional nightspot Moon atop the building. Excellent restaurants here include Garduno's for cheap Mexican and Alizé for high-end French. Spacious, modern guestrooms with lots of amenities have **great views** from the tall, narrow towers. Palms also offers a tattoo parlor, live music venue, movie theater and a spa. Free shuttles connect Palms with the Forum Shops and Fashion Show Mall. *Info:* www.palms.com. Tel. 702/942-7777 or 866/942-7777. 4321 W. Flamingo Rd., between Valley View and Arville, 1 mi. east of the Strip. 794 rooms.

Rio $$

Rio's "suites" are actually oversized rooms with separate sleeping and sitting areas. Still, at 620 sq. ft., they're some of the most spacious rooms in town. The rooms are gorgeous, with **floor to ceiling glass windows** and lots of little amenities. The hotel's Carnivale atmosphere is conducive to partying, with one of the liveliest bar and club scenes around. The hotel boasts **over a dozen restaurants of nearly every style and flavor** imaginable, including two award-winning buffets. The entertainment lineup is stacked shows and lounges. Along with the Palms, this corridor of Flamingo Road posts a **mean one-two punch** for party people. Free shuttles are offered to Caesars Palace, Bally's and Harrah's. *Info:* www.riolasvegas.com. Tel. 702/252-777 or 800/752-9746. 3700 W. Flamingo Rd., between I-15 and Valley View, 3/4 mi. west of the Strip.

Orleans $

The spirit of the Big Easy is alive and well at the Orleans, a very popular locals' casino whose appeal has crossed over to tourists thanks to **budget pricing, cheerful public spaces and oversized, comfortable accommodations**. Most rooms have separate sitting areas, some even boast four-posters. The Orleans also has a **bowling alley**, a child care center and an arena that hosts everything from football and ice hockey to concerts and circuses. We strongly recommend the Orleans for **budget-conscious travelers who still want the perks** of a Strip casino. *Info:* www.orleanscasino.com. Tel. 702/365-7111 or 800/675-3267. 4500 W. Tropicana Ave. at Arville, 1 1/4 mi. west of the Strip. 1,426 rooms.

BEST EATS
Alizé $$$$
Andre Rochat outperforms even his namesakes at this gem atop

the Palms. Superb haute French cuisine is featured at this truly elite spot. The two-story wine cellar houses nearly 7,000 bottles, some over 200 years old. You'll also find over a hundred cognacs, top-notch service, beautiful décor and a spectacular 56th floor view. *Info:* Palms – 4321 W. Flamingo Rd. Tel. 702/951-7000. Dinner nightly. Reservations suggested.

Café Martorano $$$
Thanks to the storied Mafia past of Las Vegas, the city boasts countless great Italian restaurants. Some of them have more wiseguy cred than others. How does Steve Martorano's joint stack up? He catered every Sopranos season wrap party. His joint is jumping, with eye-popping portions of flavorful South Philly style food, including an $18 cheesesteak appetizer, outrageously good shrimp Scampi and many more great dishes. As for the atmosphere, it's pure party – Martorano dashes between his sauté pans and an Apple laptop from which he mixes music and controls the visual stimulation, which includes scenes from classic mob movies. We once witnessed a surreal moment where he played the pivotal Ezekiel 25:17 scene from *Pulp Fiction*, and the entire restaurant went silent, gaping as Samuel L. Jackson delivers one of the most famous and foul-mouthed monologues in movie history. This is the kind of place that virtually guarantees stories the next day. *Info:* Palms – 4321 W. Flamingo Rd. Tel. 702/942-7778. Dinner nightly. No reservations.

Little Buddha $$$
Little Buddha adds French influence to the Asian menu. This Palms restaurant is another visually enticing, popular celebrity hangout. Besides sushi, the pan-Asian menu here is quite tempting. The Maui onion crusted mahi mahi and the boneless Kobe short ribs are particularly noteworthy, although the surroundings are better than the food or service. *Info:* Palms – 4321 W. Flamingo Rd. Tel. 702/942-7778. Dinner nightly. Reservations suggested.

N9ne Steakhouse $$$
The Vegas branch of a Chicago steakhouse, everything's high quality and well prepared although no new culinary ground is broken. What seems to be the major drawing card is N9ne's

champagne and caviar bar. This is one of the best places in Vegas to spot celebrities. *Info:* Palms – 4321 W. Flamingo Rd. Tel. 702/951-7000. Dinner nightly. Reservations suggested.

Nove Italiano $$$
The upsacale Italian from Chicago-based N9ne Group crowns the Palms' new Fantasy Tower with elegant simplicity, featuring an extensive selection of seafood crudos, pastas, Caesar salads tossed at tableside, and more. The house specialty is the Spaghetti Nove, piled high with lobster, shrimp, crab, scallops, calamari and basil. The rest of the pasta dishes are more traditional, with contemporary twists that make this restaurant an interesting alternative to the same-old same-old Italian. *Info:* Palms – 4321 W. Flamingo Rd. Tel. 702/951-7000. Dinner nightly. Reservations suggested.

Rosemary's $$$
In only a few years Rosemary's has become one of the city's most popular and exceptional restaurants. The menu is American but shows distinctive French, Italian and other influences. All the desserts are simply delectable but the standout has to be Rosemary's crème brulée. The knowledgeable and gracious staff doesn't overdo it. An extensive wine list is featured as well. *Info:* 8125 W. Sahara Ave. Tel. 702/869-2251. Lunch served weekdays, dinner nightly. Reservations suggested.

VooDoo Steak $$$
Another in the Rio restaurant juggernaut, this attractive rooftop dining room with blacklit bayou décor and the city's best views serves Creole and Cajun fare: spicy, rich and seafood-centric. Innovative dishes include grits-stuffed poblano peppers and stuffed blue crabs in red pepper sauce as well as updated classics like Maine lobster Thermidor and seafood gumbo risotto. *Info:* Rio – 3700 W. Flamingo Rd. Tel. 702/777-7800. Dinner nightly. Reservations suggested.

Buzio's $$
Buzio's is an acclaimed New England style seafood restaurant with some innovative fusion on the expansive menu. Bouillabaisse, cioppino, and Thai green curry are savored in the brass-

and-dark-wood dining room. Traditionalists choose Chilean sea bass, lobster, crab or other deliciousness from the deep. The oyster bar is a local favorite and patio seating is available. *Info:* Rio – 3700 W. Flamingo Rd. Tel. 702/777-7293. Dinner nightly. Reservations suggested.

Hash House a Go Go $
Though it's a lengthy drive from the Strip, we'd venture to Hash House every weekend. Sassy waitstaff serve up reasonably priced drinks and huge portions of superb food. It's hard to know where to start. Their awesome bloody Mary and the tangerine mimosa are great eye openers to accompany a chorizo hash or a salmon, pesto and brie scramble. At lunch, try a one pound stuffed burger. Their sage fried chicken, chicken pot pie and hand-hammered pork tenderloin get well-deserved raves. *Info:* 6800 W. Sahara Ave. Tel. 702/804-4646. Dinner served nightly. Breakfast and lunch served weekdays, brunch served weekends. Reservations optional.

Best Graveyard/ Breakfast Specials

West Strip Vicinity

• The Vegas Club offers $2.99 graveyard specials between 11pm and 6am for: two oversized pancakes with bacon or sausage; or eggs, potatoes and toast with your choice of New York steak, bacon, sausage or corned beef hash.
• Suncoast's Café Siena also has breakfast specials from midnight-9am Mon-Fri, for $1.95. Choose from two pancakes with two eggs, bacon or sausage; two buttermilk biscuits with gravy or two eggs with bacon, potatoes and toast.
• Wildfire Casino, offers all-you-can-eat pancakes for $1.99, 24 hours a day.
• On the Strip, Circus Circus has a $3.95 graveyard special at the Pink Pony.
• Del Taco is open 24 hours and overnight sells big honkin' one-pound breakfast burritos for about three bucks.

Ping Pang Pong $
The Gold Coast does cater to a large Asian clientele so they opted to go the authentic route, with positive results. Dinner is served here until the wee hours of the night, making it an excellent spot for an alcohol-soaked nightcap, if you're not expecting Ameri-

East
Strip
Vicinity

Downtown

canized Chinese. *Info:* Gold Coast – 4000 W. Flamingo Rd. Tel. 702/367-7111. Dinner nightly. Reservations optional.

RUB BBQ $

Pitmaster Paul Kirk is better known as the "Kansas City Baron of BBQ," a title he's earned by winning over 400 awards for his mastery of the delicate art and science of smoking meats. The burnt ends and St. Louis ribs are house specialties, while the pastrami is unlike any you'll find at your favorite deli. Start with Frito pie, house-cured and triple-smoked bacon or cornmeal-dusted fried dill pickles, but leave room for dessert – deep fried Oreos and cobblers make satisfying codas for your meal. *Info:* Rio – 3700 W. Flamingo Rd. Tel. 702/777-7293. Lunch and dinner nightly.

Thai Spice $
They've been packing in locals here since 1994 for dishes like Nevada chicken, served in a panang-style sauce, Thai-spiced BBQ chicken, baked Siamese duck, chili beef and catfish curry. Spring mint chicken is a house specialty. Its location is quite convenient, and lunch specials are as cheap as any. *Info:* 4433 W. Flamingo Rd. Tel. 702/362-5308. Lunch and dinner served daily. Reservations optional.

DOWNTOWN

BEST SLEEPS
Golden Nugget $$$
Amidst an ambitious $100 million, two-year expansion and re-modeling, Golden Nugget has **old-school class and European elegance** in the casino, with crystal chandeliers, fresh flowers and marble. The oversized rooms have always been kept up to date, with plentiful features and custom bath amenities. Owners Landry's Restaurants added a spectacular pool with a waterslide that goes right through a shark tank, several excellent restaurants, a remodeled showroom, a new sports book and poker room – plus a whole lot more. The Carson Street Café is **downtown's best 24-hour joint**, and the buffet is better-than-average. The new Gold Diggers lounge has a great vantage

overlooking Fremont Street. *Info:* www.goldennugget.com. Tel. 702/385-7111 or 800/846-5330. 129 E. Fremont St. between First and Casino Center. 1,907 rooms.

Downtown

Main Street Station $$
This is one of our favorite downtown haunts. Ornate stained glass, antiques and glittering lights dominate the décor, making it one of the warmest spots in the neighborhood, with bright and cheerful rooms resembling a Victorian garden. The casino is spacious for downtown and is filled with good cheer and helpful staff. The **rooms are a great value**, and the facilities are top-notch. We especially like the **Triple 7 Brewpub**, serving decent sushi in addition to typical bar fare and microbrews. Note: this is not a Station casino. *Info:* www.mainstreetcasino.com. Tel. 702/387-1896 or 800/713-8933. 200 N. Main St. at Stewart. 406 rooms.

El Cortez $
A year ago, we never would have considered including this historic hotel in a best-of book – but their **new renovations** have made this a perfectly acceptable stay – and with rates starting below $25, "perfectly acceptable" is a steal. Especially when a room comes with a funbook that includes free slot play, dining discounts, table match plays and more. *Info:* www.elcortezhotelcasino.com. Tel. 702/385-5200. 600 E. Fremont St. at 6th St.

BEST EATS
Hugo's Cellar $$$
This is one of the most elegant restaurants to be found downtown, located at the everyman Four Queens. Prime rib and steaks aged 21 days are excellent but Hugo's also serves a variety of traditionally prepared fish and seafood. The room's name comes from its extensive private wine cellar. The service is attentive without being overbearing. *Info:* Four Queens – 202 Fremont St. Tel. 702/385-4011. Dinner nightly. Reservations suggested.

Downtown

Best Cheap Shrimp Cocktails

- **Golden Gate** is often imitated but never duplicated, its deli offering a heaping tulip glass of shrimp for 99 cents, with housemade cocktail sauce, no veggies, no filler. There's also a $2.99 with jumbo shrimp, but why bother?
- **The Plaza** snack bar also has a 99 cent shrimp cocktail, but don't be a lamer. Just cross the street for the Golden Gate's.
- **Arizona Charlie's Boulder** has its own 99 cent shrimp cocktail.

Vic & Anthony's Steakhouse $$$
The gourmet room at the Golden Nugget is a classy affair – a dimly lit, plushly appointed steakhouse featuring various cuts of USDA Prime grain-fed beef, along with a dazzling array of appetizers ranging from Blue Point oysters and Beluga caviar to Maple Glazed Quail. It's intimate but at the same time has a palpable energy and a vibe that recalls the cool of the Rat Pack effortlessly. *Info:* Golden Nugget –129 E. Fremont St. between First and Casino Center. Tel. 800/634-3403. Dinner nightly. Reservations suggested.

Binion's Ranch Steakhouse $$
No other restaurant downtown can match the sweeping vista provided by the 24th floor vantage at this Vegas gem. Come here for steak and lobster. In a welcome change from most other steakhouses, dishes are not à la carte, but accompanied by vegetables and potato. *Info:* Binion's – 128 E. Fremont St. Tel. 702/382-1600. Dinner served nightly. Reservations suggested. Business casual attire.

Carson Street Café $
The 24-hour café at the Golden Nugget is one of the best in town. This pleasant, cheery sidewalk-style spot offers a vast menu of eclectic something-for-everyone fare and consistently friendly service. During peak hours the service can slow, but the restaurant generally does a fairly good job of managing its crowds. *Info:* Golden Nugget – 129 E. Fremont St. Tel. 702/385-7111. Breakfast, lunch and dinner served daily.

El Sombrero Café $

Downtown is rife with inexpensive Mexican and Latin American restaurants, and El Sombrero is a particularly good choice with 50 years of history under its belt, drawing a loyal, vociferous crowd including politicians and celebrities. The menu is simple, emphasizing their fiery colorado and verde chiles. Generous portions and sub-$10 prices make this a place to bust your belly without busting your budget. *Info:* 807 S. Main St. Tel. 702/382-9234. Lunch and dinner served Monday through Saturday.

> **Best 24-Hour Cafes Off the Strip** — Downtown
>
> • **Carson Street Cafe** – Golden Nugget
> • **Mr. Lucky's Cafe** – Hard Rock Café
> • **Grand Cafe** – Station Casinos (various)
> • **24 Seven** – Palms
> • **Jerry's Famous Coffee Shop** – Jerry's Nugget

Florida Café $

Of the decent Cuban restaurants scattered throughout Las Vegas, none is quite as surprising as this family-owned place located at a Howard Johnson on a seedy section of the Strip. Classic dishes like ropas viejas and leg of pork are served with hearty black beans and rice. *Info:* Howard Johnson – 1401 Las Vegas Blvd. S. Tel. 702/385-3013. Breakfast, lunch and dinner served daily.

Rincon Cirillo $

How did so many excellent Cuban restaurants end up in Las Vegas? This one's just a couple blocks north of Florida Café, with similar menu offerings. If your party is three or more, opt for the excellent and cheap paella. Otherwise, you can't go wrong with bistec criollo, pressed Cuban sandwich or the rich potaje de frijoles Colorado, a ham and red bean stew. Don't expect much in the way of atmosphere though. *Info:* 1145 Las Vegas Blvd S. Tel. 702/388-1906. Lunch and dinner served Tuesday-Sunday.

Triple 7 Restaurant & Brewery $

The brewpub at Main Street Station crafts quality beverages, offering a selection of five award-winning beers. The food is well-prepared and reasonably priced bar food for the most part, but

Downtown

Henderson,
Lake Las
Vegas,
South of the
Strip

Best Off-Strip Buffets

• **Feast Around the World ($)** – Green Valley Ranch: Upscale, gorgeous, especially tempting at brunch, which includes champagne and eye openers. One of the best in town at any price.

• **Feast Buffet ($)** – Sunset Station or Red Rock: Almost identical to the Green Valley buffet, but a little more affordable.

• **The Buffet ($)** – Golden Nugget: Downtown prices, Strip quality.

• **Garden Court Buffet ($)** – Main Street Station: Avoid it on steak night, but otherwise enjoy good selection and an upbeat staff.

the restaurant also has a sushi and oyster bar. Open until 7am nightly, $1 beers and breakfast specials make this an excellent late-night option. *Info:* Main Street Station – 200 N. Main St. Tel. 702/387-1896. Lunch, dinner and late-night breakfast served daily.

Upper Deck $
Located at the edge of Fremont Street, the Vegas Club is a spacious and airy casino with an ostensible sports theme, carried through to the hotel's 24-hour café, which features palatable stadium fare. It's known for its burgers, voted the best in the city by AOL Cityguide. The Big Daddy is a pound and a half of beef with all the fixings. Now that's what you call mad cow! *Info:* Vegas Club – 18 Fremont St. Tel. 702/385-1664.

HENDERSON, LAKE LAS VEGAS, & SOUTH OF THE STRIP

BEST SLEEPS
Loews Lake Las Vegas $$$$
Lake Las Vegas is admittedly a haul from the Strip, 27 miles drive down the Beltway and through Henderson. At the end of the road are first-class accommodations with a "destination resort" feel worlds away from the Strip madness. This Moroccan-influenced Loews, formerly a Hyatt Regency, is as nice as the finest property on the Strip. The two signature pools here are gorgeous, recalling temple ruins, while Spa Moulay and the hotel's kid's club offer

broad appeal. The focal point of the hotel is the 320-acre Lake Las Vegas, the captivating body of water around which the community is built. You can explore the lake with a rental kayak, pedal boat or canoe, or golf on one of two 18-hole masterpieces by Jack Nicklaus and Tom Weiskopf. In the rooms, you'll find terry robes, 37" flat screen TVs, organic Bloom toiletries, coffeemakers, high-speed Internet and much more. *Info:* loewshotels.com. Tel. 702/567-1234 or 800/233-1234. 101 MonteLago Blvd., 7 mi. from where I-215 and I-515 meet, off Lake Mead Pkwy. 493 rooms.

Henderson, Lake Las Vegas, South of the Strip

Ritz-Carlton Lake Las Vegas $$$$

Another Lake Las Vegas lodging choice is one of the finest hotels in all of Nevada, the sunny, refined Ritz-Carlton. The buildings form a crescent around the lake, echoing the Mediterranean theme of the shoreline village. The **service** here is a key selling point, with its competent, eager staff going well above and beyond the call of duty. Rooms feature lake or **mountain**

views, and offer spacious and beautiful accommodations to discriminating travelers. The Ritz-Carlton Club level ups the ante yet again, featuring food presentations throughout the day in a private lounge with its own concierge staff. The 30,000 sq. ft. Spa Vita di Lago is a **world-class facility**. The adjacent MonteLago Casino offers elegant surroundings for strong games. Ritz-Carlton guests have golf privileges at the courses at Lake Las Vegas Resort. *Info:* www.ritzcarlton.com/en/properties/LakeLasVegas/. Tel. 702/567-4700 or 800/686-2759. 1610 Lake Las Vegas Pkwy., Henderson, 7 mi. from where I-215 and I-515 meet, off Lake Mead Pkwy. 349 rooms.

Green Valley Ranch $$$

Green Valley Ranch is one of the best known locals' casinos thanks to its starring role in the fascinating *American Casino* reality show. You'll find luxurious accommodations, an absolutely beautiful casino floor, an ultralounge and lots of great restaurants. The **rooms here are four-star**, with robes, slippers,

coffee makers and down comforters. GVR can go head to head with any of the Strip properties, offering a **gorgeous premium spa** that sets certain rooms below overhead pools through which filtered sunlight shimmers down. The Tuscan-influenced hotel almost seems like a separate entity, but you're never far from the action. The swimming pool here is stunning; there's also a movie theater, a high-end outdoor shopping district, tennis courts, a vineyard and even a helipad. Some of the rooms here have breathtaking views of the Strip and the Las Vegas Valley. Overall GVR is **one of our strongest recommendations**. *Info:* www.greenvalleyranchresort.com. Tel. 702/617-7777 or 866/782-9487. 2300 Paseo Verde Dr. at Green Valley Pkwy., just off I-215 in Henderson. 497 rooms.

Sunset Station $$
Sunset Station is the nicest of the non-premium Station casinos, and as an in-between option, offers much of the same aesthetically pleasing atmosphere and primo dining as the higher-end, without charging an arm and a leg for the rooms. The **rooms are much better than average**, with pleasant light shades in Southwest and Mediterranean styles. Sonoma Cellar offers award-winning steaks and California wine, and there's also a Hooters. Entertainment options include a bowling alley, movie theater and Club Madrid's **fun 80s night**. Live bands often perform at the poolside amphitheater. The recently remodeled Feast Buffet here is **quite good, and cheap.** *Info:* www.sunsetstation.com. Tel. 702/547-7777 or 888/786-7389. 1301 W. Sunset Rd., Henderson, about 7 mi. east of the Strip.

Fiesta Henderson $
The casino floor here is **one of the most cheerful in town**, resembling a Mexican festival. We're big on the Fiestas in general because they cater to a very wide range of spending levels without making anyone feel out of place. Fiesta is an especially good choice for low-rollers, with tons of penny slots and full-pay video poker from

nickels to quarters. The rooms are **dirt cheap but quite nice**. The downside to this place is its location: not as far as Lake Las Vegas but just as remote, necessitating a decent drive to get to any shopping or dining options. *Info:* henderson.fiestacasino.com. Tel. 702/558-7000 or 800/388-8334. 777 W. Lake Mead Pkwy., Henderson at I-215/I-515. 224 rooms.

Henderson, Lake Las Vegas, South of the Strip

BEST EATS

Hank's Fine Steaks & Martinis $$$
Hank's is a fine steakhouse (with a good smattering of seafood dishes on the menu as well) with high quality, unobtrusive service. The restaurant is very attractive, with a glitzy look from polished metal, a large onyx bar and a Czech crystal chandelier. The martinis have their own menu. *Info:* Green Valley Ranch – 2300 Paseo Verde Pkwy., Henderson. Tel. 702/617-7515. Dinner served nightly. Reservations suggested.

Michael's $$$
If there was but one restaurant in town that **epitomized the old Vegas of high-roller lore**, this is it. This beautifully decorated Victorian room features **attentive, deliberately paced service**, giving you time to appreciate the crudités, the bread baskets, the spectacular steak and seafood entrees, and the platter of chocolates and fruit that are brought out after the

Best Steak Bargains

• **Monterey Room** – Gold Coast : $9.95 gets you a 16 oz. T-bone, baked beans, salad, onion rings, potato wedges, garlic bread, and a 12 oz. draft beer. Available 24 hours.
• **Mr. Lucky's** – Hard Rock Hotel: 777 Gambler's Special - $7.77 gets you a steak and three grilled shrimp combo platter. It's not on the menu, so you'll have to ask for it
• **Victorian Room** – Bill's: $10.95 for a 10 oz. prime rib with salad, onion rings and potato. They also have an 8 oz. top sirloin with all the fixings for $13.95. Both available 24 hours.
• **Courtyard Café** – Orleans: 16 oz. T-bone, dinner salad, onion rings, French fries and bread for $10.25, 24 hours a day.
• **Restaurant at Ellis Island** – Ellis Island: $4.95 for a 10-ounce steak plus potato, bread and veggies, 24/7.

Henderson,
Lake Las
Vegas, South
of the Strip
_____
Summerlin,
North Las
Vegas

meal. For dessert, try bananas Foster and cherries Jubilee prepared tableside. Tableside prep makes even a pedestrian Caesar salad memorable. Old-school to the max, super-pricey, and probably something every Vegas visitor should do once but never needs to do twice. *Info:* Barbary Coast – 3595 Las Vegas Blvd. S. Tel. 702/737-0555. Dinner nightly. Reservations required. Dress code.

Café Tajine $$
Steakhouse fare with Moroccan influences, as you might guess from its vibrant décor. Savor chick pea soup, prawns with spiced dates and spit-roasted, citrus-glazed chicken, and straightforward steaks and chops. *Info:* Loews Lake Las Vegas – 101 MonteLago Blvd., Henderson. Tel. 702/567-1234. Breakfast, lunch and dinner served daily.

Sushi Mon $$
Ask any sushi aficionado in Henderson for a recommendation, and you'll hear "Sushi Mon." Their all-you-can-eat sushi meal includes appetizer and dessert. Take out and à la carte are also available. They also feature a wide selection of premium chilled sake from various regions of Japan. Innovative rolled sushi is their forte. *Info:* 9770 S. Maryland Pkwy. Tel. 702/617-0241. Lunch and dinner daily.

Lucille's Smokehouse $
Live blues and BBQ! What more could you ask for? Lucille's offers the usual array of hickory-smoked meats: hot links, pork, chicken, ham, Angus beef, and three different kinds of ribs as well as an impressive selection of sandwiches, including portabella, marinated sirloin, and po'boys. It's a little pricey, but we can't argue with the quality. Blues musicians perform on weekends. *Info:* The District at Green Valley Ranch – 2245 Village Walk Dr., Henderson. Tel. 702/257-7427. Lunch and dinner served daily.

SUMMERLIN & NORTH LAS VEGAS

BEST SLEEPS
JW Marriott Las Vegas Resort & Spa $$$$
The JW Marriott has consistently been named one of the top golf

resorts in the US. Guests get priority tee times at the adjacent TPC and Badlands golf courses. The Aquae Sulis spa is a most welcome amenity here, as is the bustling and bright Rampart Casino, on-site but independently owned and operated (by the Cannery folks). The rooms are spectacular, with plush bedding, premium sound, and marble bathrooms with double vanities, whirlpool tubs and separate shower stalls. The whole place has a Spanish revival architecture sort of feel to it, and feels very much like a non-gaming luxury resort. The Strip and Downtown are easily accessible via a 15 minute drive. *Info:* www.jwlasvegasresort.com. Tel. 702/869-7777 or 877/869-8777. 221 N. Rampart Blvd., off Summerlin Pkwy. 541 rooms.

Red Rock $$$
Forget the Strip. This is THE casino you need to see to believe. Bellagio, Wynn, Mirage – **Red Rock trumps them all**. It combines the boundless amenities and strong gaming of a locals' casino with the design sensibilities of a top-tier boutique. The most striking thing about this $1 billion casino is its gorgeous public spaces, which echo the strata and colors of the nearby namesake Red Rock National Conservation Area. Innovative fountains, elegant typography, and untold millions of dollars worth of crystal chandeliers are nothing short of stunning.

The rooms are **practically space-age** in their sleek modernity, with some of the most striking décor we've ever seen. Large windows provide excellent views either of the mountains or the Strip. The resort's A3 (Anytime, Anywhere, Anything) service essentially lets leisure travelers enjoy the convenience and luxury of having a host at your beck and call, a perk enjoyed by casino guests for years. The three-acre pool and beach complex is a focal point of the hotel, and you'll find almost as many hot bodies at Cherry, its nightclub. The

other nightspot here is the Rocks Lounge, featuring the 21st century's Steve and Eydie, a duo named Zowie Bowie. They perform a diverse array of high-energy covers here three nights a week.

Station casinos are known for their food, and this one is no exception – **the highlight here is Salt Lick BBQ**, an out-of-this-world joint lured here from Austin. You can smell it from halfway across the property. But don't stop there. We're enthusiastic about just about all of the restaurants here, including unusual food court options like Capriotti's Sandwiches, Fatburger and Rubio's. A 16-screen movie theatre, state-of-the-art bingo parlor and full-service spa round out the amenities. *Info:* www.redrockstation.com. Tel. 702/797-7777 or 866/767-7773. 10973 W. Charleston Blvd. at CR 215 (Las Vegas Beltway), about 11 miles west of the Strip. 414 rooms.

BEST EATS
Austin's Steakhouse $$$
Austin's delivers. Diners rave about the flavorful seasonings and sauces that accompany expertly cooked cuts of prime beef. This well-rounded restaurant also earns high marks for its appetizers, soups, salad and their practically mandatory sides. *Info:* Texas Station – 2101 Texas Star Ln. at Rancho Dr., North Las Vegas. Tel. 702/631-1033. Dinner served nightly. Reservations suggested.

T-Bones Chophouse $$$
Red Rock, being the first billion-dollar casino built off the Strip, would be remiss without at least one spectacular gourmet room. As the name indicates, T-Bones specializes in bone-in chops, steaks and seafood. Try the Jumbo Jackpot platter: Maine lobster, oysters, prawns, sweet Maryland crab and crab craw. The wine loft contains 7,500 bottles, and the poolside patio is the perfect martini spot. *Info:* Red Rock – 11011 W. Charleston Blvd. Tel. 702/797-7595. Dinner served nightly. Reservations suggested.

Agave $$
This Summerlin cantina features attractive décor, authentic Guadalajaran light fixtures, a strong selection of tequila-based specialty drinks (made from 100 different tequilas), and a bold menu. Agave serves unusual and tasty variations on classics, like

freshly made guacamole with jumbo lump crab meat, chiles rellenos stuffed with rock shrimp, goat tacos, and blue corn chicken enchiladas. *Info:* 10820 W. Charleston Blvd. Tel. 702/214-3500. Lunch and dinner served daily.

Ceres $$
Is it a coffee shop? Is it a gourmet room? Ceres straddles the line, offering affordable comfort food with occasional flashes of gourmet brilliance. Its setting is striking and soothing, overlooking the hotel's extensive water features. American and Continental dishes populate the menu, varying from textbook executions of classic dishes like crab cakes, to intriguing twists like a rich cream-based onion soup. *Info:* JW Marriott - 221 N. Rampart Blvd. Tel. 702/869-7381. Breakfast, lunch and dinner daily. Reservations optional.

Salt Lick BBQ $
The heavenly aroma of the Salt Lick can be detected long before you walk through the doors of Red Rock. This BBQ joint has been an Austin landmark since 1969. Ribs, brisket, pork and even turkey are dry-rubbed and smoked in house. It's one of the best barbecues in this town or any other. *Info:* Red Rock – 11011 W. Charleston Blvd. Tel. 702/797-7576. Lunch and dinner served daily.

Best Cheap Hotdogs

• **Mermaids** downtown features Nathan's dogs for 99 cents.
• **Slots-A-Fun** offers belly-bomber 1/2 lb. hot dogs for 99 cents, 50 cents more if you don't have a Circus Players card. Try not to think about the sort of meat that costs $1.98 a pound – including the bun.
• The **Gold Coast**, **Suncoast** and **Orleans** each have 75 cent hot dog stands.

Summerlin,
North Las
Vegas

Boulder
Strip

BOULDER STRIP

BEST SLEEPS
Sam's Town $
Sam's Town is quite possibly the most popular locals' casino. The hotel's facilities are actually quite nice. Some rooms look out onto

the hotel's lobby, the large atrium known as Mystic Falls Park. There's a **cool laser/light show** here a few times a night. The restaurants here are generally good and unassuming, offering diverse options to a diverse customer base. Sam's Town offers **free shuttle transportation** to downtown and the Strip. *Info:* www.samstownlv.com. Tel. 702/456-7777 or 800/897-8696. 5111 Boulder Hwy. at Nellis, one block south of Flamingo. 650 rooms.

BEST EATS
Guadalajara $
Excellent value for your dining dollar. Authentic Mexican food is served in great quantities by a friendly and efficient wait staff all amid a delightful, vibrant atmosphere. The salsa bar has a staggering array of choices, from tropically sweet to flavorfully fiery. *Info:* Boulder Station – 4111 Boulder Hwy. Tel. 702/432-7777. Lunch and dinner served daily. Reservations optional.

7. BEST ACTIVITIES

Few cities in the world boast the depth and variety of things to do as Las Vegas. The first thing that comes to mind, of course, is **gaming**. While a certain subset of Vegas visitors (and residents) never make it past the slot machines or craps tables, that's certainly not the be-all, end-all of Las Vegas.

Between **craveworthy restaurants, omnipresent shopping, spas, golf, art museums**, and dozens of other little and not-so-little attractions, this town truly has something for everybody. We'll show you some of our favorites in the following pages.

For those of you who do gamble, we'll point you in the direction of the best places to play, regardless of your game of choice.

GAMBLING

Gambling is the lifeblood of this crazy-ass city. Most people come to Vegas unprepared for the experience. They just figure they'll sit down at a table and let the money pour in. Usually quite the opposite happens. **Gambling, like anything else, takes preparation and foreknowledge.**

If you want to learn more about how the games are played, or about winning strategies, refer to the chapter later in this book written by **Avery Cardoza**: *How to Win at Gambling*. Cardoza is a world-renowned professional gambler and writer. But his is only one side of the story.

In this section, we'll share some of the wisdom of the "house." Jay Fenster is a gaming industry insider who can show you the best places to play (and why all blackjack games, craps tables and roulette wheels are not equal) and how to get the most out of your gambling dollar.

HOW CASINOS WORK – DISPELLING THE MYTHS
Myth #1: Casinos can't be trusted to play honest.
A common refrain heard about casinos is, "I don't trust slot machines/video poker games, how do I know the machines don't cheat?" This is nothing more than paranoid urban myth. The **Nevada Gaming Commission** is one of the strictest regulatory agencies in the country. They keep fastidious, stringent tabs on casinos' business practices. Casinos caught cheating would lose their gaming license. Period. End of casino, end of story. Besides, *they don't need to cheat.*

Why not? The answer is simple: **the house edge**. With very, very few exceptions, every bet that you can place at a casino has a built in "house edge" – that is, the payoff for a bet is less than the bet's true odds of hitting. The easiest way to explain this is via roulette. If you bet on red or black, the payoff is even money. Seems reasonable, right? There's 18 red and 18 black numbers. But there are also one or two green 0 and 00 numbers, which make the actual odds of winning that bet 18 in 37 or 38, not 18 in 36. That "little" difference means that for every $100 bet on red or black, you can expect to lose $5.40 on a double-zero wheel.

Understanding the house edge is critical to playing savvy. One of the best sources of information on house edges, and the explanation behind them, can be found on www.wizardofodds.com. If you're a probability and statistics buff, you'll devour this site. If not, its plain layman's terms make it accessible for everyone.

Myth #2: You can beat the house with a betting system.
All "betting systems" are frauds. There is no way that you can alter the way that you bet in such a way that can help you overcome the house edge. One, the Martingale, advocates doubling your bet every time you lose. A bare minimum of common sense reveals how this can ruin you in a hurry. Beware of charlatans offering ways to beat the casino simply by changing the way you place bets.

Myth #3: There is no way to improve your odds of winning.
This is another way of saying that everything's random. But Blackjack and baccarat players who learn to count cards can shave a modest amount off the house edge. However, casinos will kick you out for it.

Some craps players practice "setting the dice" for hours every day: holding and releasing the dice in a certain way to gain more control over the outcome.

Both skills take a lot of time and practice to master, not to mention, they take the fun out of the games. It's particularly nerve wracking trying to count cards in a live play setting.

Myth #4: Slot machines have winning and losing cycles.
Slot machines are frequently misunderstood. Players sometimes perceive them as having "cycles" where they'll get hot and pay out a lot, and then cool down and mercilessly suck cash out of your wallet. Such cycles are a fiction.

Every slot machine (and video poker, reels and keno), has a computer chip containing a **random number generator** (RNG), which constantly spits out thousands of numbers every second. The split-second that you press the button to start the slots spinning, the machine grabs whatever random number is active. Each number corresponds to a particular outcome: whether it's Bar-Bar-Nothing, a bonus feature, or a progressive jackpot. There are no "near misses." You either hit or you don't. What comes up on the reels is merely the visual manifestation of what the RNG reads when you push that button.

The key word is "random." The RNG doesn't know if you hit the progressive on the last spin or if you've lost for the past hour. The RNG has no memory. On any given machine, you're just as likely to hit a jackpot as you were on your last spin, or each of your last 100 spins, or each of your last 10,000 spins.

That being said, **not all machines are the same**, even if you're sitting in a bank of ten identical games. Some may be programmed to hit bigger or more frequently than others. There's generally no way to tell which are which just by looking at them, even by observing who wins more. Anyone can make a killing on a tight machine if they press the button at the right instant.

Also, it's important to remember that even over a lifetime, you may never achieve the "long term" payback of a machine. The "long term" refers to some theoretical, infinite number of spins, and it may take decades to actually reach that number.

Myth #5: Casinos try to fool you into forgetting what time it is.
The era of windowless, clockless casinos is over. Casino operators know that people wear watches. They don't "trick" people into gambling by making them forget the time. Natural light has become an increasingly common and attractive feature in newer casinos. People come to gamble. They'll play when they want to and leave when they're done.

Myth #6: They pump oxygen onto the casino floor to keep people gambling longer.
Pure urban myth. Think about how many lit cigarettes you see in

casinos. Pure oxygen? Lit cigarettes? Do the math. Casinos do, however, pipe in pleasant aromas and keep the air conditioning cold to keep people awake and alert.

Myth #7: I can get high-roller treatment by just looking like a high roller.
Not in the age of computers. Sophisticated software helps casinos identify fairly accurately how much each given customer is worth to them, and reward them accordingly. To take advantage of the spoils, you have to get into the system. Sign up for a player's club card at every casino at which you gamble. Jean Scott's books, *The Frugal Gambler* and the subsequent *More Frugal Gambling*, provide excellent insight into how these systems work and how to get the most out of them.

Working the system for "discretionary comps" is a lot harder than it used to be, and tends to be a lot more marginal than anything else. If you're interested in nibbling around the edges in this manner, we recommend *Comp City* by Max Rubin.

Myth #8: I don't use a player's club card because the machines don't pay out as much to people with cards.
This one defies all logic. Why would any business punish its most loyal customers? People don't return to casinos they find unlucky. The RNG is completely separate from the player's club software. Your card tracks your wins or losses but has no influence over the outcome of your bet. If you don't use a card, you're punishing yourself by reducing your access to comps, cashback and promotions.

BEST PLACES TO PLAY
Many of the casinos offer the same game at numerous tables, but not all are the same. Rules vary from one to another, as will table minimum and maximum bets. Usually, **casinos give more favorable rules to higher-limit games**. Many games are the same from one casino to the next. Some may offer various random side bets, but we urge you to avoid these, as they always provide a bigger house edge than the main game.

Blackjack

What to look for: Make sure natural blackjacks pay 3:2. Most single-deck blackjack in Las Vegas and even many multi-deck games on the Strip pay 6:5, making it much harder to beat the house even on the short-term, adding 1.5% to the edge.

The **following rules favor the player**, so look for them:
• Dealer stands on soft 17.
• Payer can double after split.
• No late surrender.
• Aces can be re-split.

If you're a card-counter, avoid games with continuous shuffle machines. Hand-dealt games are preferable, followed by multi-deck shoe games. Casinos are defensive about card counting and reshuffle early.

Where to find it: There's a single-deck, $25 minimum game at **Binion's** with all the player-favorable rules we mentioned, including 3:2 blackjack payouts. 3:2 single-deck games can also be found at **El Cortez** and the **Western**, although these are not among the nicer casinos in town by any stretch of the imagination.

MGM Mirage properties tend to have the best blackjack rules on the Strip for big bettors. Some of the best tables in town, with a miniscule 0.19%-or-less house edge, include **double-deck games** at **Bellagio, Mirage, Slots-A-Fun, Venetian** and the **high-limit areas** at the **Las Vegas Hilton** and **Treasure Island**.

Wynn's high-limit area has the only six-deck game in town with these same player-friendly rules. Other six-deck games with good rules (.26% house edge) can be found at Bellagio, Caesars Palace, Mandalay Bay, MGM Grand, Mirage, Venetian and the high-limit areas at Luxor, Monte Carlo, New York-New York, Palms, Planet Hollywood, Red Rock, Treasure Island and Wynn.

Craps

What to look for: Look for the most favorable odds. 3x/4x/5x is standard, so don't waste your time playing with 2x odds. If you play the field bet, some casinos pay triple on the 2 or 12, reducing the edge by a few points.

Proposition bets are awful bets, with a double-digit house advantage. But some players like to make them nonetheless. Generally downtown craps tables pay 30-to-1 for the 2 and 12, or 15-to-1 for the 3 and 11. Some Strip casinos pay 29-to-1 and 14-to-1, respectively, giving these bets a whopping 16.67% house edge, the worst on the table. Most of the high-end casinos on the Strip actually offer "downtown odds."

Where to find it: Casino Royale offers the best odds in town, 100x. The **Stratosphere** offers 10x, you can find 5x at the **Sahara**.

Downtown, **Main Street Station** offers 20x odds and the **El Cortez** 10x. Many other downtown craps tables offer 5x.

Sam's Town offers 20x odds. All **Station casinos** except GVR and Red Rock offer 10x, as do the **Cannery**, both **Fiestas**, the **Hilton** and the **Silverton**. 5x odds are offered at **Arizona Charlie's**.

Roulette
What to look for: Games with a single zero (0), as opposed to a double zero (0 and 00), cut the house edge in half. Some players are confused and angry when they can't find their beloved 00, not realizing the bankroll impact. A $10 bettor will lose an extra $13 an hour on a 00 wheel.

Roulette games with European rules have a single zero and return half of even-money bets when the zero hits, for a house edge of only 1.35%.

Where to find it: Single zero roulette wheels are located at **Caesars Palace**, the **Hilton, Monte Carlo, Paris, Stratosphere** and **Venetian**.

European rules can be found, with higher limits, at **Bellagio**, **Mandalay Bay**, **MGM Grand**, **Mirage**, **Rio** and **Wynn**.

Poker Rooms

It used to be that poker rooms in Las Vegas were an albatross around the neck of the casinos. Then, the **World Poker Tour** and the **World Series of Poker** exploded onto television. Now, almost every casino has a poker room. Some of the older casinos have just railed off sections of casino floor, but others have custom-built attractive, comfortable rooms with amenities like food service and plasma TVs.

We can't publish all the details on games, limits and amenities of every poker room in town, but we can share with you some of our favorites, and point you in the direction of a more dedicated resource. Visit www.allvegaspoker.com for trip reports and user reviews of every poker room in town.

Where to find it: Our favorite poker rooms in Las Vegas are at **Caesars Palace**, **MGM Grand**, **Wynn**, **Red Rock** and **Bellagio**.

Slot Machines & Video Poker

It used to be that table games accounted for two-thirds of the income a casino would bring in, and slot machines were a diversion for high rollers' wives. Times have changed. In the twelve months ending May 2006, Clark County casinos won $10.25 billion on machine games, compared to $3.57 billion on the tables.

There are upsides and downsides to playing slot machines. The upsides: **you have a shot at a big jackpot**, you can play at your own pace, there's no skill factor, you don't have to be intimidated playing a game you don't know, and generally you are better reimbursed for your action in the form of comps and cashback.

The downside, and it's a big one: **you're much more likely to lose**, both in the short term and the long run. When you win at the slots, you can win big, but it takes a lot of losers to pay for one big score. Even the best-paying slot machines have a higher house edge than blackjack, baccarat, craps, and roulette.

Personally, we avoid the slot machines. We know, however, that they are extremely popular. So rather than urging you to do the same, we'll try to educate you to can make choices putting you in the best position for a winning session.

Slots
The amount that slot machines pay back is directly proportional to the denomination of the machines. The reasoning is fairly intuitive. A quarter slot takes up the same amount of space in a casino as a dollar slot. But if someone's playing both machines at full tilt, the quarter slot machine is only bringing in 25% as much coin-in as the dollar slot. So to be as profitable, the quarter slot needs to keep more of each bet.

So the simplest thing that you can do to improve your performance at the slot machines is to **go up in denomination**. It's not always that hard. Playing full coin on a penny video slot can cost up to $3 a spin! If you're doing that, bump up to dollar slots, bet that same $3 per spin, and win much more money in the long term.

Geography also has an impact on what you can expect to win. While we have no insight into which casinos have the best payback, the Nevada Gaming Control Board reports the casinos' wins, breaking them down by game and neighborhood. See the chart on the next page for the breakdown.

Note the **astronomical house advantage on Megabucks**. These popular progressives with multimillion dollar payoffs are bigtime sucker bets. The jackpots only hit a couple of times a year, but in between players just lose, lose, lose. Avoid Megabucks.

Locals' casinos generally provide better return on slots than tourist-oriented places, again for an intuitive reason: they de-

Casino Win Percentage in Slots

Casino Win Percentage by Slot Denomination and Area
(12 months ending May 2006)

	1¢	5¢	25¢	$1	$5	$25	Megabucks
Downtown	11.07	8.79	5.62	4.76	5.22	2.39	11.76
Las Vegas Strip & Vicinity	10.80	10.60	8.38	6.08	5.28	3.83	11.56
North Las Vegas	9.02	6.49	3.94	3.15	3.53	N/A	13.69
Boulder Strip	9.58	6.12	3.79	4.14	4.97	6.13	11.79

pend on repeat business from people who can visit every week or month. People simply won't keep coming back where they lose. While hardly scientific, the *Review-Journal* Best of Las Vegas survey has found the **Palms** and **Sunset Station** duking it out in the best paying slots category for the past five years.

Video Poker

Video poker is the only game in a casino where a knowledgeable player has the ability to beat the house in the long term. How is this possible? Like a slot machine, a video poker game is driven by a RNG that randomly picks five cards out of a 52-card deck each time you bet. There's a finite number of combinations that can be drawn from those 52 cards. Therefore, with a little applied math, based on a machine's paytable, the exact theoretical payback of a machine can be determined.

"Full pay" video poker is hard to find: especially on the Strip, most video poker games have short paytables making long term winning difficult if not impossible. But they do exist, mostly in older hotels but sometimes where you'd least expect them.

Jacks or Better, the most basic video poker game around, can often be found in a full-pay version (99.5%). While it's not a positive game in the long run, it doesn't have a lot of peaks and valleys, enabling a player to make their bankroll last. At many Strip casinos, full-pay Jacks or Better is the best available option, but at some higher-end places you'll only find it in $5 or higher denominations. It's the best paying game that you'll find at **Bellagio, Excalibur, Luxor, MGM Grand, Mirage, New York-New York, Palazzo, Terrible's, Venetian** and **Wynn**.

One of the best-paying and most popular games is **Deuces Wild**, where twos are wild cards. The full-pay version returns over 100.7%. Deuces Wild is popular not only because of its high payback but also because of its low variance, so you don't need as big of a bankroll to withstand the ups and downs of normal play as you do for other games. Besides "full-pay" deuces wild, there are variants called Loose Deuces and Double Deuces (sometimes called Downtown Deuces when the royal flush pays 4,700 coins) that are also positive expectation games, but have a much

Don't Play Slots at ...

• **Next to bathrooms, show entrances or buffet lines inside casinos.** These machines get a lot of impulse buyers, and so nobody really seems to care about the payback.
• **Bartop video poker.** Paytables on these machines are usually pretty pitiful, with occasional exceptions.
• **The Airport!** No, no, no, a thousand times no. These are sucker magnets, keeping twice as much of each bet as anywhere else in town.
• **Anywhere that doesn't have a player's club.** If you're not using a player's club card every time you play a slot machine, you're not getting your money's worth.

higher variance and so require a much larger stake.

Full-pay Deuces Wild can no longer be found on the Strip. Off-strip, there's a progressive at the **Palms**, and plenty of full-pay Deuces games at all **Station and Fiesta casinos,** the **Gold Coast and Suncoast, Cannery, Silverton** and **Sam's Town.** Double Deuces Wild games (100.9%) can be found at **El Cortez, Vegas Club** and **Sam's Town** (101.0%).

Double Bonus Poker is another popular game with a positive (100.2%) long-term payback. Here, four-of-a-kinds are big winning hands, so you pretty much live or die based on scoring quads. Many people consider Double Bonus more exciting than the better-paying Deuces Wild, because the big (250 coins or more) jackpots for a four-of-a-kind hit more frequently than the 1,000-coin mini-jackpot you get for quad 2's playing Deuces.

Double Bonus can be **found at many locals' casinos** (including all Stations, Fiestas and Arizona Charlie's) and downtown. **Stratosphere** is the only Strip casino to offer a full-pay version, the nearby **Hooters, Palms, Sam's Town** and **Silverton** do feature this game.

Slot operations departments are constantly changing inventories, so for a complete and up-to-date listing of full-pay video poker machines, with locations, visit vpFREE, a website where volunteer casino monitors track the presence or absence of these coveted machines. Their website can be found at members.cox.net/vpfree.

PLAYER'S CLUBS

The best way to maximize the benefits of gambling is join the player's club at every casino at which you gamble. **Club cards provide benefits** both in the short- and long-term. Here's how they work.

When you sign up for a player's club, the casino takes your name, address, birthday and other very basic information. In exchange, you get a card and occasionally, some kind of gift. Some casinos give you free play.

You insert your club card in a slot or video poker machine when you begin to play. You get a certain number of "points" for every dollar you pump into the machines. These points can then be redeemed for complimentary meals, shows or merchandise, or even cashback in some cases.

Some casinos offer **point multiplier days**, where you earn anywhere from 2 to 10 times the usual points when using your card. Sometimes these are promoted far and wide to the general public, sometimes casinos only offer them directly to players. In either case, these days are a great chance to maximize your return and can even turn a negative-expectation game into a positive play, when you add the value of cashback/comps. Point multiplier days are listed in the Player's Edge column in the *Review-Journal* every Friday and on the Las Vegas Advisor website.

GETTING RATED

The process is a little bit different at table games, since they're not tracking each and every bet you make, as would happen on a slot machine. When you sit down at a table, present your card to the dealer or the pit boss immediately. As you play, the pit boss will occasionally observe your bets. Each game has an average number of bets per hour, so they plug that into the equation: your average bet, times bets per hour, times the hours played, times the house advantage, equals your worth.

Not all casinos rate all table players. Some state on their cards to present for rating when you're betting at least $15, 20, or 25 per hand. It never hurts to ask.

Since the method for determining player comps is an inexact science for table games, **the system can be "worked" somewhat**. Some people bet big when the pit boss is watching and then take their bets down when he's not. Others engage the dealer in conversation to slow the pace. Here's an obvious but sometimes overlooked tip guaranteed to make your bankroll last longer: **play at a full table rather than an empty one**.

COMPS

Comps are a big part of the Vegas mystique. The fact that high rollers are treated as such injects a desirable romanticism to an industry that is, under the surface, merely applied mathematics.

The value of comps you get back is a percentage of your "average daily theoretical value" (ADT). As a general rule of thumb, you can expect to get back **approximately 10-40% of your ADT** in comps. The actual amount varies by game and casino.

Depending on the casino, you may be able to swipe your player's club card at the point of sale and deduct the points directly from your account. Sometimes you'll have to return to the player's club and ask them for a comp slip. Comps based strictly on your point redemption are called "earned comps."

You can also sometimes ask for, and receive, additional comps above and beyond what you've earned. After you've been playing for a while, you can ask a casino host, slot ambassador or pit boss for a comp (mostly food). If you've been playing for a long enough time, they'll generally give you what you ask for, regardless of whether you've earned it. These are called "discretionary comps," and they're not charged against your points.

While comps and cashback are nice perks, the biggest advantages of a slot card won't be apparent until you get home. Many players get offers for free or "casino rate" rooms. You don't have to be a high roller to get these. Some casinos start throwing freebies at customers worth as little as $10 per day. **Besides room offers, some casinos will send free show tickets, tournament invites or other value-added items.** These are called "marketing comps" and usually they won't be counted against your point balance, although you should double-check to avoid any nasty surprises.

COUPONS & FUNBOOKS

One way to make a dent in the house edge is through the use of coupons and funbooks. **Funbooks are special offers given to player's club members or hotel guests.** They can include free drinks, 2-for-1 entrees, gift shop discounts, and sometimes matchplay coupons. These work simply: bet $5 in cash or chips with a $5 matchplay coupon. If you win, you get paid $10. These turn blackjack, craps, and even roulette into positive expectation games, but only for as long as your coupons last.

Don't Be a Sucker!

Almost every bet in a casino favors the house slightly, but some bets have odds stacked so badly against the player that they're always bad news. Avoid the following if you are concerned about the odds:

• Baccarat – the tie bet has a house edge of more than 14%.
• Blackjack – insurance has a house edge between 5.88% and 7.47% - more decks means a higher edge.
• Caribbean Stud – the $1 progressive side bet has a house edge around 26%.
• Craps – the center of the craps table no-man's land, so avoid it. The proposition bets have edges from 11.11% to 16.67% - ten times higher than a pass line bet.
• Keno – without a doubt, the worst-paying game in any casino. The house edge is anywhere from 20-35%, depending on the casino.
• Let It Ride – the $1 bonus bet is one of the biggest sucker bets in any casino, with a house edge ranging from 13.77% to a whopping 36.52%.
• Slots – Megabucks. 'Nuff said.
• Sports betting – teasers have a wide range of house edges starting around 10% and reaching the mid-40s. Futures are even worse.

Some casinos offer **WinCards**. For $10, you get $15 in promotional chips (that must be played until lost, on even-money bets only) and wallet-sized reference cards to playing craps, blackjack or roulette. It's not hard to turn $15 in chips back into at least your original $10, let alone something bigger. You can usually do this once per casino, every one, two or six months, depending on the casino. At press time, some of the casinos offering WinCards included Hard Rock and Luxor (each offering $30 for $20), Santa Fe Station, Cannery, Excalibur and the Westin.

Another excellent source for coupons is the *American Casino Guide*. Published annually, it **contains hundreds of coupons** of all sorts from casinos across the country. The 2008 edition included offers for $10 free slot play at El Cortez, Venetian and Four Queens, plus matchplays and dining deals all over town. The book pays for itself in short order, especially for people who aren't already slot club members. Their website is americancasinoguide.com; there you'll find the **Vegas Values report**, an updated weekly list of casino promotions.

The **Las Vegas Advisor Pocketbook of Values** (sometimes called the PoV) is another popular and valuable resource, packed with match plays, multipliers, food, drink and room offers – including an all-purpose $50 comp at the Palms. Annual memberships to LVA including the PoV start at $37. Visit www.lasvegasadvisor.com for details.

SHOPPING

A number of casinos offer full-scale malls and shopping arcades of their own. Below are our picks for the best shopping in Vegas.

BEST HIGH-END SHOPPING
The Forum Shops at Caesars
Three expansions have increased the roster of stores here to over 160, including such high-end and in-demand shops as Juicy Couture, Gianni Versace, Louis Vuitton and Kate Spade. There's

also 13 restaurants here, including two Wolfgang Puck restaurants – Spago and Chinois, BOA Prime Grill, the Cheesecake Factory, Sushi Roku, and Palm. *Info:* 3500 Las Vegas Blvd. S. north of Flamingo. Tel. 702/893-4800. Open 10am-11pm Sun-Thu and 10am-midnight Fri-Sat.

Miracle Mile, Planet Hollywood
The nice thing about Miracle Mile is its accessibility. This is an attractive mall that's still affordable. Renovations currently in progress will replace the Arab-style décor with a sleek, modern look. Miracle Mile features diverse dining, like La Salsa and Commander's Palace, and multiple shows running at the V Theater, Krave Nightclub and the new Steve Wyrick Theater. *Info:* 3663 S. Las Vegas Blvd at Harmon. Tel. 702/932-1818. Open 10am-11pm Sun-Thu and 10am-midnight Fri-Sat.

Wynn Esplanade
The Wynn introduces several retailers who have never before opened stores in America, including Oscar de la Renta and Jean Paul Gaultier. *Info:* 3131 Las Vegas Blvd. S. at Spring Mountain. Tel. 702/770-7000. Open 10am-11pm Sun-Thu, 10am-midnight Fri-Sat.

Fashion Show Mall
The only mall on the Strip with department store anchors, Fashion Show features Saks Fifth Avenue, Dillard's, Nieman Marcus, Robinsons-May and Nevada's only Nordstrom. With over 250 stores, it's the biggest mall in Vegas. *Info:* 3200 Las Vegas Blvd. S. at Spring Mountain. Tel. 702/369-0704. Open 10am-9pm Mon-Fri, 10am-8pm Sat, and 11am-6pm Sun.

Grand Canal Shoppes, Venetian & Palazzo Shoppes, Palazzo
Connected by waterways and grand halls, these two upscale malls include Barney's New York, Jimmy Choo, Burberry,

Mikimoto, bebe, Lladro and Sephora. *Info:* 3355 Las Vegas Blvd. S. south of Spring Mountain. Tel. 702/414-4500. Open 10am-11pm Sun-Thu, 10am-midnight Fri-Sat.

BEST SHOPPING BARGAINS

Las Vegas realizes that not everybody is in the market for Louis Vuitton. So you'll find three expansive outlet mall centers where you can pick up all your favorite brands at reduced prices.

Las Vegas Premium Outlets

Near downtown, the Premium Outlets are an upscale, outdoor arcade with 120 stores including Banana Republic, Elie Tahari, Calvin Klein, A | X Armani Xchange, Nautica and Polo Ralph Lauren. *Info:* 875 Grand Central Pkwy., off I-15 exit 41B. Tel. 702/ 474-7500. Open 10am-9pm Mon-Sat, 10am-8pm Sun.

Fashion Outlets Las Vegas

Ironically, it's not in Vegas at all, but 45 minutes south in Primm. Here you'll find 100 designer outlets, including Coach, Burberry, Versace and Michael Kors. Put off by the drive? $15 gets you round-trip transportation via the Shoppers' Shuttle as well as $800 in discounts. *Info:* 32100 Las Vegas Blvd. S., Primm (I-15 exit 1). Tel. 702/874-1400. Open daily 10am-8pm.

Las Vegas Outlet Center

This indoor shopping center south of Mandalay Bay features 130 stores including Tommy Hilfiger, Adidas and Van Heusen. The stores and clientele are not as upscale as its uptown sister property. *Info:* 7400 Las Vegas Blvd. S. at Warm Springs Rd. Tel. 702/ 896-5599. Open 10am-9pm Mon-Sat, 10am-8pm Sun.

Fantastic Indoor Swap Meet

Flea markets more your style? Try "the world's largest swap meet," with hundreds of merchants peddling everything from guns and knives to china, jewelry and art. Open weekends. *Info:* 1717 S. Decatur Blvd. at W. Oakey St. Tel. 702/877-0087.

BEST PLACES TO BUY ART

The **Forum Shops** are home to some of the finest art galleries in Las Vegas, including the **Galleria di Sorrento, Elysium Gallery,**

The Art of Peter Max, and the **Galerie Lassen**. Caesars Palace also has the **Galerie Michelangelo**, near the entrance to the Palace Tower. Another excellent option is the **Passman Gallery** in the Masquerade Village at Rio and the Grand Canal Shoppes.

Miracle Mile has **Crystal Galleria, Oh My Godard, Gallery of Legends** and **Thomas Kinkade**. You'll find **Lladro, Passman Gallery,** the **Entertainment** The spacious **Gambler's Galleries** and **Regis Galerie** at Grand Canal Shoppes. You can also try the **Centaur Gallery** at Fashion Show for Rembrandts, Picassos and more. Most of the galleries in the Downtown Arts District are not just for seeing, but for shopping as well.

Best Antique Shopping

* Red Rooster Antique Mall – 307 W. Charleston Blvd. Tel. 702/382-5253
* Antiques at the Market – 6665 S. Eastern Ave. Tel. 702/307-3960.
* Antique Mall of America – 9151 Las Vegas Blvd. S. Tel. 702/933-2791
* The Antique Mall – 1495 E. Flamingo Rd. Tel. 702/270-9910
* The Funk House – 1228 S. Casino Center Dr. Tel. 702/678-6278

BEST PLACES TO BUY JEWELRY

Every casino seems to have jewelers, as do all of the local malls. **Jewels of the Nile** in the Luxor and **Tiffany & Company** or **Fred Leighton**, both in the Bellagio, are among the best. The Forum Shops has **Hyde Park Jewelers**, and the Grand Canal Shoppes has half a dozen including **Ca'd'Oro** and **Venezia**. Miracle Mile boasts **Ancient Creations** and **Clio Blue Paris**. Don't overlook Wynn Esplanade, with **Wynn & Company Jewelry** and **Graff Jewelers**. Rio has several fine jewelers including **Diamonds International**.

BEST PLACES TO BUY GAMBLING PARAPHERNALIA

If you're looking for something to bring home, how about a slot machine, poker table or maybe just some authentic chips. Some states restrict the purchase of slot machines, store personnel can give you details.

The spacious **Gambler's General Store** (800 South Main Street, Tel. 702/382-9903) is the best of the bunch, a supermarket of gambling goods including books, strategy cards and training software. The **Gambler's Bookshop** (630 S. 11th Street, Tel. 702/382-7555) has been outfitting gamblers with knowledge since 1964.

If you're more interested in souvenirs, visit **Showcase Slots & Antiquities** (4305 S. Dean Martin Dr., Tel. 702/740-5722 or Miracle Mile, Tel. 702/733-6464).

BEST PLACES TO BUY NATIVE AMERICAN GOODS & SOUTHWESTERN CRAFTS

There are a few places to buy this stuff, but not many: **Turquoise Chief**, 1334 Las Vegas Blvd. South; **Nava Hopi Gallery**, Galleria at Sunset Mall; **West of Santa Fe** in the Forum Shops, and **El Portal Gifts**, downtown on the Fremont Street Experience. En route to Hoover Dam **Buck's Trading Post** has an excellent selection (1300 Nevada Highway, Boulder City).

BEST PLACES TO BUY WESTERN WEAR

You'll find more than footwear at **Cowtown Boots**, 1080 E. Flamingo Rd., and the **Boot Barn**, 7265 Las Vegas Blvd. S. Several local favorites are **Shepler's** (with three locations: at Sam's Town, 3025 E. Tropicana Avenue, and 4700 W. Sahara Avenue); **Corral West Ranchwear**, 5436 Boulder Highway or 3129 N. Rainbow Blvd.; and **Miller's Outpost** with six locations including the Fashion Show, Meadows and Galleria Malls.

BEST PLACE TO BUY SOUVENIRS

Just about every hotel has a gift shop with logos on anything. You can also get generic Las Vegas stuff in scores of gift shops scattered on the Strip and on Fremont Street. A gift shop billing itself as the world's largest is **Bonanza**, 2400 Las Vegas Blvd. S. at Sahara. We can't verify that, but the selection is impressive.

ENTERTAINMENT & NIGHTLIFE

For some, Vegas is the entertainment capital of shlock. For others, no other city compares. The quality and quantity of bars, lounges, shows of all sorts, music and the like guarantees something for everyone.

BEST BARS
Double Down Saloon
No frills, a jukebox with everything from the Cramps to Frank Sinatra, and ass juice. Yes, ass juice. Dive bar defined. *Info:* 4640 Paradise Rd. Tel. 702/791-5775.

Beauty Bar
A vintage salon atmosphere is home to live bands and Britpop, new wave and 80s dance parties. *Info:* 517 Fremont St. Tel. 702/646-2168.

Art Bar
Paintings on consignment, an Elvis shrine, and a hipster-free crowd. *Info:* 1511 Main St. Tel. 702/437-2787.

Celebrity
Live music and all the hipsters you won't find at Art Bar. *Info:* 201 N. 3rd St. Tel. 702/384-2582.

Ice House Lounge
Art deco meets state of the art at this stylish watering hole and restaurant. *Info:* 650 S. Main St. Tel. 702/315-2570.

BEST BROADWAY IMPORTS
Mamma Mia (Mandalay Bay)
ABBA's undisputed king of Broadway in Vegas breaks every entertainment taboo, giving you your money's worth. *Info:* Tel. 877/632-7400. Performances are 7:30pm Sun-Thu, 6 and 10pm Sat. Tickets are $45, $75 and $100.

Phantom – The Las Vegas Spectacular (Venetian)

The Andrew Lloyd Weber classic is customized to appeal to the short attention spans and high expectations of Vegas visitors. *Info:* Tel. 866/641-7469. Performances are Wed-Mon at 7pm, with additional 10pm performances on Wed, Sat. Tickets are $75, $100, $125, and $150.

Monty Python's Spamalot (Wynn)

Monty Python fans know what to expect from this wackjob comedy "lovingly ripped off" from their Holy Grail movie. *Info:* Tel. 702/770-WYNN or 888/320-7110. Performances at 8pm Sun-Wed and Fri, 7 and 10pm on Sat. Tickets are $69-99, making this – surprisingly – one of the best entertainment values in Vegas.

Tony n' Tina's Wedding (Rio)

This dinner show has been running strong for over four years, blurring the line between performer and observer. The performance comes with an Italian buffet, champagne toast and wedding cake. *Info:* Tel. 702/777-7776. Performances at 7pm nightly. Tickets are $86.85 and $137.50.

Menopause The Musical (Las Vegas Hilton)

This sleeper hit will likely be a fixture at the Hilton for quite some time. *Info:* Tel. 800/222-5361. Performances are at 7pm Tue-Sat with matinees at 2pm Sun, Wed, Thu, 4pm Sat and 5pm Sun. Tickets are $49.50.

BEST HEADLINERS

Elton John (Caesars Palace)

His powerful baritone sounds as good as ever and his stage show is unbelievable. *Info:* Tel. 888/4-ELTON-J. Performances are at 7:30pm for several weeks out of the year. Call or check online for current dates. Tickets range from $100 to $250.

Wayne Brady (Venetian)

He can sing, he can dance, he can act – and this hilarious triple-threat has the charm to make his old-school Vegas variety show a hit. Cover songs, improv comedy routines and audience interaction recall the days of the Rat Pack. *Info:* Tel. 702/414-9000. Performances Thu-Mon at 9pm. Tickets are $49-149.

Lance Burton (Monte Carlo)
Lance Burton performs magic the old-fashioned way, with style. *Info:* Tel. 702/730-7160. Performances Tue-Sat at 7pm, with additional 10pm performances on Tue and Sat. Tickets are $60.50-$72.55.

Penn & Teller (Rio)
If you've ever wanted to see grown men shoot one another in the face or throw a bunny in a wood chipper, line up. *Info:* Tel. 702/740-4277. Performances at 9pm Wed-Mon. Tickets are $75.

Best Free Attractions

- Masquerade Show in the Sky (Rio)
- Sunset Stampede (Sam's Town)
- Fountains of Bellagio
- Fremont Street Experience (Downtown)
- Volcano (Mirage)

Toni Braxton (Flamingo)
Perhaps the Strip's unlikeliest headliner. But the sexy R&B diva could earn a new following here. *Info:* Tel. 702/733-3333. Performances at 7:30pm Tue-Sat. Tickets are $65-100.

BEST PRODUCTION SHOWS
Cirque du Soleil – O (Bellagio)
Water, water everywhere in this dazzling production. *Info:* Tel. 702/693-7111. Performances at 7:30 and 10:30pm Wed-Sun. Tickets are $93.50-$150.

Donn Arden's Jubilee! (Bally's)
Busby Berkley style dance, Cole Porter music, performed on a grand scale. *Info:* Tel. 800/237-SHOW. Performances at 7:30 and 10:30pm Sat-Thu. Tickets are $65-82.

Cirque du Soleil – Mystère (Treasure Island)
Las Vegas' first Cirque show is one of its best, and its easiest ticket score. *Info:* Tel. 800/392-1999. Performances at 7:30 and 10pm Wed-Sat, 4:30 and 7:30pm on Sun. Tickets are $60, $75 and $95.

Le Reve (Wynn)
Imagine Cirque du Soleil's "O," without the whimsy. This show from Cirque mastermind Franco Dragone captures the darker

side of the human condition to create a show wth a refreshingly honest tone. *Info:* Tel. 702/770-WYNN or 888/320-7110. Performances at 7 and 9:30pm Mon, Thu, Fri, Sun; 8 and 10:30 pm on Sat. Tickets are $99-159.

Blue Man Group (Venetian)
This avant-garde performance enthralls some but just confuses others. *Info:* Tel. 866/641-SHOW. Performances at 7:30pm nightly, with an additional 10:30pm performance on Sat. Tickets are $93.50 and $121.

BEST LIVE MUSIC VENUES
The Joint (Hard Rock)
Cutting-edge acts make this their stop of choice in Las Vegas. *Info:* Tel. 702/474-4000.

House of Blues (Mandalay Bay)
Features touring acts and weekly events. Classic rockers and emo kids alike flock to this place. *Info:* Tel. 702/632-7600.

The Pearl (Palms)
Some of the biggest acts in music play this state-of-the-art venue, home of the 2007 MTV Video Music Awards. Ticket prices can be staggering. *Info:* Tel. 702/942-7777.

Theater for the Performing Arts (Planet Hollywood)
This 7,000-seat remnant from the original Aladdin remains one of the city's most sought after venues. *Info:* Tel. 702/785-5000.

Mandalay Beach (Mandalay Bay) – Their summer concert series brings in mostly nostalgia acts to the hotel's spectacular pool venue. *Info:* Tel. 877/632-7800.

BEST NIGHTCLUBS
PURE (Caesars Palace)
The standard-bearer and celebrity favorite, includes the Pussycat Dolls burlesque show. *Info:* Tel. 702/731-7873.

Tao (Venetian)
Includes an ultralounge, dancefloor and a good pan-Asian restaurant. *Info:* Tel. 702/388-8588.

Body English (Hard Rock)
Especially wild on Sundays when the debauched Rehab crowd staggers in.*Info:* Tel. 702/693-5000.

Tryst (Wynn)
Oh, that waterfall. *Info:* Tel. 702/770-3375.

Jet (Mirage)
The one place on this list that doesn't make you feel like you're not cool enough to get in. *Info:* Tel. 702/792-7900.

SPORTS & RECREATION

Few other major cities in America can match the variety of great activities here in Las Vegas. Recreational enthusiasts can partake in **outdoor activity at any time of the year.** It's possible to ski the snowy slopes of Lee Canyon and water ski on Lake Mead in the same day. The winters are mild enough to get out on the golf course and even the summer, with its dry heat, doesn't deter too many people. We should, however, remind and caution those who aren't accustomed to the heat to take it slowly and try, whenever possible, to restrict strenuous activity to the morning hours.

BEST BICYCLING
Head out to Red Rock Canyon or the Lake Mead National Recreation Area. Bike lanes are common throughout Vegas and many of the Valley's residential communities have bike paths. These abound in Summerlin and Henderson, which has miles of trails already in use and many more on the drawing board. For information, contact the **Henderson Department of Parks and Recreation,** Tel. 702/565-2063. You can also join organized bike rides offered by the **Las Vegas Valley Bicycle Club,** Tel. 702/897-7800.

Relive the most exciting part of the Tour de France with the services of **Downhill Bicycling Tours,** Tel. 702/897-8287. They'll bus you 18 miles from Las Vegas to an 8,000-foot elevation and from there you return by bike, all either downhill or on level ground.

Much of the area surrounding Las Vegas has terrain well suited to mountain biking. Try **Bootleg Canyon,** in Boulder City off of US Highway 93 via Yucca Road. The Canyon has a number of well maintained trails varying in difficulty. Rent mountain bikes or learn how to use them at the **Blue Diamond Bike Outpost,** Tel. 702/875-4820. Guided biking trips through Bootleg Canyon are offered by **Boulder City Outfitters,** Tel. 702/293-1190.

BEST BOATING
Boating choices are pretty simple: close by, there's **Lake Mead.** There are six marinas to choose from within the National Recreation Area. For those without their own boat, the **Lake Mead Lodge,** 322 Lakeshore Road, Boulder City, Tel. 702/293-3484, is very accessible and has a good selection of rentals. Kayak trips in smaller coves of Lake Mead can also be arranged. Try **Boulder City Outfitters,** Tel. 702/293-1190.

A 90-minute drive from Vegas, boating can be done on Lake Mohave or the Colorado River, accessible from Laughlin. Call or visit the **Laughlin Visitor Center,** 1555 S. Casino Drive, Tel. 702/ 298-3321 or 800/LAUGHLIN.

BEST BOWLING
The biggest and best bowling alleys in the Las Vegas area are located in some of the locals' casinos. Although none are on the Strip itself, several are close by. All are open 24 hours.

Red Rock
Private VIP lanes and cosmic bowling are big draws at this brand-spankin'-new alley in the northwestern part of the valley. *Info:* 10973 W. Charleston Blvd Tel. 702/797-PINS. 72 lanes.

Sunset Station
One of the newest, the largest and the nicest. Cheerful and modern décor, with shades of Chihuly in the can't-miss glass pin sculpture. *Info:* 1301 W. Sunset Rd., Henderson. Tel. 702/547-PINS. 72 lanes.

Sam's Town
It's not "cosmic bowling," it's "The Extreme Bowling Experience." Fog machines, laser lights and special effects add a real nightclub feel, weekends between 11:45pm and 4am. *Info:* 5111 Boulder Hwy. Tel. 702/454-8022. 56 lanes.

Orleans
The Orleans alley is a perennial favorite, named the city's best by *Review-Journal* readers seven times in the past ten years. *Info:* 4500 W. Tropicana Ave. Tel. 702/367-4700. 70 lanes.

Gold Coast
The closest bowling alley to the Strip. *Info:* 4000 W. Flamingo Rd. Tel. 702/367-4700. 72 lanes.

BEST ECO-TOURS
If you're interested in something more unusual than the standard bus tour, should consider one of the following:

ATV Action Tours
Specializing in highly personalized SUV trips for two to ten people, destinations include the Extra-Terrestrial Highway, Area 51, and ghost towns. *Info:* Tel. 702/566-7400 or 888/288-5200.

Desert Eco-Tours
A variety of tours to destinations near and relatively far. *Info:* Tel. 702/648-8388.

Desert Fox Tours
Offers desert tours in a Hummer. *Info:* Tel. 702/361-0676.

Pink Jeep Tours
Even flashier than a Hummer: a pink jeep or SUV. A variety of tours near and far include Grand Canyon, Valley of Fire, Red Rock and the off-the-beaten track Buffington Pockets and more. *Info:* Tel. 702/895-6777 or 888/900-4480.

Rebel Adventure Tours
Rebel offers tours by Hummer, raft, or mountain bike. *Info:* Tel. 702/380-6969 or 800/817-6789. Make your arrangements through Allstate Ticketing and Tours, Tel. 800/634-6787.

BEST PLACES TO GOLF

The Vegas area has some of the finest golfing in the Southwest. There are currently the mind-boggling total of almost 70 major golf clubs, both private and public, including some good courses in outlying areas like Mesquite and Primm. Note that access to the **par-70 Wynn Country Club** is strictly limited to hotel guests. And even then you'll have to shell out $500 per person.

We don't have nearly enough space to do more than list area golf courses, which doesn't do you much good: instead, pick up a copy of Vegas Golfer or use their online course guide at www.vegasgolfer.com. Another good online option is www.lasvegasgolf.com.

To ensure getting a spot on the links, use a golf reservation service. A couple of the better ones are **Las Vegas Golf Adventures**, Tel. 702/898-4899 or 800/841-6570 and **Las Vegas Preferred Tee Times**, Tel. 702/450-8111.

BEST PLACES FOR HIKING

Some of the area's best hiking and rock climbing are at **Red Rock Canyon National Conservation Area**. There are several developed trails of varying lengths and difficulty. Organized hikes are conducted on a regular basis. For reservations, call 702/363-1922. The **Lake Mead National Recreation Area** also has good hiking and intense challenges. Get trail information at the Alan Bible Visitor Center on US 93 south of Boulder City.

A great place for easier hiking (much of it can be done by walkers)

is on the **River Mountains Trail**. A large section in Henderson is already open. When the 30-mile long trail system is completed you can walk from Las Vegas all the way to the Hoover Dam.

BEST PLACES FOR HORSEBACK RIDING

Red Rock Canyon is the venue of choice. Horses can be rented there from **Cowboy Trail Rides**, Tel. 702/387-2457 or at nearby **Bonnie Springs Ranch**, Tel. 702/875-4191. A little further away are **Mount Charleston Riding Stables**, Tel. 702/872-7009. The weather is a lot cooler up there.

Two other nearby ranches offer trail rides and other equestrian activities: the **Sagebrush Horse Ranch**, Tel. 702/645-9422 in the Spring Mountains; and the **Sandy Valley Ranch**, Tel. 702/631-0463. Both have packages including cowboy-style lunch.

BEST HOT AIR BALLOONING

We suggest **A Great American Balloon Company**, Tel. 877/933-6359, or **Adventure Balloons**, Tel. 702/247-6905. Each offers a variety of standard and customized tours with features like a champagne toast, sunrise and sunset flights, and hotel pick-up.

If ballooning sounds a little placid for you, try out the **Las Vegas Soaring Center**, Tel. 702/874-1010, located in nearby Jean. It offers a variety of programs including one and two-passenger sail planes and rides in old fashioned open bi-planes. Prices begin at $25.

BEST RAFTING

Head to Boulder City for a three-hour raft tour with **Black Canyon River Adventures**. The trip begins at the base of Hoover Dam and winds past stunning canyon lands. The trip ends at Willow Beach, where you will be transported back by bus. *Info:* The expedition depot is located at the Hacienda Hotel & Casino on US 93 just south of the Alan Bible Visitor Center. Tel. 702/294-1414 or 800/455-3490. Reservations are suggested. The price is $73 per person including lunch, and $45 to $70 for children. Hotel pickup is available for an additional fee of about $30.

BEST SKATING

Another thing you wouldn't expect in Las Vegas, ice skating is quite popular. Roller skating too. Try **Crystal Palace Skating Centers** (4680 Boulder Hwy., Tel. 702/458-7107; 3901 N. Rancho Dr., Tel. 702/645-4892); **Las Vegas Ice Center**, (9295 W. Flamingo

Rd., Tel. 702/253-9832); or **SoBe Ice Arena at Fiesta Rancho** (2400 N. Rancho at Lake Mead Blvd. Tel. 702/631-7000).

BEST SKIING
You can take advantage of some good cross-country and alpine skiing in season in the Mount Charleston area of the Toiyabe National Forest. The **Las Vegas Ski & Snowboard Resort at Lee Canyon**, State Highway 156; Tel. 702/385-2754, is located just under 50 miles from the Strip. They have double chair lifts on each of four runs. Base elevation is 8,500 feet. In addition, you can go cross-country skiing in the national forest on Mt. Charleston. Contact the forest service office: Tel. 702/873-8800.

BEST SKYDIVING
Skydive Las Vegas at the Boulder City Airport provides a 20-minute lesson before taking you up 13,000 feet, where you jump into a 45-second free-fall before opening your chute and taking the six minute ride back to earth. Tel. 702/759-3483 or 800/875-9348. A virtually identical program is offered by **Sin City Skydiving**, Tel. 702/300-8508. Free transportation is provided.

At **Flyaway Indoor Skydiving**, you can experience simulated flight in a wind tunnel after receiving instruction. *Info:* 200 Convention Center Drive Tel. 702/731-4768 or 877/545-8093. Cost is $60 per person. Open daily from 10am till 7pm.

BEST SWIMMING
As you might expect, the casino resorts of Las Vegas boast some incredible swimming pools, with all kinds of amenities and atmosphere. The best of the bunch include:

Mandalay Bay
The 11-acre Mandalay Beach has a 1.6 million gallon wave pool, a topless beach club, two restaurants, cabanas and opium beds. In the summer big-name concerts are featured.

Hard Rock
The site of the notorious Rehab party, Hard Rock's pool features a white sand bottom, swim-up blackjack, underwater music, a dance floor, and the hippest, hottest crowd in town.

Caesars Palace
The Garden of the Gods is an opulent, inviting facility with lush landscaping and the ultraluxe Venus Pool Club, offering topless bathing, high-end food, a traveling mojito/margarita cart and decadent service features.

Palms
The brand new $40 million three-pool complex features swim-up blackjack, in-pool cocktail service and poolside massages. The pool's also used as a concert venue.

Rio
VooDoo Beach features five Jacuzzis, a sand-bottom pool, and two full-service bars.

If you prefer a real beach, drive out to the Lake Mead National Recreation Area's **Boulder Beach**. It's open all year but the water and air can be kind of chilly during the winter. **Harrah's Laughlin** also has a private white sand beach on the Colorado River.

Most hotels close their pools during the short winter. You can count on all of them being available at least from April through October, though.

BEST TENNIS
There are no fewer than 350 tennis courts in and around the city. Many of the hotels offer tennis courts for their guests. Hotels with their own courts include Alexis Park (2), Bally's (8), Caesars Palace (3), Flamingo (4), Las Vegas Hilton (6), Plaza (4), Riviera (2) or Tropicana (4).

BEST SPECTATOR SPORTS
Auto Racing
The **Las Vegas International Motor Speedway**. The 1,500 acre complex hosts prestigious auto racing events including the famous NEXTEL Cup Series. *Info:* 7000 Las Vegas Blvd. N., Tel. 800/644-4444, is located off I-15 exit 54

Baseball
The **Las Vegas 51s** of the triple-A Pacific Coast League take to the

diamond just a few blocks north of downtown at Cashman Field, 850 Las Vegas Blvd. N.; Tel. 702/386-7200. The season runs from April to September.

Basketball
The 2007 NBA All Star Game was held at the Thomas & Mack Center, this will be the first time a teamless city has hosted the annual exhibition. Given the chaos that surrounded that weekend, it's unlikely that Vegas will get its own franchise anytime soon. There is a minor league basketball team, the American Basketball Association's **Las Vegas Slam**. *Info:* Tel. 702/895-3900, who plays at Cox Pavilion at UNLV.

Boxing
Las Vegas is "the Mecca of boxing." Popular venues include the MGM Grand Garden Arena, Roman Plaza Amphitheater at Caesars Palace, the Special Events Center at Mandalay Bay and the Thomas & Mack Center on the UNLV campus. In recent years, mixed martial arts events like UFC pay-per-views have also popped up here, supported by the Maloofs and the Fertittas.

Equestrian Events
The **South Point** is the first Las Vegas hotel with its very own Equestrian Center. There is seating for 4,400 people and stalls to accommodate up to 1,200 horses.

Football
If you go for high-scoring indoor football on a small field then watch the **Gladiators** of the Arena Football League. They play their regular season at the Thomas & Mack Center from February through May. *Info:* Tel. 702/731-4977.

Hockey
The **Las Vegas Wranglers** of the ECHL have established a loyal following, thanks in part to creative promotions like their Dick Cheney hunting vest giveaway. They play October through April at the Orleans Arena, a pleasant 7,000-seat facility. *Info:* Tel. 702/471-7825.

Rodeo
The biggest event of the year is the **National Finals Rodeo,** taking place during the early part of December. The most important competitions are held at the Thomas & Mack Center and other venues. Rooms and tickets should be booked as far in advance as possible.

Volleyball
The men and women of the AVP Pro Beach Volleyball Tour come to the Roman Plaza Amphitheater at Caesars Palace every September for the **Gods and Goddesses of the Beach** tournament.

College Sports
The **University of Nevada-Las Vegas (UNLV)** conducts a full schedule of men's and women's intercollegiate sports. The most popular here are men's basketball and football. The Runnin' Rebels play basketball at the Thomas & Mack Center. The football team uses Sam Boyd Stadium, 7000 E. Russell Road, just off of Boulder Hwy. Football tickets are reasonably priced and good seats are usually available. Basketball tickets are a different story. *Info:* For information and tickets for all UNLV sporting events, contact the Thomas & Mack box office, Tel. 702/895-3900.

8. HOW TO WIN AT GAMBLING

by Avery Cardoza
www.cardozabooks.com
Best-selling author of 21 gaming books and advanced strategies

You can win in Vegas! Sometimes with luck, sometimes with skill— but the smart player, the one who learns the skills necessary to win, has the best chance of beating the house. In this chapter, we'll give you those basic skills and show you how to be a winner!

While no one can guarantee whether you'll win or lose, you'll have the best chances to come home with money if you read this section carefully. Pay attention and good luck!

To buy Cardoza Publishing books, visit the website listed above, or stop by **Cardoza Publishing Books** at 5473 S. Eastern Ave. (between Tropicana and Russell), Tel. 702/870-7200 or 800/577-WINS.

BLACKJACK

Blackjack is a game you can beat! With proper play, you can reduce the casino's edge to nearly zero and give yourself the best shot at winning. In this section, we'll give you the basic strategies to play the casino tough.

Object of the Game

The object of blackjack is to beat the dealer. This can be done by having a higher total than the dealer without exceeding 21 points, or if the dealer's total exceeds 21 (this is called **busting**, assuming the player hasn't busted first).

Decks of Cards — The Basics

Las Vegas casinos use one, two, four, six and sometimes as many as eight decks of cards in their blackjack games. Each deck used in blackjack is a standard pack of 52 cards. Suits have no relevance; only the numerical value of the cards count. Cards are counted at face value, 2 = 2 points, 3 = 3 points, except for the Ace, which is valued at 1 or 11 points at the player's discretion, and the **picture cards,** the J, Q, K, all of which count as 10.

Entering a Game

To enter a blackjack game, sit down at any unoccupied seat at the blackjack table, and place the money you wish to gamble with near the betting box in front of you. The dealer will exchange your money for chips.

Multiple Deck

Hitting **Standing**

Multiple Deck — Hitting and Standing

The Player's Options

Each player is dealt two cards, as is the dealer. The player receives both cards face down; the dealer receives one card face down, the other face up. After examining your cards and the dealer's exposed (face-up) card, the player has several options.

He can **stand**, take no more cards; **hit** or **draw**, take an additional card or cards; **double down**, double his bet and take one more card only; **split**, take cards of equal value and split them into two separate hands; or if offered, **surrender**, forfeit the hand along with half the bet.

A player may draw cards until he is satisfied with his total; however, once his total exceeds 21, his hand is **busted**, and he's a loser, regardless of what subsequently happens to the dealer's hand.

The Dealer's Rules

The dealer, however, has no such options, and must play by prescribed rules. Once the players have played out their hands, it's the dealer's turn. He turns over his hidden card for all to see, and must draw to any hand 16 or below and stand on any total 17-21. The dealer has no options and cannot deviate from these rules. In some casinos the dealer must draw to a **soft 17** — a total reached when the Ace is valued at 11 points.

Payoffs

The bettors only play against the dealer and must have a higher point total without exceeding 21 to win. Winning bets are paid at even money. When both hold the same total, it is a **push**, a tie, and nobody wins.

Blackjack Master Strategy Chart

The Master Strategy Chart below gives you an extremely accurate game against both single and multiple deck games in Las Vegas. For multiple deck games, make the plays as shown. For single deck games, make the following changes: where there is a single asterisk (*), double down, and where there are two asterisks (**), split.

Blackjack: Master Strategy Chart
–Dealer's Upcard–

	2	3	4	5	6	7	8	9	10	A
7/less	H	H	H	H	H	H	H	H	H	H
8	H	H	H	H	H	H	H	H	H	H
9	H*	D	D	D	D	H	H	H	H	H
10	D	D	D	D	D	D	D	D	H	H
11	D	D	D	D	D	D	D	D	D	H*
12	H	H	S	S	S	H	H	H	H	H
13	S	S	S	S	S	H	H	H	H	H
14	S	S	S	S	S	H	H	H	H	H
15	S	S	S	S	S	H	H	H	H	H
16	S	S	S	S	S	H	H	H	H	H
A2	H	H	H**	D	D	H	H	H	H	H
A3	H	H	H**	D	D	H	H	H	H	H
A4	H	H	D	D	D	H	H	H	H	H
A5	H	H	D	D	D	H	H	H	H	H
A6	H*	D	D	D	D	H	H	H	H	H
A7	S	D	D	D	D	S	S	H	H	H
A8	S	S	S	S	S	S	S	S	S	S
A9	S	S	S	S	S	S	S	S	S	S
22	H	H**	spl	spl	spl	spl	H	H	H	H
33	H	H	spl	spl	spl	spl	H	H	H	H
44	H	H	H	H	H	H	H	H	H	H
55	D	D	D	D	D	D	D	D	H	H
66	spl	spl	spl	spl	spl	H	H	H	H	H
77	spl	spl	spl	spl	spl	spl	H	H	H	H
88	spl	spl	spl	spl	spl	spl	spl	spl	spl	spl
99	spl	spl	spl	spl	spl	S	spl	spl	S	S
1010	S	S	S	S	S	S	S	S	S	S
AA	spl	spl	spl	spl	spl	spl	spl	spl	spl	spl

H = Hit   S = Stand   D= Double   spl = Split
*In multiple deck games, hit only - do not double or split.

If the dealer busts, all remaining players (those who have not already busted) win and are paid out at **even money**, $1 paid for every $1 bet.

Players who get dealt a **blackjack**, an ace and any 10-value card (10, J, Q or K), get paid 3:2 ($3 for every $2 bet) unless the dealer gets a blackjack also, where it's a push. If the dealer gets a blackjack, he wins only what the player has bet.

Insurance
When the dealer shows an Ace as the exposed card, the player is offered an option called **Insurance**. It's a bet that the dealer has a 10-value card underneath for a blackjack. The player is allowed to bet up to one half of his original bet, and gets paid 2 to 1 if he is correct. This is always a bad bet and should not be made unless you're a card counter.

Winning Strategies
Dealer Pat Hands: 7-Ace as Upcard — When the dealer shows a 7, 8, 9, 10 or Ace, hit all hard totals of 16 or less.

Dealer Stiffs: 2-6 as Upcard — When the dealer shows a 2, 3, 4, 5 or 6, he will frequently bust. The player should stand on all hard totals of 12 or more. Exception — Hit 12 vs. dealer upcards of 2 or 3.

Player Totals of 11 or Less — On point totals of 11 or less, always draw (if you do not double down or split).

Player Totals of Hard 17 or More — On point totals of hard 17 or more, stand.

Doubling and Splitting — Play aggressively, taking full advantage of doubling and splitting options, as presented in the master strategy chart on the following page.

CRAPS
Craps is the most exciting of the casino games. The action is fast, and a player catching a good roll can win large sums of money quickly. In this section we'll show you the basics of play and how to be a winner at the game of casino craps.

The Basics of Play

The game of craps centers around the craps **layout**, made of green felt covering listing the bets available. On this layout wagers are made and the dice are rolled. In this very popular and action-packed game, the players make bets against the house, which books these bets, and receives paybacks ranging from even-money to payoffs as high as 30 to 1, depending on your bet.

The equipment of the game is simple; a craps layout and table, two standard six-sided dice, numbered from 1 to 6, the chips or cash used by the players, and a few accessories used by the house to mark and move the action along. Casino craps is run by two **dealers** who collect and pay off bets; a **stickman**, who calls the game and passes the dice to the player; and a **boxman**, who sits in the middle of the action, lording over the chips, and supervising the proceedings.

To enter a game, simply find a space at the craps table. Exchange your cash for chips from one of the dealers working the table, or if you already have chips or want to play cash, you're ready to go.

The Basics

Play starts when one of the players, known as the **shooter**, chooses two dice from the dozen or so offered to him by the stickman, shakes them up and rolls them the length of the table. This first roll by the shooter, called the **come-out roll**, can determine immediate winners or losers if it is a 2, 3, 7, 11, or 12, or it will establish a **point**, any of the other throws possible — 4, 5, 6, 8, 9, or 10. Here's how it works.

Players making **pass line** wagers, betting that the shooter will pass, or win, are hoping that the come-out roll is a 7 or an 11, an automatic winner for them. If the roll instead is a 2, 3 or 12,

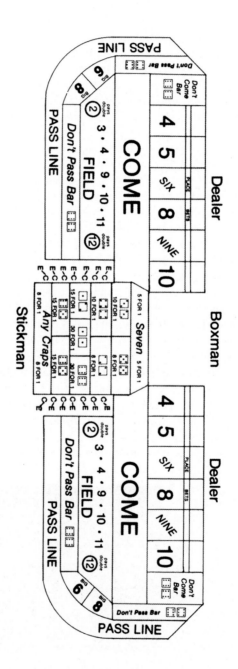

Nevada Craps Layout

the shooter is said to have **crapped out**, and that's an automatic loser for pass line bettors. These wagers are made by placing bets in the area marked *Pass Line*.

Players making **don't pass** wagers, betting against the dice, are hoping for just the opposite. A 7 or 11 thrown on the come-out roll is an automatic loser for them, while the 2 and 3 are automatic winners. The 12, if rolled, is a tie for don't pass bettors (In some casinos it's the 2 instead that's a tie and the 12 is a winner.) These wagers are made by placing bets in the area marked *Don't Pass*.

Any other number thrown on the come-out roll, the 4, 5, 6, 8, 9, and 10, becomes the **point**. Once a point is established, there are only two numbers that matter to pass or don't pass bettors — the 7 and the point. If the 7 is thrown before the point is thrown a second time, pass line bettors lose and don't pass bettors win. And if the point repeats before the 7, then the opposite is true; the pass line bettors win, and the don't pass bettors lose. All other throws are immaterial. For example, if the point is a 6, rolls of 12, 3, 8, and 10 are completely inconsequential. It's only the 7 or the point, the 6, that affects these wagers.

The **shoot**, as this progression of rolls is called, will continue until the point repeats, a winner for pass line bettors, or until a 7 is rolled, called **sevening-out**, a loser on the pass line but a winner for don't pass bettors. The very next roll will be a new come-out roll, and a new shoot will begin.

The shooter will continue to roll the dice until he either sevens out or voluntarily gives up the dice. And then, in a clockwise direction, each successive player gets a chance to be the shooter, or that player may decline and pass the privilege to the next player. There is no benefit (nor downside) to being a shooter. The only requirement a shooter has, other than throwing the dice, is to make either a pass or don't pass bet.

Winning pass and don't pass bets pay even-money. For every dollar wagered, a dollar is won.

The Bets
In addition to the pass and don't pass bets discussed above, the player has a wide choice of bets available. We'll look at these below.

Come & Don't Come Bets
Come and don't come bets work exactly like the pass and don't pass except that these bets can be made only *after* the come-out roll, when a point is already established. (Pass and don't pass bets can be made only on a *come-out roll*.)

The throw of a 7 or 11 on the first roll is an automatic winner for come bets while the throw of a 2, 3, or 12 is an automatic loser. Don't come bets work the opposite way; a 7 or 11 on the first throw is an automatic loser, and the 2 or 3 is a winner. The 12, or in some casinos the 2 instead, is a tie for don't come bettors, just like on the don't pass.

Any other throw, the 4, 5, 6, 8, 9, or 10 establishes a *come point*. Once that occurs, only the 7 and the point are consequential rolls for come and don't come bettors. Come bettors win when the point repeats before the 7 is thrown, and lose if the 7 occurs first, while don't come bettors win if the 7 is thrown before the point repeats.

For example, if the first throw after the placing of a come bet was a 5, throws of 11, 2, 9 and 8 have no effect on this bet. Should the next roll be a 7, the come bettor will now lose that point, while don't come bettors with established points will win. (Incidentally, the 7 will make losers on all *established* pass and come points, and winners on *established* don't pass and don't come points.) Newly placed come bets though, before a point is established, would be winners on that throw of a 7.

These bets are made by placing the wagers in the area marked *Come* or *Don't Come*, and pay even-money on winners.

Free Odds Bets
Free odds bets, so named because the casino enjoys no edge on them, are the best bets available to the player, and should be a part of every player's winning strategy. To make a free odds bet, the

player must first have placed a pass, don't pass, come or don't come wager, since the free odds are made in conjunction with these bets.

Free Odds: Pass Line

After a point is established (a 4, 5, 6, 8, 9, or 10), the pass line bettor is allowed to make an additional wager, called a **free odds** or **single odds** bet, that his point will repeat before a 7 is thrown. He may bet up to the amount wagered on his pass line bet and does so by placing the chips behind that wager. For example, if $10 is bet on the pass line, the player may bet $10 as the free odds wager.

On points of 4 or 10, the casino will pay 2 to 1 on a free odds win, on points of 5 or 9, it will pay 3 to 2 and on points of 6 or 8, it will pay 6 to 5. Notice that these are the exact odds of winning. For example, if the point is a 6, there are five ways to win (5 ways to roll a 6) and six ways to lose (six ways to roll a 7) — 6 to 5 odds. So if the player bet $10 on a free odds point of 8, he would win $12 on that bet, getting paid the true odds of 6-5.

Free Odds: Don't Pass Line

Works the other way. Free odds bettors wager that the 7 will be thrown before the point repeats. Since the odds favor the bettor once the point is established, there being more ways to roll a 7 than any other number, the don't pass free odds bettor must **lay odds**, that is, put more money on the free odds bet than he will win.

The allowable free odds bet is determined by the *payoff*, not the original bet. The bettor is allowed to win only up to the amount bet on the don't pass line.

We'll assume a $10 don't pass bet, which means the player can win only up to $10 on the free odds bet. On points of 4 or 10, the player must lay $20 to win $10; on points 5 and 9, he must lay $15; and on points 6 and 8, he must lay $12 to win that $10.

To sum up, the player must give 1 to 2 odds on points of 4 and 10, 2 to 3 odds on points of 5 and 9, and 5 to 6 odds on points 6 and 8. Don't pass free odds bets are made by placing the wager next to the don't pass wager in the don't pass box.

Free Odds: Come & Don't Come Bets
These bets work the same as the free odds on the pass (corresponds to the come bet) and don't pass line (corresponds to the don't come) except they can only be made *after* the come point is established.

The only other difference is that the free odds bet is not in play on the come-out roll, though the come bet itself is. (The free odds on the don't come, pass and don't pass bets are always in play.)

You make these wagers by giving your chips to the dealer — they'll place the bets for you.

Triple Odds Up to 100x
Most casinos off 3x, 4x, 5x, and sometimes up to 100x odds. These work just like the free odds bets described above except that even more money can be bet. For example, if 3x odds are offered, triple the money could be wagered as a free odds bet.

Place Bets
These are bets that a particular point number, the 4, 5, 6, 8, 9 or 10, whichever is bet on, will be rolled before a 7 is thrown. The player can make as many place bets as he wants, and bet them at any time before a roll. Place bets of 4 or 10 are paid at 9 to 5, on 5 or 9 are paid at 7 to 5 and 6 or 8 are paid at 6 to 5. These bets are not in play on the come-out roll.

Big 6 & Big 8
These are bets that the 6 (Big 6) or 8 (Big 8) are rolled before the 7. Winning bets are paid off at even money.

Field Bet
This is a one roll bet that the next roll of the dice will be a number listed in the field box — a 2, 3, 4, 9, 10, 11 or 12. Rolls of 2 and 12 pay double, all others in the box pay even money. Rolls of 5, 6, 7 and 8 are losers. This bet can be made anytime. (In some casinos, the 2 or 12 may pay triple.)

One Roll Bets
These bets are about the worst you can find in a casino. They're

found in the center of the layout and are made by giving the chips to the dealer.

The **Any 7** is a bet that the following roll will be a 7 and pays the winner 4 to 1; **Any Craps** is a bet that the following roll will be a 2, 3 or 12, pays 7 to 1; **2 or 12** is a bet that the next roll will be a 2 (or 12). You can bet either or both, pays 30 to 1. **3 or 11** is a bet that the 3 or the 11, whichever is chosen, will come up next. Pays 15-1.

The **Horn Bet** is a four-way bet that the next roll will be a 2, 3, 11 or 12. Pays off 15-1 on the 3 or 11 and 30-1 on the 2 or 12. The other three losing chips are deducted from the payoff.

Whenever the numbers 4, 6, 8 and 10 are rolled as doubles, the roll is said to be thrown **hardways**. Betting *hardways* is a wager that the doubled number chosen comes up before a 7 is thrown, or before the number is thrown *easy* (not as a double). Bets on hardways 6 or 8 pay 9 to 1, and on hardways 4 or 10, pay 7 to 1.

Right & Wrong Betting
Betting with the dice, pass line, and come betting, is called **right betting**. Betting against the dice, making don't pass and don't come bets, is called **wrong betting**.

Betting right or wrong are equally valid methods of winning, to almost identical odds.

Winning Strategy
To get the best chances of beating the casino, you must make only the bets that give the casino the least possible edge.

You can see from the chart that bets vary in house edge from the combined pass line: double odds wager where the house has but a 0.6% edge to the horn bet where the house edge can be as high as 16.67%!

To win at craps, **make only pass and come bets backed up by free odds wagers or don't pass and don't come bets, and back these wagers up with free odds bets**. These bets reduce the house edge to the absolute minimum, a mere 0.8% in a single odds game or 0.6% in a double odds game if this strategy is followed.

House Edge in Craps Chart

Bet	Payoff	House Edge
Pass or Come	1 to 1	1.41%
Don't Pass, Don't Come	1 to 1	1.36%
Free Odds Bets*	***	0.00%
Single Odds**	***	0.8%
Double Odds**	***	0.6%
Place 4 or 10	9 to 5	6.67%
Place 5 or 9	7 to 5	4.00%
Place 6 or 8	7 to 6	1.52%
Field	2 to 1 on 12	
	1 to 1 other #s	5.56%
Field	3 to 1 on 12	
	1 to 1 other #s	2.78%
Any Craps	7 to 1	11.11%
Any 7	4 to 1	16.67%
2 or 12	30 for 1	16.67%
	30 to 1	13.89%
3 or 11	15 for 1	16.67%
	15 to 1	11.11%
Hardways 4 or 10	8 for 1	11.11%
6 or 8	10 for 1	9.09%

*The free odds bet by itself.
**The free odds bet combined with pass, don't pass, come and don't come wagers.
***The payoffs on the free odds portion of the bets vary. See discussion under free odds for payoffs.

By concentrating our bets this way, we're making only the best bets available at craps, and in fact, will place the majority of our bets on wagers the casino has absolutely no edge on whatsoever! This is the best way to give yourself every chance of beating the casino when the dice are hot and you've got bets riding on winners.

Try to keep two or three points going at one time by making pass and come bets if you're a right bettor, or don't pass and don't come bets if you're a wrong bettor and back all these bets with the full free odds available.

Money management is very important in craps, for money can be won or lost rapidly. However, try to catch that one good hot streak, and if you do, make sure you walk away a winner.

SLOTS
The allure of slot machine play has hooked millions of players looking to reap the rewards of a big jackpot!

There are two types of slot machines. The first type, the **Straight Slots**, pays winning combinations according to the schedule listed on the machine itself. These payoffs never vary.

Players' Clubs

There's hardly a hotel/casino in Las Vegas that doesn't have a **players' club**. You sign up at their casino club desk and get a card that looks like a credit card. Each time you play at slots or video poker you put the card in the machine and earn points for as long as you play. The **points can be redeemed for free meals, gift items, room discounts and, increasingly, for cold cash.** The general rule is that you add up points quicker on the higher denomination machines.

Is this a great deal or what? Absolutely! If you come to Vegas regularly, you can accrue all sorts of benefits being a member of the players clubs. And not only do these points count in conjunction with table game play, but in many of the bigger casinos, the points are linked across casinos in the same ownership group. There is no cost to join, and often, immediate benefits for your efforts — various goodies, benefits, and bonus sign-up points. In addition, you get on the players clubs' mailing list and can benefit from special offers (such as free or deeply discounted rooms) that the casinos run throughout the year.

The second type of machine is called **Progressive Slots.** These too have a standard set of payoffs listed on the machine, but in addition, and what sometimes makes for exciting play, it has a big jackpot which progressively gets larger and larger as each coin is put in. The jackpot total is posted above the machine and can accumulate to enormous sums of money!

Playing the slots is easy, no more complicated than getting your money in the machine and either pulling the slots handle (or pressing the "SPIN REELS" button) to activate the reels. But there is more to this game that pulling handles and pressing buttons, and we'll go over these things in this chapter.

Your goal is quite simple. You want the symbols on the reels to line up directly behind the payline in one of the winning combinations listed on the machine. While any winning combination is good, what you really want is the big jackpot. Let's see what we can do about that!

Playing the Slots
The easiest way to play the slots is by inserting bills directly into the machine and playing off the credits. The device that accepts your money is called a **bill acceptor**. The machines will normally accept $1, $5, $20, $50 and even $100 bills.

These bills get converted directly into credits on the machine and allow you to play carefree as long as you still have credits available. There are still older machines on the floors that will accept coins, but as I said earlier, they are fast becoming a relic of the past. Let's take a closer look at paying by credits.

Playing by Credits
Once you have credits, playing slots couldn't be easier. On every machine, you'll see a play button marked "PLAY MAX COINS," "PLAY THREE COINS," "PLAY FIVE CREDITS," or similar buttons. The buttons might also be marked as "PLAY MAX CREDITS," "BET MAX COINS" or "PLAY ALL CREDITS."

Pressing the play button automatically spins the reels if you have credits available. That is it! Unlike the older generations of slot machines, you have no fuss with constantly putting in coins or pulling handles. Once you have established credits on a machine, all you need to play is one finger! Now that is easy. You can also choose to lay one coin at a time by hitting the PLAY ONE CREDIT or PLAY ONE COIN button as well.

Winning Slots Hint

When playing a slot with multiple paylines, **insert the full number of coins** so that all paylines get activated.

Experienced slots players love the PLAY button for its ease of play and speed use that button as if it were a speed dial. They'll run through multiple plays faster than a player on an old machine could get off even one spin of the reels. The casinos love this feature as well for it allows gamblers nonstop play at speeds not possible before. And this means more action per hour.

The play button is typically found on the right side of the machine, the area most convenient for easy play. You can expect this button to be large and easily visible.

Coin Denominations
Slot machines come in a variety of coin denominations with larger coin amounts available at casinos attracting high rollers and smaller coin amounts available in sawdust and grinder joints. The most popular machines are the 25¢ and $1 machines, found in most locations. The latest trends in slot machine play feature a return of the penny slots! Yes, **the 1¢ machines are back**, except unlike the old versions that cracked you for a penny a pull, the new ones allow multiple "penny plays" and can actually be more expensive per round of play than higher coin versions.

House Percentages in Slots
Slots is the only game offered in the casino where you can't figure out the house edge. The payback percentage could be 93%, 99%, 96%, or any other percentage, but you would have no way of knowing this as a player. The percentages are not posted anywhere nor is the frequency of occurrence of any one symbol made available.

So how do you figure out the casino's edge on a particular slot machine? You don't!

You may see a casino advertise 99% return on slots, but the question is: Which machine or machines have that return? There is no way to *know* where a good machine might be, however, in the strategy section, we'll show you ways to locate the better -paying machines just the same.

Winning Slots Strategies

Surprisingly, **there are lots of strategies you can pursue** for such a simple game. And following our advice, you'll do much better than the average player and at times, under the right conditions, you may actually find yourself looking at a jackpot!

There is only room to briefly touch upon a few ideas here, but for those players serious about their slots play, I recommend my slots book, *Secrets of Winning Slots* (available from our website at www.cardozabooks.com), which is loaded with information about slots strategies and the machines in general.

The first rule is to **concentrate your action at casinos that cater to serious slots players**. If a casino is looking to attract serious business, it's got to give these players something to whoop about so that it can keep them as steady players. In the old days, this meant having machines with a good payback. Nowadays, it also means having an aggressive players club rich with rewards for their good players. With all else equal, you would much rather **play at a casino with a more aggressive players club program**, one that will get you to the slots rewards quicker. And of course, you would rather play at a casino that has better paying machines.

So how do you get a sense of when a casino is good for slots players? If the casino is buzzing with slots players, that's a good sign. On the other hand, an empty mausoleum-like atmosphere doesn't bode well. Regular players will return to places where they win and avoid places that seem to suck their bankrolls dry.

What kinds of places are these? If you want to get good odds, avoid playing slot machines in the following places like the plague: laundromats, bars, grocery and convenience stores, gas stations, the airport, and the like, places whose slot machines will swallow your money as fast as you can feed them.

Choosing the right location within a casino is often important as well. That slot machine in or near the bathroom can be counted on to have the worst payback in the entire casino. Think about it: Who is going to be hanging around a bathroom very long for the purpose of gambling? (If you can think of someone that might, well, what can I tell you?) Slots lining a restaurant or buffet line are generally set with lower percentages to catch the impulse coins that go into these machines.

Slot machines pay proportionately more on their jackpots if the maximum coins are played, thus a very important principle to keep in mind is to **play the maximum number of coins allowed**. The big jackpot payouts in slots only earn out to their full potential when all coins are played, so you don't want to miss losing a big payday because you weren't playing the machine properly.

On non-progressive machines, there is often a payout difference as well on the bigger money payout. For example, one coin might pay 800, two coins 1600, and three coins, 4,000. That's a big difference.

KENO
There are 80 numbered squares on a keno ticket which correspond exactly to the 80 numbered balls in the keno cage. A player may choose anywhere from one number to fifteen numbers to play and does so by marking an x on the keno ticket for each number or numbers he or she so chooses.

The Basics
Twenty balls will be drawn each game and will appear as lighted numbers on the keno screens. Winnings are determined by consulting the payoff chart each casino provides. If enough numbers are correctly **caught**, you have a winner, and the chart will show the payoff. The more numbers caught, the greater the winnings.

Bets are usually made in 70¢ or $1 multiples, though other standard bets may apply, and a player may bet as many multiples of this bet as he desires as long as the bet is within the casino limits.

5 Spot Straight Ticket

Marking the Ticket
The amount being wagered on a game should be placed in the box marked *Mark Price Here* in the upper right hand corner of the ticket.

Leave out dollar or cents signs though. $1 would be indicated by simply writing 1- and 70¢ by .70. Of course, any amount up to the house limit can be wagered. Underneath this box is a column of white space. The number of spots selected for the game is put here. If six spots were selected on the ticket, mark the number 6, if fifteen numbers, mark 15.

This type of ticket, which is the most commonly bet, is called a **straight ticket**.

Split Tickets

A player may also play as many combinations as he chooses. **Split tickets** allow a player to bet two or more combinations in one game. This is done by marking two sets (or more) of numbers from 1-15 on a ticket and separating them by either a line, or by circling the separate groups. Numbers may not be duplicated between the two sets.

On split tickets in which several games are being played in one, the keno ticket should be marked as follows. In addition to the x's indicating the numbers, and the lines or circles showing the groups, the ticket should clearly indicate the number of games being played.

For example, a split ticket playing two groups of six spots each would be marked 2/6 in the column of white space. The 2 shows that two combinations are being played, and the 6 shows that six numbers are being chosen per game. If $1 is bet per combination, we would put a 1- and circle it underneath the slashed numbers to show this, and in the *Mark Price Here* box, we would enter 2, to show $2 is being bet—$1 per combo.

Winning Strategy

Keno is a game that should not be played seriously, because the odds are prohibitively against the player. The house edge is typically 20% and higher—daunting odds if one wants to win in the long run.

One thing to look out for are casinos that offer better payoffs on the big win, so a little shopping might get you closer to a bigger payoff. For example, some casinos will pay $50,000 if you catch all the numbers while another pays just $25,000. Why not play for the $50,000?

Keno is a great game to test out your lucky numbers. Picking birth dates, anniversaries, license plate numbers, and the like offer a big pool of possibilities to see which ones will really pay off. If you know your lucky numbers, you may just give them a whirl and see if you can't walk away with a $50,000 bonanza!

ROULETTE

Roulette offers the player a multitude of possible bets, more than any other casino table game. All in all, there are over 150 possible combinations to bet. While roulette still gets some table action in Las Vegas, it is not nearly as popular as the *single zero* European game which offers the player much better odds than the American double zero game.

The Basics

Roulette is played with a circular wheel containing 36 numbers from 1 to 36 and a betting layout where players can place their wagers.

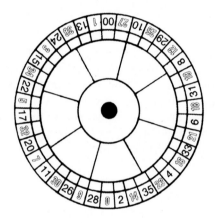

The American Wheel

The Play of the Game

Play begins in roulette with the bettors placing their bets on the layout. The wheel is spun by the dealer who will also throw the ball in the opposite direction from which the wheel is spinning. When the ball is about to leave the track, the dealer will announce that bets are no longer permitted.

When the ball has stopped in a slot, the outcome is announced, and the dealer settles bets. Let's now look at the bets available at roulette:

The Bets

Single Number Bet—A single number bet can be made on any number on the layout including the 0 and 00. To do so, place your chip within the lines of the number chosen, being careful not to touch the lines. Otherwise you may have another bet altogether. Payoff is 35 to 1.

Split Bet — Place the chip on the line adjoining two numbers. If either number comes up, the payoff is 17 to 1.

Trio Bet — The chip is placed on the outside vertical line alongside any line of numbers. If any of the three numbers chosen are hit, the payoff is 11 to 1.

4-Number Bet — Also called a **square** or **corner** bet. Place the chip on the spot marking the intersection of four numbers. If any come in, it is an 8-1 payoff.

5-Number Bet — Place the chip at the intersection of the 0, 00 and 2 to cover those numbers plus the 1 and 3. If any of these five land, the payoff is 6-1. It is the only bet not giving the house an edge of 5.26%. It's worse — 7.89%!

6-Number Bet — Also called a **block** bet. Wagers are placed on the outside intersecting line that separates the two sets of three numbers chosen. The payoff is 5-1.

The Roulette Layout

		0		00
1 to 18	1st 12	1	2	3
		4	5	6
EVEN		7	8	9
		10	11	12
◇	2nd 12	13	14	15
		16	17	18
◆		19	20	21
		22	23	24
ODD	3rd 12	25	26	27
		28	29	30
19 to 36		31	32	33
		34	35	36
		2-1	2-1	2-1

Columns Bet — A chip placed at the head of a column, on the far side from the zero or zeros, covers all 12 numbers in the column and has a winning payoff of 2-1. The 0 and 00 are not included in this bet.

Dozens Bet — A bet on 1-12, 13-24 or 25-36. They're called the first, second and third dozen respectively. The winning payoff as in the column bet is 2 to 1.

Even Money Bets
You can also bet:

Red-Black — There are eighteen black and eighteen red numbers. A player may bet either the red or the black and is paid off at 1 to 1 on a winning spin. Bets are placed on the black or white diamond.

High-Low — Numbers 1-18 may be bet (low) or 19-36 (high). Bets are paid off at 1 to 1. Bets are placed in these particular boxes.

Odd-Even — There are 18 even numbers and 18 odd numbers. Winning bets are paid at 1 to 1. Bets are placed in the odd or even box on the table.

Roulette Payoff Chart

Roulette Bets	#	Payoff
Single Number	1	35-1
Split Bet	2	17-1
Trio	3	11-1
4-Number (Corner)	4	8-1
5-Number	5	6-1
6-Number or Block	6	5-1
Columns Bet	12	2-1
Dozens Bet	12	2-1
Red or Black	18	1-1
High or Low	18	1-1
Odd or Even	18	1-1

 # column is the amount of numbers covered by the bet.

Winning Strategy
It must be stated clearly: the casino has the mathematical edge over the player in roulette. No betting strategy or playing system can overcome those odds. Except for the five number bet  which is at 7.89%, all bets at roulette give the house a 5.26% advantage.

You can have fun at roulette and come home a winner if you catch a good streak. Money management is all-important – protect your losses and quit when ahead. Betting strategies can work – in the short run – and provide the player with a fun, working approach to winning. And really, that's what the game is all about.

VIDEO POKER
Video poker is loosely based on draw poker. You get five cards to start and can keep or exchange any or all of these cards to form a new five card hand. Your goal is to get a five card poker hand in the combinations listed on the front of the machine. The higher ranked the poker hand, the greater the payout.

The Basics
The game is simple to play, but you must make the right decisions on which cards to hold to maximize your winning chances. That is the skill element. The fun element comes in when your good play turns into winnings. You have a wide variety of variations to choose among, from the standard Jacks or Better machines found in most places, and the popular Deuces Wild games, to a widening choice of spin-offs and variations.

Getting Started
The typical video poker game uses a 52-card deck, dealt fresh after each hand. There are other variations that use multiple decks and extra cards such as wild cards, but the principles are the same.

To start, you need to insert money into the machine. Almost all modern machines have bill acceptors, devices that accept $1, $5, $10, $20, $50, and $100 bills. Once the bills are accepted into the machine, the equivalent amount of credits will be posted on the machine for your bankroll. For example, if you insert a $20 bill into the bill acceptor on a quarter machine, 80 credits will be posted.

Wins and losses will be added or deducted from your credits. If you start out with 80 credits and bet five coins, then five credits will be deducted from your total credits and the machine will show "75" credits. A win of 45 credits will boost your total to 120 credits and "120" will appear in the credits area.

Playing by Credits

With credits on the machine, getting your cards dealt is as easy as hitting a button. On every machine, you'll see a button marked "PLAY MAX COINS," "PLAY FIVE CREDITS," or a similar play button. Pressing this button deals five cards to you and deducts five credits from your credit total. Thus, if you had 100 credits to start, pressing PLAY FIVE CREDITS would reduce your total to 95 credits. You now have your initial five card hand.

There is also a button on the machine that allows you to play one credit at a time. This button may be marked "PLAY ONE CREDIT," "PLAY ONE COIN," or the like. Since the maximum number of coins are not being played, you also have to hit the DRAW/DEAL button for the cards to be dealt.

If less than the maximum amount of coins are inserted, you'll need to press the button marked DRAW/DEAL to receive your cards. Once you have established credits on the machine (by winning hands), until you hit the CASH OUT button, you will be playing by credits anyway and using the "PLAY MAX COINS" or "PLAY FIVE CREDITS" to deal cards.

Your Initial Five Card Hand

You start out with a five card hand. You may keep one, some, all, or none of these cards. It's your decision. There are five hold buttons, one underneath each card. To keep a card, press the button marked "HOLD" underneath the corresponding card you wish to keep. Thus, for each card you want to keep, you must press the hold button.

"HELD" will appear on the screen underneath each card or cards so chosen. The other cards, the ones you wish to discard, will not be kept by the machine.

What happens if you press the wrong hold button by accident or change your mind? No problem. Press the corresponding button again. If the card indicated "HELD," the "HELD" will disappear and the card will not be held by the computer. If you change your mind, press the button one more time and again "HELD" will appear on the screen indicating that the card will be kept on the draw.

Until you press the draw button, it is not too late to change your strategy decision.

Keeping/Discarding All Five Cards
You may keep all five original cards by pushing the hold button under each card, or discard all five original cards by pressing the DRAW/DEAL button without having pressed any of the hold buttons.

Discarding all your cards is often the correct strategy in video poker and we'll discuss when to do so in the winning strategies section.

The Final Hand
To discard the cards you don't want to keep and receive your new ones, you now press the DRAW/DEAL button again. Cards that had "HELD" underneath will remain, while those cards not chosen to be held will be replaced by new ones. This set of cards is your final hand.

If your hand is a winner, the

Winning Video Poker Hint

If you get dealt a great five card hand that you want to keep, such as a straight or even a royal flush, remember to press the hold button underneath each and every one of the cards before pressing the DEAL/DRAW button – or you will lose the hand on the card exchange!

machine will flash "WINNER" at the bottom of the screen. Winning hands are automatically paid according to the payoffs shown on the machine and will be added to your total number of credits.

The Cash Out Button
When you are finished playing and want to leave the machine, you'll want to take your money with you of course. You can retrieve your credits at any time by pressing the CASH OUT button. Your winnings will be sent tumbling into the well below in a noisy racket as metal meets metal.

Important Tip: If you have won more money than is in the machine or more than it can pay out, press the service button, then sit tight and do not leave the machine until an attendant comes to pay you the rest of the money you've won.

The Winning Hands
Typically, the minimum winning hand in video poker is a pair of jacks or better, though that varies by machine type. For example, Deuces Wild machines require at least a three of a kind for a payout and Pick Five machines pay out for hands as low as a pair of sixes.

The chart below describes the winning hands for the Jacks or Better based variations. Hands are listed from weakest to strongest.

On wild card machines, you will see additional listings for five of a kind hands (made possible because of the wild cards) and two types of royal flushes.

The more valuable royal flush is the natural royal flush which doesn't use any wild cards to form it. The natural is harder to get and will pay more. The other type of royal flush is the wild royal flush, which uses at least one wild card to form the five card royal flush.

There are also payouts for other types of hands, such as the Bonus Quad machines where specified four a kind hands will receive a higher payout amount than other types of four of a kinds hands, but these will be clearly listed on the machines themselves.

Winning Hands in Video Poker

Jacks or Better - Two cards of equal value. Jacks or better refers to a pairing of Jacks, Queens, Kings or Aces.

Two Pair - Two sets of paired cards, such as 3-3 and 10-10.

Three of a Kind - Three cards of equal value, such as 9-9-9.

Straight - Five cards in numerical sequence, such as 3-4-5-6-7 or 10- J-Q-K-A.

Flush - Any five cards of the same suit, such as five hearts.

Full House - Three of a kind and a pair, such as 2-2-2-J-J.

Four of a Kind - Four cards of equal value, such as K-K-K-K.

Straight Flush - A straight all in the same suit, such as 7♥, 8♥, 9♥, 10♥, J♥.

Royal Flush - 10♦, J♦, Q♦, K♦, A♦, all in the same suit.

Progressives/Non-Progressives
Video poker machines can be played as either Flat-Top (or Straight) machines, where there are set payoffs on all the hands won, or as Progressives, where the progressive jackpot constantly increases until the royal flush is hit.

On both type of machines, all the payoffs are proportionate for the winning hands. Thus, a winning payoff on two coins played will be exactly double that for the same winning hand with one coin played.

The one exception is for the royal flush, where a winning payoff on a non-progressive machine typically gives you a 4,000 coin return when all five coins are played. One, two, three and four coins pay respectively, 200, 400, 600 and 800 coins for the royal.

The progression would normally take you to a 1,000 coin payoff, but there is a bonus for playing the full five coins and that is the 4,000 coin payoff. It is the same on a Progressive machine, where to get the full benefit of the Royal Flush jackpot, you need to play the full five coins.

That is why it is always important to play all five coins whether playing the Straight machines or the Progressives.

Important Tip: Always insert the full five coins to get the best odds at video poker.

Payoffs – Jacks or Better: 9/6 Machine

Coins Played	1	2	3	4	5
Royal Flush	250	500	750	1000	4000
Straight Flush	50	100	150	200	250
Four of a Kind	25	50	75	100	125
Full House	9	18	27	36	45
Flush	6	12	18	24	30
Straight	4	8	12	16	20
Three of a Kind	3	6	9	12	15
Two Pair	2	4	6	8	10
Jacks or Better	1	2	3	4	5

Winning Strategy
The big payoff in video poker on the jacks or better machines is the royal flush – a whopping 4,000 coins are paid for this score when five coins are played.

On progressive machines, if five coins are played, the total could be a great deal higher, possibly as high as $3,000 (12,000 coins) on a quarter machine. It's rare but it happens!

The royal doesn't come often. With correct strategy, you'll hit one every 40,000+ hands on the average. This doesn't mean, however, that you won't hit one in your very first hour of play!

Jacks or Better: 9-6 Flattop Strategy

1. Whenever you hold **four cards to a royal flush**, discard the fifth card, even if that card gives you a flush or pair.

2. Keep a **jacks or better pair** and any higher hand such as a three of a kind or straight over three to the royal. **Play the three to a royal** over any lesser hand such as a low pair or four flush.

3. With **two cards to a royal**, keep four straights, four flushes, and high pairs or better instead. Otherwise, go for the royal.

4. Never break up a **straight or flush**, unless a one card draw gives you a chance for the royal.

5. Keep **jacks or better** over a four straight or four flush.

6. **Never break up a four of a kind, full house, three of a kind** or **two pair** hands. The rags, worthless cards for the latter two hands, should be dropped on the draw.

7. The **jacks or better pair** is always kept, except when you have four cards that could result in a straight flush or royal flush.

8. Keep **low pairs** over the four straight, but discard them in favor of the four flushes and three or four to a royal flush.

9. When dealt **unmade hands**, pre-draw hands with no payable combination of cards, save in order; four to a royal flush and straight flush, three to a royal flush, four flushes, four straights, three to a straight flush, two cards to the royal, two cards jack or higher and one card jack or higher.

10. Lacking any of the above, with no card jack or higher, discard all the cards and draw five fresh ones.

These strategies are not applicable to 8/5 or other paytables.

Meanwhile, you'll be collecting other winners such as straights, full houses and the like. With proper play, all in all, you can beat the video poker machines.

To collect the full payoff for a royal flush, proper play dictates that you always play the full five coins for each game. Of course, those that want to play less seriously can play any amount of coins from 1 to 5.

LET IT RIDE
The Basics
Let it Ride is played on a blackjack-style table with a single standard pack of 52 cards. On the flat side of the table is the dealer who performs all the normal dealer functions. Across from the dealer, along the oval edge are as many as seven players.

There are three betting circles in front of each player's seat. These circles are laid out next to each other, horizontally, in front of each player's position. Going left to right, they are marked "1," "2" and "$" respectively. These are the spots where the three mandatory bets are placed by each participating player. There is one additional bet spot as well, a red button located in front of each player, where an optional $1 wager can be made on the Let it Ride Bonus Bet.

You get dealt three cards and will use these three cards in combination with the two community cards shared by all players to form a final five card hand that either qualifies for a payout, which is a winner, or doesn't qualify for a payout, which of course, is a loser.

There are no draws of additional cards, bluffing of opponents, or strategy decisions as in regular draw poker. Here, your only decisions besides the initial bets made, are whether to take down two of the three mandatory starting bets in the game, or whether to let them ride.

There is no competition against other players as in regular poker or against the dealer as in Caribbean Stud Poker. In Let it Ride, the goal is solely to draw a hand strong enough to qualify for a payout.

The Play of the Game
Before any cards are dealt, you must place three bets in equal amounts on each of the three betting circles in front you. For

example, if $5 is wagered on the circle marked "1," the same $5 must be bet on the other two circles, the one marked "2," and the one marked "$." Additionally, a $1 wager may be made on the Tournament or Bonus spot.

There is normally a minimum $5 bet on each circle, though sometimes smaller minimums may be found.

The dealer will deal three down cards to each player and two face down cards that will be placed in the two rectangular boxes in front of his own position. These two cards are community cards that will be shared by the players to form their final five card holding.

The dealer himself does not get any cards. You are not competing against the dealer nor other players. As in video poker, you are simply trying to get a hand strong enough to qualify for a payout. The rules of the game disallow you from showing your cards to other players at the table. This rule exists because casinos don't want players to gain any untoward advantage that may help them make better playing decisions.

The Player's First Option
Each player in turn, after looking at his or her three down cards, has the option of playing for the bet in circle "1," that is, *letting it ride,* or withdrawing that bet from play and having it returned to his or her bankroll.

Letting a bet ride is done by placing the cards under or in front of the cards in the circle marked "1."

If you wish to remove your bet from play, simply scrape the table with the cards. This motion will prompt the dealer to remove your bet from the first circle and return it to you. You should not physically take back your own bets. Let the dealer perform that function.

The Player's Second Option
After all player's have made their decisions on bet circle "1," the dealer turns over one of the two community cards in front of him. Now you know four of the five cards that will be used to form your

final hand. As in the first round, you are faced with the decision to let your bet in circle "2" ride, or to take it down and put it back into your bankroll. You may remove this bet even if you chose to let your bet in circle "1" ride.

The Showdown
After all players have made their betting decisions, the dealer will turn over the second community card. The two community cards along with your three cards will form your final five card hand. Unlike the previous two rounds, the bet in circle "3" cannot be removed. This bet is for keeps and will be settled by the dealer along with the bets, if any, that you have riding in the other betting circles.

If you hold at least a pair of 10's or higher ranked poker hand, you will qualify for payouts according to a payout schedule that will be posted at the table.

Winning hands pay out on all spots containing bets. For example, if you hold a pair of Jacks, which pays 1-1, and have $5 bet on each of the three spots, you would win $15 total, $5 for each bet spot. Thus, $30 gets returned to you, $15 in winnings plus the original $15 wagered. If only spots "2" and "3" contained $5 bets, then $20 gets returned to you, $10 in bets and $10 in winnings.

Typical Payoff Schedule
Payout schedules for winning hands can vary from casino to

Typical Let it Ride Payoff Schedule

Royal Flush	1,000-1
Straight Flush	200-1
Four of a Kind	50-1
Full House	11-1
Flush	8-1
Straight	5-1
Three of a Kind	3-1
Two Pair	2-1
Pair of 10's or Better	1-1

casino. The following paytable is a standard one found in casinosand features a 1000-1 payoff on a royal flush. You get compensated more for big wins on this schedule and less for the full house and flush wins.

$1 Bonus Bet
You have the option to make a separate $1 bet which will go toward an additional payout pool. There is a Bonus spot on the table to accommodate this wager and it is made by placing $1 in the circle marked for it.

The Bonus payout is fixed according to a set schedule and is paid out on the spot. There are many bonus paytables in effect for winners of the Let it Ride Bonus. The most liberal payouts will give the house a 3.05% edge on the Bonus bet with the worst giving the casino an edge as high as 35% or more. The following chart shows one type of paytable.

$1 Bonus Payout	
Royal Flush	$20,000
Straight Flush	$2,000
Four of a Kind	$200
Full House	$75
Flush	$50
Straight	$25
Three of a Kind	$5
Two Pairs	$4
10's or Better	$1

The Winning Strategies
The main strategy considerations in Let it Ride center around the bets that have been made in the first two betting circles, "1" and "2," where you have a choice of letting one or both of these bets ride or bringing them down and playing only for the bet in the third circle. Thus, there are two decisions to make, one for each circle.

The first decision occurs when you decide to either let the bet ride in circle "1" or bring it down. We'll call this the *Three Card Betting Strategy*. The second decision occurs when the dealer exposes the community card and you decide the fate of the bet in circle "2." This is the *Fourth Card Playing Strategy*.

THIRD CARD BETTING STRATEGY

You already know three of the five cards that will comprise your final hand, and this of course, gives you a good indication of where the hand may be headed. Below are the six categories of Let it Ride poker hands where the best play is to let the bet ride in circle 1.

Hands You Will Play

Let your bet ride with these three card hands:

1. Three of a Kind: You have an automatic winner with at least a 3-1 payoff on all your bet spots.

2. Pair of 10's or Higher Pair: You already have at least a 1-1 payoff and can't lose.

3. Three to a Straight Flush or Royal Flush: You have shots here for the royal flush, straight flush, flush, straight, and high pair (plus three of a kind and two pair).

4. Three Flush with Two Cards 10 or Higher and a Straight Possibility: You have two high cards, which can pair, and the possibility of the straight. An example is Q♣, J♣, 9♣, or K♥, J♥, 9♥.

5. Three Flush with J 9 8, 10 9 7 or 10 8 7: These three hands can be thought of as a three card flush with one high card and one gap.

6. 10 J Q or J Q K: You have possibilities for pairs, three of a kinds, and open-ended straight possibilities.

Hands You Won't Play

Unless you have one of the hands in the categories listed in the above section, remove your bet from the first circle. Do not play any hands that are not listed in the Hands You Will Play section.

FOURTH CARD BETTING STRATEGY

After the dealer exposes one of the two community downcards, you now have knowledge of four of the five cards that will make up your final hand. As with the third card betting strategy, you'll only play hands with a positive expectation of winning. There are three categories below.

Hands You Will Play

Let your bet ride with the following four card hands.

1. Pair of 10's or Higher

You already have a winning hand. This category includes all made hands such as three and four of a kinds, full houses, straights, flushes, and of course a straight and royal flush.

2. Four to a Royal Flush or Straight Flush

There are good possibilities for a big score and you definitely want your bet on the table.

3. Four to a Flush or Open-Ended Straight

One more card and there is a payout. An open-ended straight is a straight where you can fill the straight with straight cards at either end, such as a 9 and a 4 if you held the cards 5 6 7 8. Since the hand 5 6 7 9 can only be filled one way, with an 8, it is not considered an open-ended straight (it is an *inside* straight) and would not be played.

Hands You Won't Play

Lacking any of the combinations listed above, take down the bet and have it returned to your bankroll.

Strategy Overview

The best percentage that can be achieved at the Let it Ride table game is a house edge of about 3.5% against you for the basic bets. This is assuming that you use the optimal strategy presented here and avoid the $1 bonus bet, which gives the house an even larger edge.

POKER: A GENERAL OVERVIEW

Welcome to the great American game of poker! In this section you'll learn how to play and win at Texas hold'em. One quick reading and you'll be on your way to playing this great game and perhaps lots of profits!

The Basics

Poker is a betting game requiring two or more players. It is played with a standard pack of fifty-two cards consisting of thirteen ranks, ace through king in each of four suits (hearts, clubs, diamonds, spades). The ace is the best and highest card, followed in descending order by the king, queen, jack, 10, 9, 8, 7, 6, 5, 4, 3 and then the **deuce** or 2, which is the lowest ranked card. The king, queen and the jack are known as **picture cards** or **face cards**. The four suits in poker have no basic value in the determination of winning hands.

Cards are referred to in writing by the following commonly used symbols: ace (A), king (K), queen (Q), jack (J), and all others directly by their numerical value: 10, 9, 8, 7, 6, 5, 4, 3, and 2. When the cards are held together in various combinations, they form hands of different strengths. These are called **hand rankings** or **poker rankings**.

There are many variations of poker, but they all have these four things in common:

1. Players receive an equal number of cards to start.

2. There will be a wager after these cards are received; players that match the wager can continue playing the hand, players that don't match the wager, will sit out. You have to pay to play!

3. More cards are usually dealt, with players having an option to wager more money following each round of cards.

4. The winner of each hand will be the player with the best hand or the last one standing because all opponents have refused to match his bets.

Each player in poker plays by himself and for himself alone against all other players. Playing partners is illegal and is considered cheating.

Object of the Game
Your goal in poker is to win the money in the **pot**, the accumulation of bets and antes in the center of the table. You can win in two ways.

The first way is to have the highest ranking hand at the **showdown** — the final act in poker, where all active players' hands are revealed to see who has the best one. The second way is to be the last player remaining when all other players have dropped out of play. When this occurs, there is no showdown, and you automatically win the pot.

Basic Game Formats
Poker can be played in two basic forms — as cash games or in a tournament format. While tournaments get all the television coverage, the more popular games being played in cardrooms are actually the cash games. Let's take a quick look at each one:

Cash Games
In a **cash game**, the chips you play with represent real money. If you go broke, you can always dig in to your pocket for more money. If you give the poker room $100 in cash, you get $100 worth of chips in return. If you build it up to $275, you can quit and convert your chips to cash anytime you want. Your goal in a cash game is to win as much money as you can, or if things are going poorly, to minimize losses.

Tournaments
In a **tournament**, every player starts with an equal number of chips and plays until one player holds them all. Your goal in a tournament is to survive as long as you can. At the very least, you want to survive long enough to earn prizes, usually money, and in the best case scenario, to win it all, become the champion, and win the biggest prize. As players lose their chips, they are eliminated from the tournament. Unlike a cash game, where the chips are the equivalent of cash money, **tournament chips** are only valuable in the tournament itself and have no cash value.

Betting Structures

Poker has three different types of betting structures: limit, pot-limit, and no-limit. These structures don't change the basic way the games are played, only the amount of money that can be bet. The big difference between the three structures is the strategy.

The amount you can bet changes the hands that you should play, when you should play them, and how much you should risk in any given situation. Here's a brief look at each structure.

Limit Poker

In **limit** poker, the most common game played in cardrooms and casinos for cash, all bets are divided into a two-tier structure, such as $1/$2, $3/$6, $5/$10, $10/$20 and $15/$30, with the larger limit bets being exactly double the lower limit. These are the only bets permissible. In the sections on the individual games, we will go over exactly when the upper level of betting comes into effect and how that works.

No-Limit Poker

No-limit hold'em is the exciting no-holds barred style of poker played in the World Series of Poker main event and seen on television by millions weekly on the World Poker Tour and stations such as the Travel Channel and ESPN. The prevailing feature of no-limit poker is that you can bet any amount up to what you have in front of you on the table *anytime* it is your turn. No-limit is usually associated with Texas hold'em, but this style of betting can be played in any variation.

Pot-Limit Poker

Pot-limit is most often associated with hold'em and Omaha, though this betting structure, like no-limit, can be played with any poker variation. The minimum bet allowed in pot-limit is set in advance while the maximum bet allowed is defined by the size of the *pot*. For example, if $75 is currently in the pot, then $75 is the maximum bet allowed.

Types of Poker Games

Poker is typically played as **high poker**, that is, the player with the best and highest five card combination at the showdown wins the money in the pot. Of course, in each variation, the pot can also be won by a player when all of his opponents fold their hands at any point before the showdown, leaving one player alone to claim the pot — even though he may not actually have held the best hand!

The order in which cards are dealt or how they are displayed is irrelevant to the final value of the hand. For example, 7-7-K-A-5 is equivalent to A-K-7-7-5. Note that all poker hands eventually consist of five cards, regardless of the variation played. Hands are shown from lowest ranked to highest.

High-Card Hands – A hand containing five unmatched cards, that is, lacking any of the combinations shown below, is valued by its highest ranking card. Example: 3♠, 9♦, Q♦, 4♥, J♠.

One Pair – Two cards of equal rank and three unmatched cards. If two players hold competing one-pair hands, then the higher ranked of the pairs — aces highest, deuces lowest — wins the pot. If two players have the same pair, then the highest side card would be used to determine the higher-ranking hand. Example: 5♠, 5♥, 8♦, J♠, K♣.

Two Pair – Two pairs and an unmatched card. The highest pair of competing two-pair hands will win, or if the top pair is tied, then the second pair. Example: 6♦, 6♠, J♠, J♦, 2♥.

Three of a Kind – Three cards of equal rank and two unmatched cards. **Example: Q♠, Q♦, Q♥, 7♠, J♦.**

Straight – Five cards of mixed suits in sequence, but it may not wrap around the ace. If two players hold straights, the higher straight card at the top end of the sequence will win. Example: 8♣, 9♠, 10♦, J♠, Q♣.

Flush – Five cards of the same suit. If two players hold flushes, the player with the highest untied card wins. Suits have no relevance. Example: K♦, 10♦, 9♦, 5♦, 3♦.

Full House – Three of a kind and a pair. Example: 5♦, 5♠, 5♥, 9♣, 9♥.

Four of a Kind - Four cards of equal rank and an odd card. Example: K♥, K♠, K♦, K♣, J♥.

Straight Flush – Five cards in sequence, all in the same suit. If two straight flushes are competing, the one with the highest card wins. Example: 7♦, 6♦, 5♦, 4♦, 3♦.

Royal Flush –A-K-Q-J-10 of the same suit. Example: A♥, K♥, Q♥, J♥, 10♥.

The Dealer
The **dealer** is responsible for shuffling the cards after each round of play so that they are mixed well and in random order. In a casino or cardroom, the dealer is not a participant in the betting or play of the game. His role is simply to shuffle and deal the cards, point out whose turn it is to play and pull bets into the pot after each round of cards. And at the end, he will declare the winner, push the pot over to the winning player, reshuffle the cards, and deal out the next round.

In all variations, the order of dealing and play always proceeds in a clockwise direction.

The Player's Options
When it is your turn to play, the following options, which apply to all forms of poker, are available to you:

1. Bet: Put chips at risk, that is, wager money, if no player has done so before you.

2. Call: Match a bet if one has been placed before your turn.

3. Raise: Increase the size of a current bet such that opponents, including the original bettor, must put additional money into the pot to stay active in a hand.

4. Fold: Give up your cards and opt out of play if a bet is due and you do not wish to match it. This forfeits your chance of competing for the pot.

5. Check: Stay active in a hand without making a bet and risking chips. This is only possible if no bets have been made.

The first three options — bet, call, and raise — are all a form of putting chips at risk in hopes of winning the pot. Once chips are bet and due, you must match that bet to continue playing for the pot or you must fold. Checking is not an option. If no chips are due, you can stay active without cost by checking.

If a bet has been made, each active player — one who has not folded — is faced with the same options: call, fold, or raise.

When a bet has been made, it no longer belongs to the bettor; it becomes the property of the pot, the communal collection of money that is up for grabs by all active players.

Betting continues in a round until the last bet or raise is called by all active players, at which point the betting round is over. A player may not raise his own bet when his betting turn comes around. He may raise only another player's bet or raise.

What Betting Is All About
You'll make bets for one of three reasons:

1. You feel your hand has enough strength to win and you want to induce opponents to put more money into the pot.

2. You want to force opponents out of the pot so that the field is narrowed, since fewer players increases your chances of winning.

3. You want to induce all your opponents to fold so that you can win the pot uncontested.

Minimum & Maximum Bets: Limit Poker
The minimum and maximum bets in limit games are strictly regulated according to the preset limits. For example, $3/$6 and $5/$10 are two common limits. The number of raises allowed in

a round are also restricted, usually limited to three or four total according to the house rules. The exception to this rule comes into play when players are heads-up, in which case, there is no cap to the number of raises that can be made.

Minimum & Maximum Bets: No-Limit Poker

In no-limit cash games and tournaments, there is typically no cap to the number of raises allowed, though there are cardrooms that still impose the three- or four-raise rule. There is also no limit to how high a bet or raise can be. Players may raise as often as they like and for all their chips.

The minimum bet in no-limit must be at least the size of the big blind while the minimum raise must be at least equal to the size of the previous bet or raise in the round. For example, a $10 bet can be raised $30 more to make it $40 total. If a succeeding player reraises, he would have to make it at least $30 more — since that is the size of the last raise — for $70 total.

How to Bet

A bet is made by either pushing the chips at least six inches in front of you — an action which speaks for itself — or by verbally calling out the play, and then pushing the chips in front of you. Simply announce, "I call," "I bet," "I raise," or whatever clearly indicates your desire, and then push your chips out on the felt. Note that if you announce a check, bet, raise, or a fold, it is binding and you're committed to the action.

To check, tap or knock on the table with your fingertips or hand or announce "I check" or "check." To fold, push your cards or toss them *face down* towards the dealer. It is illegal to show your cards to active players who are competing for the pot.
You should wait for your turn to play before announcing or revealing to any opponents what decision you will make. It is also improper and illegal to discuss your hand or another player's hand while a game is in progress.

The Rake

One of the biggest differences between casino poker and private poker games is that in casino games the house gets a cut of the action, called a **rake**, as its fee for hosting the game. In low limit games and online, the rake can be anywhere from 5% to 10%, usually with a cap of $3 to $5 per pot. In higher limit games, the house typically charges players by time.

TEXAS HOLD'EM

Your final five-card hand in **Texas hold'em**, or **hold'em**, as the game is more commonly known, will be made up of *any* combination of the seven cards available to you. These include the **board**, five cards dealt face-up in the middle of the table, cards which are shared by all players, and your **pocket cards** or **hole cards**, two cards dealt face-down that can be used by you alone. For example, your final hand could be composed of your two pocket cards and three cards from the board, one of your pocket cards and four from the board, or simply all five board cards.

At the beginning of a hand, each player is dealt two face-down cards. Then each player gets a chance to exercise his betting options. Next, three cards are dealt simultaneously on the table for all players to share. This is called the **flop**, and it is followed by another round of betting. A fourth board card, called the **turn**, is then dealt, and it too is followed by a round of betting. One final community card is dealt in the center of the table, making five total. This is the **river**. If two or more players remain in the hand, it is followed by the fourth and final betting round.

When all bets have concluded, there is the **showdown**, in which the highest ranking hand in play wins the pot.

How to Read Your Hold'em Hand

You have all seven cards available to form your final five-card hand — any combination of your two hole cards and the five cards from the board. You can even use all five board cards. Let's look at an example.

You Hold   **Your Opponent**

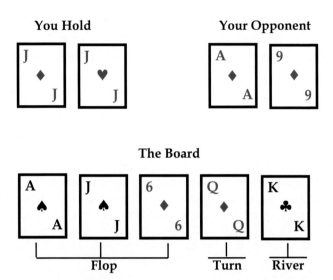

The Board

Flop   Turn   River

Your best hand, three jacks, is made using your two pocket cards and one jack from the board. This beats your opponent's pair of aces, formed with one card from his hand and one from the board.

If the river card, the last card turned up on the board, had been a K♦ instead of a K♣, your opponent would have a diamond flush (formed with his two pocket diamonds and the three diamonds on the board), which would beat your set of jacks.

The Play of the Game

All play and strategy in hold'em depends upon the position of the **button**, which is a small disk, typically plastic and labeled "Dealer." The player who has the button in front of him, who is also known as the button, will have the advantage of acting last in every round of betting except for the preflop round. After each hand is completed, the disk will rotate clockwise to the next player.

The player immediately to the left of the button is called the **small blind** and the one to his left is called the **big blind**. These two players are required to post bets, called **blinds**, before the cards are dealt.

The big blind is typically the same size as the lower bet in a limit structure, so if you're in a $3/$6 game, the big blind would be $3 and in a $5/$10 game, it would be $5. The small blind will either be half the big blind in games where the big blind evenly divides to a whole dollar, or two-thirds of the big blind when it doesn't. For example, the small blind might be $2 in a $3/$6 game and $10 in a $15/$30 game.

In limit games, on the preflop and flop, all bets and raises must be at the lower limit, and on the turn and river, all bets double and are made at the higher limit. In a $5/$10 limit game, for example, when the lower limit of betting is in effect, all bets and raises must be in $5 increments. When the upper range is in effect, all bets and raises must be in $10 increments.

In no-limit cash games, the amount of the blinds are preset and also remain constant throughout the game. In tournaments, however, the blinds steadily increase as the event progresses, forcing players to play boldly to keep up with the greater costs of the blinds. In all forms of no-limit, you an bet all your chips any time it is your turn to play.

Order of Betting

On the preflop, the first betting round, the first player to the left of the big blind goes first. He can call the big blind to stay in competition for the pot, raise, or fold. Every player following him has the same choices: call, raise, or fold. The last player to act on the preflop is the big blind. If no raises have preceded his turn, the big blind can either end the betting in the round by calling, or he can put in a raise. However, if there are any raises in the round, the big blind and other remaining players must call or raise these bets to stay active, or they must fold.

On the other betting rounds — the flop, turn and river — the first active player to the button's left will go first and the player on the button will go last. If the button has folded, the player sitting closest to his right will act last. When all bets and raises have been met on the flop and turn, or if all players check, then the next card will be dealt. On the river, after all betting action is completed, players will reveal their cards to see who has the best hand.

Betting in a round stops when the last bet or raise has been called and no bets or raises are due any player. Players cannot raise their own bets or raises.

At any time before the showdown, if all opponents fold, then the last active player wins the pot.

Limit Hold'em Strategy

In limit hold'em, where all betting is in a two-tier structure, such as $3/$6 or $5/$10, the three main factors to consider when deciding how to play a hand are the strength of your starting cards, where you are sitting relative to the button, and the action that precedes your play. There are other considerations that enter into the mix, such as the cost of entering the pot and the aggressiveness or tightness of the table, but you should always consider these three fundamental factors first.

Starting Cards

The foundation of playing winning hold'em is starting with the right cards in the right positions. In early position, play only the **premium hands** — A-A, K-K, A-K, Q-Q, J-J — and raise with them. These premium hands are the best starting cards in limit hold'em and are strong enough to raise from any position at the table. You want to get more money into the pot on a hand in which you're probably leading and protect that hand by narrowing the field of opponents.

Winning Poker Tip

Never fold the big blind unless the pot has been raised. If there is no raise, there is no cost to play and you can see the flop for free.

In middle position, play the early position premium hands listed above plus these **playable hands**: A-Q, A-J, A-10, K-Q, 10-10, 9-9, 8-8. With the hands in the playable hands group, raise if you're the first in the pot, call if players before have called, and fold if there is a raise that precedes your position. Reraise if you have a premium hand.

In late position, along with the premium and playable hands, enter the pot with these **marginal hands** if the pot has not been raised: the small pairs — 7-7, 6-6, 5-5, 4-4, 3-3, 2-2 — plus K-J, Q-J, K-J, Q-10, K-10, J-10, an ace with any other card, and suited connectors: 5-6, 6-7, 7-8, 8-9, 9-10 of the same suit. If a raise precedes you, fold the marginal hands, call with the playable hands, and reraise with premium hands. If no one has entered the pot, raise with all premium, playable and marginal hands.

All other hands not shown in the above three categories should be folded unless you're in the big blind and can see it for free.

Flop & Beyond
If you don't improve on the flop, fold if it costs you to play further into the hand. For example, if an overcard flops when you have jacks, queens, or even kings, or you miss entirely with A-K, you have to think about giving up on these hands if an opponent bets into you or check-raises. K-K is vulnerable if the flop is A-J-2.

Be careful playing flush and straight draws unless they're to the **nuts** — the best hand possible given the cards on board. For example, you don't want to play a straight draw if there is a flush draw on board.

No-Limit Hold'em Strategy
In no-limit hold'em, your entire stack of chips is at risk on every single hand — as are those of your opponents. One big mistake and they're gone. In limit hold'em, one bet is only one bet. In no-limit, that one bet could be the defining moment of your game because it could be for all your chips. And that changes the way you play hands.

Starting Hands – The Preflop: Early Position
The best starting cards in no-limit hold'em are the **premium hands** — pocket aces, kings, queens, jacks, A-K, and A-Q. In an unraised pot, bring these hands in for a **standard raise** — three times the size of the big blind — in early position. So if the big blind is at $5, make your raise $15, and if it's $10, make your raise $30.

Your goal is to narrow the field to one or two callers and either to win the pot right there when all players fold or to reduce the number of players who will see the flop.

If you have aces or kings, hopefully you'll get a caller or two, or even better a raiser. Then you'll raise right back the size of the pot or go in for all your chips if you get reraised. With queens and A-K, you can stand a raise to see the flop, but if the raise is for all your chips, you may need to let these hands go.

If you don't want your day finished with queens, you certainly don't want to go out on jacks or A-Q! If an opponent goes all-in when you hold J-J or A-Q, or even puts in a big raise, these are grounds for folding these hands.

If a player comes in raising before you, the aces and kings are automatic reraises and the non-premium hands are automatic folds. Lean towards calling with A-K and queens. If the raiser is tight, fold with A-Q and jacks; if the raiser is loose, raising or calling are both viable options. Remember that no play is set in stone in no-limit hold'em. You need to judge hands on a situation by situation basis.

Pass on all other hands from early position.

Middle Position
If there is a raise before your turn, consider folding all non-premium hands. If the raiser is tight, fold jacks and A-Q as well. If you have aces or kings, reraise and have no fear of getting all your chips in the middle. You can also reraise with queens and A-K, or you could just call.

If no one has raised in front of you, you will still play the premium hands for a raise and can add the second tier hands — eights, nines and tens, along with A-J, A-10, and K-Q — to your list of raising hands. If you get reraised by a player behind you, consider throwing second tier hands away. These hands have value but against heavy betting, they're chip burners.

Late Position
In late position, if the pot has been raised in early position, reraise with A-A, K-K, Q-Q, and A-K. If you get reraised, you may consider just calling with Q-Q and A-K, and if the raiser is tight and goes all-in, you probably want to release these hands. And

you certainly do not want to be in that reraised pot with jacks, A-Q or anything less. With aces and kings, you're always ready to play for all the marbles preflop.

If the pot is raised in middle position, reraise with the top four hands, A-A, K-K, Q-Q, and A-K. How you play jacks and A-Q is a judgment call, but it may be safer to just call and see the flop. If there has been no raiser in the pot, you can expand your starting hands to any pair, an ace with any other card, and any two cards 10 or higher, for example, Q-10 or K-J. Generally, it's best to come in raising. Most of the time, you'll win the blinds, which is good. If you get callers, you have some value to see the flop.

If you get aces or kings in late position, and you think you'll get a caller, raise. If not, it might be better to limp in. You don't get kings or aces often, and when you do, you want to make money on them.

You can also play suited connectors, such as 6-7, 7-8, 8-9, and 10-J, if you can see the flop cheaply.

The Blinds
Play the blinds according to the advice in the early position strategy section.

The Flop
If you came in raising preflop, you want to continue playing aggressively. If you're first, bet regardless of what flops. Your opponent will probably fold and you've got the pot. If he calls and you don't improve, you might consider checking on the turn. If he raises you, it's a tough call, but you'll have to consider giving up the hand unless you feel you've got better. Now, if you're second, and he checks, bet out at him.

What if he bets into you? If you miss the flop, give him the pot. Since you've shown strength preflop, his bet on the flop means you're probably second-best.

When you have what you think is the best hand, your goal is to take the pot immediately, particularly when there are straight and flush draws possible, for example, two cards of the same suit are on the board. You don't want opponents playing for another card cheaply, making it, and then destroying you on a hand that shouldn't have even seen another card. If opponents are going to beat you, make them pay to do so.

However, if you have an absolute monster like a full house or quads, you want to keep players in and extract more bets out of them. Often, that means checking and hoping a free card gives them a bigger hand.

The Turn

If you've played aggressively on the preflop and flop, and your opponent hasn't budged, you have to figure him for possible strength. It's time for you to look at what you think *he thinks* you have. If you're representing strength and playing tight, you have to give him credit for a strong hand and slow down your betting. If he checks, you check, and if you're first, check to him and see how he reacts.

The River

When you have a big hand that you're confident is the best, you want to get more chips into the pot. If you're last and there have been no bets, put the amount of chips in the pot you feel your opponent will call. If you're first, you have two options: check or bet. If your opponent is very aggressive or has been leading at the pot, you can consider checking and letting him bet, then going over the top of him with a raise to try and get more chips in the pot. You want to be careful not to move an opponent off a pot with a bet. Let your knowledge of how your opponent plays guide you.

When you have a strong hand but have doubts whether it's the best one out there, it's often better to check at the river, rather than bet and risk a big raise that you won't call. If your opponent checks, you'll see the showdown with no further cost. If he bets, you see what you want to do. Be careful about betting in an attempt to get an opponent to fold. He might raise you back or set you all in, and you'll be forced to muck your cards and give up your chips.

If you're going to bluff at the river, however, make sure it's for enough chips so that your opponent will be faced with a tough decision on whether to call.

Tournament Poker

Tournaments are a great way to have fun and hopefully, win lots of money. They can be entered for as little as $10 to as much as $25,000 in the big events! Tournaments are set up as a process of elimination. As players lose their chips, they get eliminated and the remaining competitors get consolidated into fewer tables. Eventually, only the **final table** will remain. This is where the prestige and big money is earned. Those last players will compete until one player holds all the chips—the **champion**.

Tournaments are divided into **levels** or **rounds**. Each level is marked by an increase in the blinds and after a few levels, the antes kick in, putting more pressure on players to make moves or lose their chips to inactivity. Levels may be as short as fifteen minutes in low buy-in events that are designed to be completed in as little as a few hours, or as long as ninety minutes to two hours for major multi-day events.

There are two types of tournaments—freeze-outs and rebuy tournaments. A **freeze-out tournament** is a do or die structure. Once you run out of chips, you are eliminated. In a **rebuy tournament**, you can purchase additional chips which is usually allowed only when your chip stack is equal to or less than the original starting amount and only during the first few rounds of play. Once the rebuy period ends, your tournament is over if you lose your chips.

SEVEN RULES OF WINNING POKER

1. Play with players you can beat. Don't be a patsy for players who are just too good for you.

2. Play at stakes you can afford. You can never go wrong playing at stakes within your means.

3. Fold when you're beat. Being an overall winning player has more to do with losing less when your cards don't come in the

Money Management

Being smart with your money is the key to being a winning poker player. The temptation to ride a winning streak too hard or to bet wildly during a losing streak are how gamblers beat themselves. Follow these five basic principles:

1. Play at stakes you can afford and which are comfortable for you.

2. Bankroll yourself properly. As a rule of thumb, bring thirty times the maximum or big bet in a limit game for a session of play, and fifty times the big blind in pot-limit or no-limit games.

3. Set loss limits. Restrict losses to reasonable amounts and you can never get badly hurt in any one poker session.

4. Quit when you're not at your best. If you're exhausted, annoyed, or simply frustrated by bad hands, players, or life, take a break.

5. Never gamble with money you cannot afford to lose, either financially or emotionally. Risking funds you need for rent, food, or other essentials is foolish. The short-term possibilities of taking a loss are real, no matter how easy the game may appear.

This is sound money management advice. Follow it and you can never go wrong.

running than it has to do with the pots you win when you have the best hand!

4. Play with starting cards that can win. The object in poker is to have the best hand at the showdown, which means that to win you must enter into the betting with hands that have a reasonable chance of winning.

5. Play aggressive poker. Betting and raising often causes opponents to fold, giving you a "free" pot, or makes them more them cautious playing against you on further betting rounds or hands.

6. Respect position. Your position is an important consideration in whether and how to play your starting cards and then how to proceed in future betting rounds. The deeper your position, the more playable a marginal hand.

7. Vary your play. If you're unpredictable, opponents can't get a read on you, which gives you leverage that can be turned into profits.

9. PRACTICAL MATTERS

ARRIVALS & DEPARTURES
Flying to Las Vegas
The point of entry and exit for many of the 35 million visitors to Las Vegas is **McCarran International Airport** (general information: Tel. 702/261-5211; terminal paging: Tel. 702/261-5733). McCarran is one of the busiest airports in the United States.

More than 20 airlines serve Las Vegas. McCarran is one of the most modern, attractive and efficient airport facilities in the world. Moving walkways help you negotiate the long distances between the main terminal and the gates. The C and D gates are reached from the main terminal via automated rail.

When departing Las Vegas by air don't cut your time too short. Getting to your destination gate can be a long trip and with the crowds at peak periods you may find yourself having to run, especially given today's more stringent security practices. Plan to arrive at least two hours before your scheduled departure.

Las Vegas is served by more than two dozen different airlines. There's sure to be one or more that serves your home city, likely with either non-stop or direct service. The largest carrier at

McCarran is Southwest, followed by US Airways. Other majors are Continental, Delta and United (including its budget subsidiary, Ted). jetBlue and Allegiant also offer nonstop service, and many foreign airlines fly here too.

Rental Cars

If you want to rent a car, agencies close to the airport make it easy. If you decide you want one once you check in, you're in luck, as many hotels offer rentals as well.

It's always a good idea to **book in advance, especially during weekends, major holidays and tradeshows**. Car rental prices in Las Vegas are generally lower than elsewhere in the country but do check on things such as mileage charges. Following are among the many car rental agencies you'll find in town. The local phone number is either a central reservation point for all locations or is the office nearest the airport.

Cars to Fit Your Mood

Why not rent a fantasy ride while here? Available options include Ferraris or Corvettes as well as Hummers and Escalades. Of course, it's hard to get the full power of these machines on the crowded Strip, but it's more about appearance.

- **Dream Car Rentals**, 3049 Las Vegas Blvd. S., Tel. 702/822-6392; or 3734 Las Vegas Blvd. S., Tel. 702/856-0375
- **Rent-A-Vette**, 5201 Swenson Street, Tel. 800/312-1981 or 702/736-2592
- **X-Press Rent-A-Car**, 3735 Las Vegas Blvd. S., Tel. 800/795-2277 or 702/795-4008

Taxis & Limos

The city's bus service has two lines to the airport but they aren't so convenient. A possible exception is if you are staying on Paradise Road near the Convention Center. Route 108 covers this territory and goes straight to the terminal. McCarran is close in, however, just one mile from the southern part of the Strip and about five miles from downtown.

Several mini-bus services offer the least expensive method of getting to Strip and downtown hotels, including the **Gray Line** airport shuttle, Tel. 702/739-5700, **Star Trans**, Tel. 702/646-4661 and **Bell Trans Shuttle**, Tel. 702/739-7990. They pick you up across from the baggage claim area. Make your reservations a day in advance. Prices run about $6-10.

Taxi Warning

If you're taking a taxi from the Airport to the Strip, don't let the driver use the tunnel under McCarran Airport – this is the long way around and will double your fare. **Insist that the driver use Swenson Street.**

Or, consider taking one of the many **limousine services** located in front of the terminal (about $35-40 per trip to the Strip and up to $60 downtown). The largest of these operators are **Ambassador Limo**, Tel. 702/362-6200, **Bell Transportation**, Tel. 702/385-5466, and **Las Vegas Limousine**, Tel. 702/739-8414.

More expensive limos with upgraded services are available from **Presidential**, Tel. 702/731-5577.

Taxis are also readily available at the terminal and will cost you somewhere between the shuttle and limousine prices.

Inquire with your hotel before you arrive to see if they offer free pickup from the airport. Such services used to be reserved for high rollers but they have become more common in recent years.

Driving to Las Vegas

If you're coming by car make sure that you have a full tank of gas, a spare tire and plenty of water. **Gas stations are few and far between on some stretches.** Even if your car is in great shape, bring water as emergency protection against overheating. The desert has eaten cars hardier than yours.

Driving conditions are generally excellent but you should be aware of **occasional dust storms and winter snows in the high mountain passes**. In the event of a dust storm drive cautiously with your lights on. If visibility decreases to where you cannot see clearly then pull off the road and wait for it to improve. For current local road conditions, you can call:

• **Nevada**, Tel. 877/687-6237
• **California**, Tel. 800/427-7623
• **Arizona**, Tel. 888/411-7623
• **Utah**, Tel. 800/492-2400

Bus to Las Vegas

Greyhound buses serve Las Vegas from all directions. It is by far the cheapest way to travel. The main terminal is located downtown at 200 S. Main Street near the Plaza: Tel. 702/382-5468 for the bus station, Tel. 800/231-2222 for reservations. Greyhound has additional service to other parts of Las Vegas.

Train to Las Vegas

Nope, sorry. Unless you're going to hop on a freight train hobo-style, there's no way to get here by train. The closest Amtrak stations are in Kingman, AZ and Salt Lake City.

GETTING AROUND LAS VEGAS

Las Vegas is easy to navigate. Many of the big hotels on the Strip are within walking distance from each other, as are the casinos in the smaller downtown area, though you will need transportation between those two areas and to get to surrounding areas and excursion destinations.

Walking

It's easy to walk the Strip or downtown. Though it's four miles from Mandalay Bay to the Stratosphere, plenty of places are within walking distance of one another. Of course, sometimes the weather or your energy level don't cooperate. In such instances taxis or buses fit the gap. Comfortable shoes are an absolute must.

Downtown is a couple of miles north of the Stratosphere but **the downtown casino corridor is only about five blocks long**. You don't want to walk between the two areas, as you'll traverse some of the city's more unpleasant neighborhoods.

Always be alert for traffic when crossing the Strip. The law favors drivers over jaywalkers. Fortunately, a system of **handicapped-accessible pedestrian bridges** has been built over many busy intersections, allowing cars and pedestrians to avoid one another. It also eases traffic congestion.

Bridges connect all four corners of the Strip at three major intersections: Flamingo, Tropicana and Spring Mountain/Sands. Harmon is next on the list, once the road is realigned between

CityCenter and the Cosmopolitan. At other intersections, you're on your own.

Driving

There is nothing like the flexibility of a car. This convenience becomes a necessity if you're venturing off the Strip. Las Vegas is an easy place to get around by car since the major streets are generally in a grid pattern and there are only a few important routes that you need to be familiar with. A growing network of highways makes getting to outlying areas much faster.

Las Vegas Boulevard South, aka the Strip, is the main street of interest. It runs north-south and is paralleled to the west by I-15. Another major arterial highway is I-515 (also designated as US 93/US 95) which runs from the infamous Spaghetti Bowl interchange just north of downtown to Henderson and Boulder City.

Another highway is the **Las Vegas Beltway**, portions of which are still under construction. Most of it is designated as County 215. This part runs from I-15 in North Las Vegas along the western side of the Valley before heading back east. Where it once again crosses I-15 it becomes I-215 and continues to I-515/US 93/US 95 in Henderson. It's a highway in some sections but only a temporary frontage road (with traffic lights) in others. It will take several more years before it is completed.

The major east-west thoroughfares crossing the Strip are (from south to north): Russell Rd., Tropicana Ave., Flamingo Rd., Sands Ave./Spring Mountain Rd., Sahara Ave. and Charleston Blvd. Another important route is Desert Inn Rd., which doesn't intersect the Strip, instead going underneath Las Vegas Boulevard and over I-15, making it the best route between the east and west sides of the city.

There are few greater buzzkills in Las Vegas than traffic, especially on the Strip. It's a horror to drive after about ten in the morning at least through 11pm. It is often bumper to bumper. Avoid driving on the Strip at all except for what is, among visitors, almost an obligatory nighttime cruise to see the sleepless neon city in action.

Most locals know how to access the Strip hotels without spending time in bumper-to-bumper on Las Vegas Boulevard. Just west of the Strip is  **Frank Sinatra Drive**, which provides access to Mandalay Bay, Luxor, Excalibur, New York-New York, Monte Carlo, Bellagio, and Caesars Palace. It is also accessible via I-15 northbound and Russell Road.

On the west side of I-15 is another useful alternate route, **Dean Martin Drive**. It is more of a thru street than an access road, connecting with all the major east-west routes via direct intersections (Blue Diamond Rd., Warm Springs Rd., Tropicana Ave. and Twain Ave.) and access roads (use Connector Rd. to get to Hacienda Ave./Mandalay Bay Rd. and Hotel Rio Dr. to get to Flamingo Rd.). Just north of Twain, Dean Martin goes under I-15 and intersects with his Rat Pack partner.

Together, the two roads combine to form **Industrial Road,** which continues north between the Strip and I-15, providing back access to Treasure Island, Mirage, Spring Mountain Rd. (use Fashion Show Dr.), Circus Circus, Sahara Ave. (use South Bridge Ln. for eastbound, North Bridge Ln. for west) and Wyoming Ave.

On the east side of the Strip, **Paradise Road** is the main alternate north-south route. It's a useful thoroughfare, hitting all the main east-west routes before meeting the Strip at the Stratosphere, crossing over and turning into Main Street, which takes you up to downtown. Casinos located on Paradise include Hard Rock, Terrible's, and the Las Vegas Hilton. It's also where you'll find the Convention Center. You can also access some of the east Strip casinos – specifically the Riviera and Sahara.

Further to the south, other north-south roads cut closer. **Koval Lane** provides access to Venetian, Harrah's, Ellis Island, MGM

Grand and the Tropicana. **Audrie Street** connects Flamingo Road
with Flamingo and Imperial Palace. It then ends. The street picks
up again at Harmon Ave., providing access to Paris, Planet
Hollywood and MGM Grand.

The good system of highways and broad streets keep traffic
generally tolerable, although locals complain about it all the time.
Be prepared also for long signals at major intersections. Delayed
greens and long turn signals require vigilant attention. Right
turns on red are allowed unless otherwise indicated. Be aware of
school zone speed limits. They are strictly enforced.

At least **parking is rarely a problem**. All Strip hotels have plenty
of free parking. Downtown lots are free with validation in the
casino. You don't actually even have to gamble at most of them
for them to stamp your ticket. The Strip hotel garages are always
behind the hotel itself but, due to the size of many resorts, it may
be a lengthy walk to the casino floor, theater or wherever you're
going. If you have dinner reservations or show tickets, be sure to
allow enough time to navigate the garages and walkways.

All hotels have free valet parking which avoids the walking but,
of course, the tradeoff is the tip – a buck or two. Valets aren't
always quicker than self-parking at the end of the night, but if
you're running late they can shave valuable minutes off your trip.
Expect to wait 7-10 minutes for the valet to return your car.

Buses
Buses are an easy and fairly inexpensive away to get around. The
Regional Transportation Commission of Clark County runs the
Citizens Area Transit bus system: Tel. 702/228-7433 for route
information and schedules. Trips on the Strip usually take longer
than scheduled but the system is generally reliable.

The most important route that visitors need to be aware of is **"the
Deuce"** (formerly the #301), with a route up and down the Strip.
It runs from the Downtown Transportation Center (DTC) to the
South Strip Transfer Terminal (SSTT), just off of Las Vegas Blvd.
at Sunset Road. The directional signs only indicate DTC or SSTT.
Service is frequent and the line runs 24 hours a day. The fare is $2

and exact change is required. An all-day pass is a good buy at $5. Modern double-decker buses are now used exclusively on this line, and the upper level offers a bird's eye view of the sights. At night, you'll almost certainly be stuck in traffic, so bring that camera!

One other line that you may be able to make use of is **the #402 Crosstown Express**. This line has limited stops but connects many of the city's major shopping centers. CAT has almost 40 other routes that go to just about every part of the Las Vegas Valley, although other routes generally do not have service between 1:30 and 5:30am. Frequency varies by line from about 15 minutes to an hour. All lines other than the Deuce charge $1.25. There are no free transfers between routes but if you are going to be using buses frequently during a single day then consider one of two available daily passes. The first costs $2.50 and is good for all routes except the Deuce, but you can add that for 50 cents. The other pass costs $5.00 and is valid for unlimited rides on all routes. Virtually all buses are handicapped accessible and have bike racks.

The privately owned and operated **VEGAS.com Arrow**, Tel. 702/382-1404, covers the entire Strip. It runs from Las Vegas Hilton to the north, to Stratosphere and all the way down the Strip to Mandalay Bay. The Arrow has one added convenience over the city buses: riders are dropped off at the porte-cochère of most of the hotels. This can save a fair amount of walking over CAT buses but it takes even longer to drive into and out of each hotel drop-off point. The fare is $2.50 for one-way, $4.25 for day or night passes, $10 for a 24 hour pass including the Monorail, with exact change required. The Arrow service runs from 8:30am to midnight every 15 minutes.

Free Shuttles
Many of the off-Strip hotels offer free shuttle transportation to central locations on the Strip – usually the Forum Shops and/or Fashion Show Mall. Inquire at your front desk for details.

Additionally, many off-Strip owned hotels offer transportation to their on-Strip sister properties. **Rio**, for example, offers shuttle buses to Caesars Palace, Paris/Bally's, and Harrah's. The former **Barbary Coast** is accessible via shuttle from Orleans, Gold Coast, South Coast and Suncoast. **Sam's Town** runs shuttles to Bill's, Tropicana, Harrah's, and California/Fremont.

Several hotels are connected via free trams: Mirage and Treasure Island; and then further to the south, Mandalay Bay, Luxor and Excalibur.

The Las Vegas Monorail

The Las Vegas Monorail has been fraught with mistakes and missteps. It opened in 2004 after considerable delay and much-publicized reliability issues, connecting destinations on the east side of the Strip. Stops are at the Sahara, Las Vegas Hilton, Convention Center, Harrah's/Imperial Palace, Flamingo, Bally's/Paris and MGM Grand.

 The monorail's upside is that it's a fast, convenient alternative to taxis or walking. You can get from one end to the other in 15 minutes, much quicker than peak hour driving. The downside is cost. It's now $5 per ride or $20 for six rides. Day passes are a better buy at $15, three days are $40. Service runs 7am-2am, until 3am on weekends.

They seem to have worked out most of the kinks in the system but are waging an uphill battle to reclaim public opinion and ridership, which has been steadily declining.

Taxis

Taxis are plentiful and easy to get either on the Strip or downtown. It's best to call for a taxi when you're off the Strip. On the Strip, however, they're conveniently lined up at every hotel awaiting fares. The current cost is $3 for the initial drop of the meter (the first 1/9th of a mile) and then $1.80 for each mile thereafter (20 cents for 1/9-mile), with nominal extra charges for more than three passengers. Then they also tack on 35 cents for each minute of waiting time. An additional fee of $1.20 is added on for trips from McCarran airport.

Major cab services in Las Vegas include **Ace Cab**, Tel. 702/736-8383; **Checker Cab**, Tel. 702/873-2000; **Desert Cab**, Tel. 702/386-9102; **Western Cab**, Tel. 702/736-8000; **Whittlesea Blue Cab**, Tel. 702/384-6111 and **Yellow Cab**, Tel. 702/873-2000.

Limousines are an alternative consideration. Rates start at $40 to $50 an hour, much more for some huge stretch limos or those offering extra amenities. The standard limo offers a comfortable ride and a few amenities. Stretch limos run about $65-$85 per hour and include a stocked bar, cellular phone, color TV, stereo and other amenities. See above for limo service contact numbers.

BASIC INFORMATION
Business Hours
While Las Vegas is a 24-hour town, business hours here are the same as elsewhere in the United States – generally 9 to 5.

Climate & Weather
The Las Vegas Valley sits in the middle of the desert, actually the meeting point of three deserts: the Mojave and Sonoran Deserts plus the Great Basin. Obviously, the temperature can get pretty hot. The city is surrounded by mountains, the highest peak of which is Mt. Charleston, a nearly 12,000-foot peak northwest of the city. Vegas gets 4 1/4 inches of rain per year and more than 290 days of sunshine. It is **dry, windy and hot much of the time**. The low humidity keeps most days tolerable. On 100-degree days, you'll see people driving around with their windows open.

Drinking & Gambling Laws
The minimum drinking age is 21 years. Servers can and do card and, so don't go anywhere without picture ID. The same restrictions apply to gambling. Parents should take note that Nevada gaming regulations prohibit children from loitering in the casino.

Average Temperatures & Rainfall

	Avg. High	Avg. Low	Avg. Rainfall
January	57 F	37 F	0.59"
February	63	41	0.69
March	69	47	0.59
April	78	54	0.15
May	88	63	0.24
June	99	72	0.08
July	104	78	0.44
August	102	77	0.45
September	94	69	0.31
October	81	57	0.24
November	66	44	0.31
December	57	37	0.40

You are not allowed to play if your child is present. Almost every casino is designed so that you have to pass through it in order to get anywhere. Children can walk through the casino so long as they keep moving.

Casinos operate 24 hours a day, 365 days a year. Likewise, beer, wine and hard liquor are always available, at casinos, bars, restaurants, convenience stores, grocery shops and even drugstores. Many hotels sell bottles on the premises, but the best booze bargains can generally be had at neighborhood drugstores off the Strip.

Emergencies & Safety
Coordinated emergency services (police, ambulance and fire) throughout the Las Vegas area can be reached by dialing 911.

For urgent but non-emergency situations you can dial 311. Like the 911 system, this will automatically route your call to the nearest law enforcement authorities. However, 311 is not available from cell phones and pay phones charge for its use. The Las Vegas Metro Police Department's non-emergency number is Tel. 702/229-3111. Metro handles policing duties for the entire Las

Vegas area except for Henderson and North Las Vegas, which have their own police departments.

If you need a doctor or dentist rather than a hospital emergency room, call the Clark County Medical Society, Tel. 702/739-9989, or the Clark County Dental Society, Tel. 702/255-7873 for a referral. There are **dozens of walk-in quick care medical centers** throughout the city, consult your yellow pages. There is a walk-in medical practice open to the public on the Strip at the Imperial Palace hotel.

Pharmacies on the Strip include Walgreen's (3765 Las Vegas Blvd. S., at Harmon and 3025 Las Vegas Blvd. S., at Convention Center) and CVS at 3758 Las Vegas Blvd. S., near the Monte Carlo. Walgreen's also has a downtown location on Fremont Street. In addition to filling prescriptions, these are also excellent sources for sundry items. They are all less expensive than buying the same items at any hotel.

Considering the number of tourists that come through each year, the safety record for visitors is exceptional. The police (and hotel security forces which assist them) do a good job of protecting travelers. While some simple precautions are in order, the Las Vegas Strip is probably one of the safest streets in America. On the other hand, feeling too secure is never a good idea anywhere, so use common sense (avoid panhandlers, don't wander on your own late at night, etc).

Festivals, Holidays & Conventions
The roster of annual events keeps growing. From the rodeo to poker tournaments to crafts shows, Las Vegas has plenty of things to do all year round. Beyond a couple of major events listed below, things tend to change fairly quickly from year to year. Check out the Las Vegas Convention and Visitors' Authority website (www.lvcva.com) for the latest.

Las Vegas is the world's foremost convention city. More than six million people come to town for conventions now. Few other places can match the facilities that Las Vegas possesses for the largest conventions. Besides the behemoth Las Vegas Convention Center, there's the giant Sands Convention Center and the Cashman Field Center. And the majority of the Strip hotels all have their own extensive convention facilities.

Because of the large number of hotel rooms in Las Vegas, conventions don't usually lock ordinary travelers out of the room market. However, there are exceptions. The biggest conventions are weeks to be avoided, when rooms, if you can get them at all, will be at a steep premium. The largest:

- Consumer Electronics Show (Jan) – 150,000
- APEX (Nov) – 130,000
- SEMA (Nov) – 120,000
- National Association of Broadcasters (Apr) – 100,000
- World of Concrete (Jan) – 85,000
- World Market Center (Jan) – 62,000
- ASD/AMD (Feb, Aug) – 62,000
- JCK Show (Jun) – 50,000
- American Dental Association (Oct) – 50,000

Below is our Top Ten list for the **best annual events** in Vegas:

1. CineVegas (Jun) – stars come to the Palms in force for "the world's most dangerous film festival," with premieres, panels, awards and paparazzi. www.cinevegas.com.

2. UNLVino (Jul) – in a city with more master sommeliers than anyplace else in America, you can expect great things from this wine festival, held every year since 1974. www.unlvino.com.

3. World Series of Poker (May-Jul) – believe the hype. This is the

most talked-about poker tournament ever, with amateurs, professionals and celebrities alike buying $10,000 seats at Rio's tables. www.worldseriesofpoker.com.

4. New Year's Eve (Dec) – a coordinated fireworks display is shot off from multiple hotel rooftops, lighting up the sky over the entire length of the Strip. The entire length of the Strip is closed to traffic and becomes a pedestrian street party that rivals that of Times Square.

5. Taste of Las Vegas (Sep) – Live bands, cooking demonstrations from celebrity chefs, and sample-sized tastings from some of the city's best restaurants make this event a must for foodies. www.tasteofvegas.com.

6. The Comedy Festival (Nov) – five days of performances from everybody who's anybody in comedy, held at Caesars Palace in November, including a live Comic Relief broadcast. www.thecomedyfestival.com.

7. Super Bowl Sunday (Jan) – there's as much excitement in Las Vegas as in the host city, especially at the sports books. Dozens of hotel/casinos large and small host Super Bowl parties. They are sometimes held in the sports book, but occasionally in larger special event rooms. Most viewing parties charge admission, anywhere from $15 to $100+. For your dollars you get to watch the game on giant screens, and the hotel throws in food and drinks and even entertainment in many cases. It beats watching the game on your 29-inch.

8. Las Vegas 400 (Mar) – Part of the NASCAR Nextel Cup series, this is one of the biggest events of the year, both on the racing circuit and for the city in general – hundreds of thousands of people fill the grandstand, the sports books and hotel rooms for the event. www.lvms.com.

9. NFR – National Finals Rodeo – (Dec) – the whole town is overrun with cowboys for the country's largest and most prestigious rodeo event. Events are held at the Thomas & Mack Center, South Point Equestrian Center, Orleans Arena and elsewhere. Even Legends in Concert goes all-country. www.nfrexperience.com.

10. St. Patrick's Day Block Party (Mar) – The Fremont Street Experience downtown turns green for this massive drunken street party. Of course, there's events all over town, but this is this big one.

Internet Access

Most hotels now offer in-room Internet access, in the form of wi-fi, wired connections or a WebTV-like interface. In addition, most of the major casinos have business centers with Internet access or kiosks where you can check your email, print boarding passes, etc. Expect to pay about $12 for 24 hours' worth of in-room access, or $1 a minute for business center or kiosk usage. Internet cafes and gift shops offer access for about 20-30 cents/minute.

Money

Sales tax in Las Vegas is 7.75% and is added to the cost of all purchases of merchandise with only a few exceptions. There is no sales tax on services. An additional 2% tax is levied on the cost of hotel rooms and 6% on car rentals. But the biggest tax that the state of Nevada smacks visitors with is for live entertainment, including shows, sporting events and even some restaurants. The **entertainment tax, on top of regular sales tax, ranges from 5-10%, based on venue size**. Also, casinos report to Uncle Sam any machine winnings over $1200.

Most banks are open from 9am until 5pm on weekdays (with some later hours on Friday) and from 10am to 1pm on Saturday. A few are open on Sunday.

You won't find any banks on the Strip, although there are several within a short walk of the downtown casino center. So, for Strip guests, you'll have to rely on the ubiquitous automatic teller machines (ATMs) with particularly painful fees. Many casino ATMs also issue cash advances on your VISA, MasterCard or other major credit card, whose fees make ATM surcharges look like nothing at all.

Credit cards are almost universally accepted in Las Vegas. They will always be accepted for show tickets and most restaurants (except for some fast-food outlets).

You should have no trouble using traveler's checks in casinos to buy chips. If you have good credit you may be able to take out a line of credit, but call first to line up the necessary documentation.

Visitors from abroad can exchange **foreign currency** at McCarran Airport or at most of the larger Strip hotels, although the latter may restrict this service to their own guests. However, the most favorable rates are found at Foreign Money Exchange, 101 Convention Center Drive, Tel. 702/791-3301. Their office is within walking distance of the northern Strip hotels and the Convention Center. There's also a full-service American Express travel office in the Fashion Show Mall. It's a good idea to bring traveler's checks for the bulk of your cash, or even better, rely on the plastic.

Postal Services
For stamps, visit your hotel's sundry shop or business center, or ask guest services.

Senior Citizens
Discounts for senior citizens are often available for the asking. This includes airfare, hotels, restaurants, car rental, area attractions and even some shopping. Many casinos even offer special promotions to seniors.

Whether you're seeking general information or specific activities and events for seniors, a good source is the Senior Citizens Center of Las Vegas and Clark County, 451 E. Bonanza Road, four blocks from Casino Center Blvd, Tel. 702/229-6454.

Telephones
The **702 area code** covers all of Clark County (which encompasses the entire Las Vegas area). It may be necessary to use the 702 area code prefix for some of the outlying portions of Clark County. The 1 prefix is required before all other area codes and for all toll-free calls (800, 866, 877, 888, etc.). Public telephones are easy to find. Local calls are about 35 to 50 cents for the first three minutes.

When using a telephone from your hotel room, be aware of costs imposed by the hotel. These are usually in printed material by the phone or in the guest's information booklet. If you have any questions call the front desk.

Time
Las Vegas is in the Pacific Time Zone and it observes Daylight Savings Time. Wear a watch. There really are no clocks!

Tipping

Tipping is a way of life in this city. The question of who to tip, and how much, is a vital part of Vegas protocol. Here a few rules for tipping Vegas-style.

Gratuities are not included at restaurants except for large parties. For good service a 15% tip is the norm, with 20% or more appropriate for outstanding service. Don't forget to tip your buffet server. Many people overlook them, but it's customary to leave $2-3 per person for dinner. A dollar each will suffice for breakfast and lunch. At the bar, leave a dollar for each round of drinks. The same is true for the cocktail waitress in the casino who brings you your free drink. Tip bigger, and your next drink may be stronger. Valet parking attendants also get a buck or two.

Dealers get tipped when you're winning. It's customary to throw the dealer a little something, either just a straight-up tip or as a bet on their behalf. One popular practice is placing a horn bet for the dealers when leaving the craps table. It's a sucker bet for you and it is for them too. If you want to place a bet for them, bet as if you would for yourself. Tips are also customary for hand-pays.

For taxis, the standard tip is 10%; 10-15% for limousines. Give your bellhop a dollar or two for bringing your bags to your room but $3 or more if you have a number of heavy bags. One to two dollars per day is fine for your maid.

Tourist Information

Prior to coming to Las Vegas you might want to contact the **Las Vegas Convention and Visitors Authority**, the largest official source of information, located at 3150 Paradise Road, Las Vegas, NV 89109 (Tel. 702/892-07115). They also have a room reservation service, Tel. 800/332-5333. Their website, www.visitlasvegas.com, has information on hotels, restaurants and much more. The LVCVA folks can also give you up-to-the-minute information on special events and show schedules for the time you will be in town. You can request information packets online or over the phone.

Another great resource is www.vegas.com, a commercial website where you can book everything from flights to hotel rooms to show tickets to VIP nightclub passes. The site includes broad information on just about everything the city has to offer. There is also some tourist information on the *Las Vegas Review-Journal* website (www.reviewjournal.com) but it's not nearly as up-to-date as vegas.com.

Water

Drink lots of water! We can't stress this enough. With bright sunshine and daytime temperatures above 110 degrees, you'll dry out quick. That goes double if you're drinking. **Drink lots of water!** You will dehydrate during the day, you will dehydrate at night. You will hate your life if you're not well-moistened.

Vegas tap water is, to put it gently, an acquired taste. Bottled water can get expensive in bulk, so before your trip, visit an outdoor/sporting goods store for **a filtered sports bottle**. Refill it at any tap and drink clean tasting water, pure of lead, chlorine and other contaminants. Prices vary, but you can expect to pay $1 or less per gallon, as opposed to $3 for a liter of Evian, which, of course, is "naive" spelled backwards.

INDEX

Things Change!

Phone numbers, prices, addresses, quality of service – all change. If you come across any new information, we'd appreciate hearing from you. No item is too small! Drop us an e-mail at jopenroad@aol.com, visit us at www.openroadguides.com, or write us at:

Open Road's Best of Las Vegas
Open Road Publishing
P.O. Box 284
Cold Spring Harbor, NY 11724

LOOK FOR THESE OTHER GREAT TITLES:
Open Road's Best of Arizona, $14.95
Open Road's Best of The Florida Keys, $14.95
Open Road's Best of New York City, $14.95
Open Road's Best of Southern California, $14.95
Open Road's New York City with Kids, $14.95
Open Road's Best National Parks With Kids, $14.95
Open Road's Washington, DC with Kids, $14.95
Open Road's Hawaii with Kids, $14.95

You'll find them all at huge discounts at www.openroadguides.com.